Praise for *Sidewalk Critic*

"Mumford wrote with tremendous evocative power, so that almost every paragraph is an adventure in a city you once knew or wish you had. He is the opinionated, sometimes wrongheaded, companion whose sincerity you trust, whose acute sensibility and sense of humor you seek out."
—Caroline C. Pam, *New York Observer*

* * *

"This collection of *New Yorker* pieces from the 1930s is bound to evoke a certain nostalgia.... It is a powerful reminder of what a good critic Lewis Mumford...could be." —Keith Miller, *Times Literary Supplement*

* * *

"For those of us who missed Lewis Mumford's 1930s articles in the *New Yorker* the first time around, this book provides a wonderful opportunity to 'catch up' and to consider again how this remarkable scholar could be at once so perceptive and so maddening." —Kenneth T. Jackson, editor of *The Encyclopedia of New York*

* * *

"The reviews collected in *Sidewalk Critic: Lewis Mumford's Writings on New York* are a reminder of the importance of high-quality architectural criticism.... Mumford contributed a strong and eloquent voice to an important conversation on the shape of the places we live. We could use more such voices today." —James B. Goodno, *In These Times*

* * *

"By gathering some of the best of Mumford's The Sky Line columns from *The New Yorker* of the Thirties, editor Wojtowicz does readers of our era a great service.... Wojtowicz's compact biography of Mumford is a fitting prelude to the essays of this very busy writer." —David Bryant, *Library Journal*

Doug Van
Volkenburgh
12 13

SIDEWALK CRITIC
LEWIS MUMFORD'S WRITINGS ON NEW YORK

EDITED BY

Robert Wojtowicz

PRINCETON ARCHITECTURAL PRESS • NEW YORK

Published by
Princeton Architectural Press
37 East Seventh Street
New York, New York 10003
212.995.9620

For a catalog of books, call 1.800.722.6657.
Visit our web site at www.papress.com.

"The Sky Line" is a trademark of the
New Yorker.

Editing and design:
Clare Jacobson
Copy editing and indexing:
Andrew Rubenfeld

Special thanks to: Ann Alter, Amanda
Atkins, Eugenia Bell, Nicola Bednarek,
Jan Cigliano, Jane Garvie, Caroline
Green, Beth Harrison, Mia Ihara, Leslie
Ann Kent, Mark Lamster, Anne
Nitschke, Lottchen Shivers, Jennifer
Thompson, and Deb Wood of Princeton
Architectural Press
—Kevin C. Lippert, publisher

The Library of Congress has cataloged
the hard cover edition of this book as:
Mumford, Lewis, 1895–1990
    Sidewalk critic : Lewis Mumford's
writings on New York / Robert
Wojtowicz, editor.
    p.   cm.
    A selection of essays from the New
Yorker, published between 1931 and 1940.
    Includes bibliographical references
and index.
    1. Architecture—New York (State)
—New York. 2. Architecture, Modern
—20th century—New York (State)—
New York. 3. New York (N.Y.)—
Buildings, structures, etc. I. Wojtowicz,
Robert. II. Title.
NA735.N5M79 1998
720'.9747'1—dc21   98-18843
                                          CIP
ISBN 1-56898-252-6 (alk. paper)

CONTENTS

To Richard Coons

ACKNOWLEDGMENTS

OVER the years, I have encountered people, who, upon hearing of my interest in Lewis Mumford, have asked: "Why don't you do something with the early 'Sky Lines' that he wrote for the *New Yorker?*" *Sidewalk Critic* is my response to them, while it is also an offering to those readers who will be encountering Mumford's work for the first time and those "students" of New York City who will revel in the abundance of information that follows. There is no more delightful introduction to Lewis Mumford and the city he called home for the first forty years of his life.

Special thanks are due to my friend and agent Robert E. Shepard, who convinced Princeton Architectural Press to publish this collection. My editor, Clare Jacobson, guided the project through to publication with astonishing calm and speed. Robert Arbuckle, Rachel Bones, Nancy Shawcross, Nancy Shelton, and Clay Vaughan uncovered information when I could not access it myself. Permission to republish this material was graciously provided by Elizabeth Morss, executor of the Mumford estate and Lewis and Sophia Mumford's granddaughter, and the legal counsel of the *New Yorker,* largely through the efforts of Jeanne Bauer.

Robert Wojtowicz
Norfolk, Virginia

Cap, at Duell, Sloane & Pearce, suggested doing a book of Sky Lines. I collected these hastily in the spring of 1953, to see if they held up under critical inspection. My judgement was yes & no: so I decided against it—though by this time Harcourt, after Cap's talking with Giroux, were ready, too. Since then, I have a few good ones to add: yet I hesitate, until at least I publish one or two more books on non-architectural subjects.

LM
December 29, 1953

INTRODUCTION

L EWIS Mumford (1895–1990) was the most important architectural critic produced by the United States in the twentieth century.[1] A modernist who opposed the International Style, and a contextualist long before the emergence of postmodernism, he was primarily a social critic whose views on architecture defy easy categorization. In addition, he considered his architectural criticism to be an inseparable part of a larger, organic body of thought that found expression in more than twenty books and more than a thousand articles and reviews on a staggering array of subjects. To a large extent this is the case, but buried in the back issues of the *New Yorker* under "The Sky Line" lies a trove of Mumford's best work in architectural criticism, unencumbered by weighty discourses on the tyranny of machines or the dissolution of cities.

That Mumford should have equivocated over the republication of the early "Sky Lines" at first seems rather curious. Charles "Cap" Pearce, formerly of Harcourt Brace and the *New Yorker,* and others in Mumford's publishing circle clearly saw merit in them, so why would Mumford have wanted to suppress them? Moreover, why did Mumford generally feel uneasy about his role as architectural critic? The answers lie in the peculiar circumstances of the first part of his career. Following the trail blazed by earlier American critics such as Montgomery Schuyler, Mariana Griswold van Rensselaer, and Herbert Croly, Mumford first rose to national prominence in the 1920s through a series of short books on utopian thought and American culture and through dozens of articles and reviews on an even wider range of topics. A common thread that linked many of these pieces was architecture's pivotal role as an index of civilization, a role that, according to Mumford, was in desperate need of clarification. From 1931 to 1963, his position as a regular columnist for the *New Yorker* provided him with the ideal platform for disseminating his views on modern architecture. Neither American traditionalists nor European modernists were spared his somewhat biting and often humorous criticism, as he attempted to strike a balance between internationalism and regionalism, the "technic" and the "organic," style and function.

Yet, Mumford was dissatisfied with these early literary and journalistic efforts. From the early 1930s to the early 1950s, he focussed his growing intellectual ambitions on *The Renewal of Life,* a multivolume study of Western civilization that he hoped would bring him the same international renown that had already settled on Oswald Spengler and would later greet Arnold Toynbee.[2] Using the parallel themes of technology, urbanism, and sociology, Mumford explicated an organic philosophy, synthesized from a variety of sources, that had guided his thinking since his college days. Architecture remained a unifying but background theme in this study, providing a benchmark against which he could measure the integration of form and purpose that he sought in modern life. While the first two volumes on technology and urbanism were well received, the later volumes on society—the ones in which Mumford felt he had made his most original contribution—were less successful; an inattentive public and mediocre reviews left him plagued by self-doubt. Greater acclaim awaited him following the publication of his sweeping epic, *The City in History,* but that lay several years in the future.[3]

Thus in 1953, Mumford was at a crossroads in his career. Though "The Sky Line" was appearing with less frequency in the pages of the *New Yorker,* it was as popular as ever, and its impact was being felt internationally. However, Mumford craved recognition as a social philosopher, and he would pursue this goal for the remainder of his life, even if it meant demeaning his importance as an architectural critic. Although he eventually relented to the extent of reissuing many of his post-World War II "Sky Lines" in paperback form,[4] the earlier columns—those that deal principally with New York City and its environs—have remained largely inaccessible until now.

Sidewalk Critic is not a comprehensive collection of Mumford's output for the *New Yorker.* Rather, it is a selection of his best pieces from 1931–40. Within a single column, he bounces from topic to topic, as the critic himself hopped from curb to curb in his walks about the city. The book essentially assembled itself. Several months after the death of her husband in 1990, Sophia Mumford (1899–1997) sent a folder identified only as "Old

Sky Lines" to the Mumford Papers at the University of Pennsylvania. Beneath a cover sheet, from which the introductory epigraph is taken, there lay nearly two dozen columns from the 1930s to the 1950s. Because the material in the folder was not substantial enough to form a book, and because much of the later material had been republished in other places, a revamped collection of Mumford's columns from 1931–40 was assembled; it includes, in addition to "The Sky Lines," several "Art Galleries" and two autobiographical pieces. Limitations of space would not permit the collection to be comprehensive, but it is broadly representative of his best criticism from these years. The pieces are arranged chronologically according to the fall-to-spring arts season that the magazine followed, and set under their original headings. Bibliographers should note that during this period, two editions of the *New Yorker* were published: a metropolitan edition and an out-of-town edition. Mumford's columns always appeared in the former, but only occasionally in the latter during the 1930s. Unfortunately, Sophia Mumford did not live to see this collection, to which she had given her wholehearted approval.

The subjects that Mumford tackled in "The Sky Line" range widely from the mingiest lunch counter to the grandest skyscraper, each receiving the same careful scrutiny in regards to function, scale, context, and style. On this last point he maintained a careful reserve, for he regarded much art deco architecture to be excessively ornamental while at the same time he found the emerging International Style to be needlessly barren. On the Romantic revival of past styles, only then sputtering to a halt, he had nothing but contempt, because it held no possible relevance to twentieth-century society. In many ways, Mumford's "The Sky Line" is a microcosm of the *New Yorker* of the 1930s as a whole: literate, entertaining, provocative, and thorough. Before examining Mumford's association with the magazine, however, it is useful to look briefly at his early life and career.

Lewis Mumford was born in Flushing, Long Island in 1895, the only child of Elvina Mumford, a single housekeeper. He never knew his father, Lewis Charles Mack, a businessman with whom Elvina conducted a brief affair. Mother and son lived in genteel but reduced circumstances in a series of residences on the Upper West Side of Manhattan. Elvina's mother and stepfather, Charles Graessel, also lived with them during Mumford's early childhood. Graessel, a retired headwaiter from Delmonico's, had a formative influence on his stepgrandson, particularly in his reserved urbanity and old-fashioned comportment. With Mumford in tow, Graessel paid numerous social calls around the city, opening the young boy's eyes to the teeming life of the growing metropolis.

Mumford was an avid reader and the valedictorian of his elementary school class. Stuyvesant High School presented a more competitive atmosphere and a greater intellectual stimulus; it was here that writing emerged as his chief passion and lifelong vocation. The numerous plays and screenplays that survive from Mumford's adolescence attest to his literary ambitions, but his inability to secure their production eventually resulted in his reorientation toward the more promising field of journalism. Mumford enrolled in New York's City College in the fall of 1912, where he intended to pursue a Ph.D. in philosophy. Lack of interest coupled with a tubercular spot on his lungs prompted his withdrawal in 1915, and so he never completed his baccalaureate degree.

The next few years were a period of self-study and self-improvement for Mumford. A college course in biology had introduced Mumford to the writings of Patrick Geddes, the Scottish botanist cum polymath who advocated an interdisciplinary approach to all knowledge.[5] At a time when Mumford was rebelling against academic strictures, Geddes proved to be a perfect role model—albeit a disastrous mentor—for he was an intellectual who allowed himself the freedom to explore everything within his grasp and who used cities and their surrounding regions as his laboratory. Moreover, Geddes's seemingly radical ideas about the interrelationship between biological and social evolution lay at the foundation of an organic philosophy, or "organicism," that Mumford was beginning to assemble from a wide variety of sources that included Ralph Waldo Emerson and Claude Bragdon, the American architect and theorist; this organicism would later be modified by contact with Frank Lloyd Wright. During this transitional period, Mumford also read Ebenezer Howard's *Garden Cities of To-morrow*, a landmark book in urban planning that called for the integration of city and country life in a new entity, the self-sustaining, moderately scaled garden city.[6] The garden city became Mumford's ideal urban entity thereafter.

Fortified by these new ideas, Mumford set out with pad and pencil, recording in countless notes and sketches his impressions of the New York metropolitan area during a feverish period when skyscrapers were supplanting modest commercial buildings in downtown Manhattan and whole neighborhoods were being carved out of the scraggly farmland of the outer boroughs. A ten-month interlude in the U.S. Navy interrupted Mumford's explorations, but, by the time he was discharged in 1919, he was ready to embark on his journalistic career.

Success did not come immediately, but by the mid-1920s, Mumford had held editorial appointments at the *Dial* and the *Sociological Review* and had become a regular contributor to the *Freeman,* the *New Republic,* the *Journal of the American Institute of Architects,* and the *American Mercury.* The success of his first book, *The Story of Utopias,* eased his way into New York's literary circles.[7] Four books on American culture followed in relatively quick succession, plumbing what Mumford's friend and fellow writer Van Wyck Brooks called the "usable past." *Sticks and Stones* proffered an unorthodox social history of American architecture and was hailed by many critics for its original thinking while scorned by many architects for its attack on professional conservatism.[8] *The Golden Day* and *Herman Melville* examined the American writers of the mid-nineteenth century: Nathaniel Hawthorne, Henry David Thoreau, Walt Whitman, Ralph Waldo Emerson, and Herman Melville.[9] In *The Brown Decades,* Mumford sought to excavate the writers, artists, and architects of the late nineteenth century from the usable past in order to provide role models for his contemporaries in those fields, many of whom he believed had lost their creative way.[10] Underpinning all of these writings was Mumford's constantly evolving "organicisim" and his growing pessimism that technology was threatening to displace society's equilibrium in the twentieth century.

B Y the time Mumford joined the staff of the *New Yorker* in 1931, he was a highly visible young writer whose breadth was widely admired and whose critical skills had been tested in literature, art, and architecture. He was also a social advocate who wrote extensively on the inadequacies of housing and community planning in the years following World War I and the need to plant garden cities in the United States. In pursuit of these goals, he helped to organize the Regional Planning Association of America, an informal, progressive think tank of writers, architects, and planners, many of whom he counted among his closest friends.[11] Lastly, he was the head of a small family, sustaining a modest existence on income from royalties, free-lance articles, lectures, and short-term academic appointments and holding a mortgage on a small house in Sunnyside Gardens, Queens. Mumford's wife, Sophia, had been an assistant editor at the *Dial* until the birth of their son Geddes in 1925; a daughter, Alison, joined the family in 1935. With the depression showing no signs of abating, the *New Yorker's* offer came at a very propitious time, although Mumford did not recognize this at first.

The surviving correspondence between Mumford and the *New Yorker* concerning "The Sky Line" is extensive and has only recently been made available at the New York Public Library to researchers.[12] "The Sky Line" had been a regular and controversial feature in the magazine almost since its inception in 1925. In October 1926, George S. Chappell became the column's first regular writer, appearing under the pseudonym "T-Square." A somewhat conservative critic, he is remembered chiefly for having sparked litigation with his first column over his biting criticism of the Delmonico Building in Midtown Manhattan."[13] The magazine printed a retraction sixteen months later,[14] but Chappell did not leave the staff until Mumford took his place in the fall of 1931. It seems Chappell alienated his editors over the erratic schedule of his submissions, just as they were considering a higher-profile replacement.

Mumford was a logical choice to replace Chappell, since he had written extensively on architecture for the magazine's rivals in a consistently accessible, often humorous, and thoroughly analytical manner. Securing his services, however, proved to be no easy task. The catalyst seems to have been an article that Mumford wrote for the *New Republic* in March 1931 that surveyed the city's most recent crop of skyscrapers, the exaggerated scale of which he generally despised. The piece included a long section on the emerging design of Rockefeller Center, which he deemed "the sorriest failure of imagination and intelligence in modern American architecture."[15]

Harold Ross, the irascible editor of the *New Yorker*, invited Mumford to write for the magazine the following month, but the latter was presumably unwilling to commit because of upcoming travel and other obligations.[16] In an extraordinary act of hubris, Mumford responded to the offer by submitting a writing sample by Catherine Bauer, his colleague in the Regional Planning Association of America and his current mistress. "I read Miss Bauer's piece," Ross wrote Mumford in early May. "I think she writes well and probably knows what she is talking about, but I don't think she is the qualified authority you are." Ross closed by reminding Mumford that the magazine was "willing to entertain a suggestion for a story on the Rockefeller City."[17]

The speed of the subsequent volley of letters is a startling reminder of the once-fabled efficiency of the U.S. mail, with its multiple daily deliveries. "Your note found me surrounded by three thousand words I had written this morning on Radio City," Mumford wrote in a letter to Ross the next day, "and I have just thrown them into the waste basket."[18] Not one to be defeated so easily, Ross responded the day after that. "I am very sorry," he wrote rather dryly. "I wonder if you couldn't retrieve those 3,000 words from the waste-basket and let me see them. I am not convinced there is not a story in it."[19] Mumford finally relented the next day. In a self-deprecating tone, he wrote:

> I did tear up those three thousand words: one has to do that every once in a while just as a moral exercise, to keep oneself in trim for cutting out a whole chapter. But here are a few pages, prompted by your gentle insistence, which I've just done tonight. If I had any notion that you'd want to print it, I'd remind you that it is only a first draft, and unfortunately the characteristic mumford style doesn't begin to emerge until I have sweated over the third draft. But I've done this rather to convince you of my hopelessness of doing anything: so you have my permission to put it in your waste-basket after you've glanced through it.[20]

Ross liked Mumford's piece and suggested only minor clarifications for the general reader. "With that little help to beginners injected, I should like to use the article about as it is," Ross wrote to Mumford in the middle of May. "I think what you have to say is new and important."[21]

When he submitted the revised draft toward the end of May, Mumford, perhaps recalling Chappell's misfortunes over the Delmonico Building, proposed that Ross present the piece to Raymond Hood or Harvey Corbett, two of the architects associated with Rockefeller Center.[22] Ross turned the piece over to Associate Editor Katharine S. White, who did not pursue Mumford's recommendation; nevertheless, it was carefully scrutinized by Ross, White, Assistant Editor Wolcott Gibbs, the magazine's legendary fact checkers, and the magazine's counsel, spurring another exchange of letters.[23] Mumford, who counted two attorneys among his in-laws, respected the editors' caution, which to less experienced writers might have seemed excessive.[24] "I am glad you consulted your lawyer...," Mumford wrote Gibbs. "The cost of winning a lawsuit is just as painful as the cost of losing one: so one has every reason to be decently careful in matters of phrasing."[25] The piece finally appeared in the June 20, 1931 issue under the provocative headline "Frozen Music or Solidified Static? Reflections on Radio City." While it essentially launched Mumford's association with the *New Yorker*, it would still be several months before he assumed the duties of architecture critic.

Ross and White were not about to let Mumford go after just one article. They continued their pursuit for the remainder of the summer leading into the fall, and by October, Mumford was a regular member of the staff in charge of "The Sky Line."[26] Despite his initial reluctance, Mumford settled into his new role quickly, and before the end of 1931, he had reviewed the George Washington Bridge and the Cornell Medical Center over the byline L. M. "I hope that my habit of treating buildings at a little greater length than T-Square did doesn't conflict with some holy editorial policy," Mumford wrote Ross after the first "The Sky Line" appeared in November. "In a short paragraph one can't say very much more than I like it or I don't: and I think that a few reasons one way or the other are probably helpful to the reader, if not to the architect."[27] Ross, who could be stingy with praise, commended his newfound critic on the piece. "I thought your column was excellent," Ross wrote Mumford a couple of days later, "and though I had it in mind to write you and tell you so I rarely carry out my good intentions."[28] An informal schedule was set for the spring season whereby Mumford would produce a column about every four weeks.[29]

The fall/spring season of 1931–32 was one of Mumford's most prolific as "The Sky Line" columnist. He wrote nine pieces and, beginning with the March 19 issue, signed his full name to them. Thereafter his output decreased to about four to six per season. A depressed real-estate market affected the initiation of major projects in the early part of the decade, and he compensated for this by reviewing smaller projects, building remodelings, architecture and design exhibitions, and relevant books. "At first these articles were elemental and brief...," Mumford recalled in his autobiography. "But they tested my critical competence: if I could make a discriminating esthetic judgment about the design of a modern lunchroom, I could perhaps handle Michelangelo or Le Corbusier!"[30] "The Sky Line" was never illustrated, except for small vignettes near the headline. This was a situation that Mumford actually preferred, since it forced the reader into seeking out the buildings and places that were the topics of the column.

Relations between Mumford and Ross remained cordial, even as the former began reporting to the latter's assistants for the routine editing of the columns. The two quickly began addressing each other by their surnames in their letters, a schoolboy affectation that resisted Ross's almost comic attempt to address his critic as "Lew," a name Mumford never used.[31] It became Mumford's habit to visit the buildings under review anonymously and to research and write his columns within the space of a few days, typing them at home and delivering them to the office quietly. Thus, he never formed close bonds with the other *New Yorker* editors and writers. "I wish you would look in on me next time you are in this office (where you are suspected of being an elf)," Ross wrote Mumford in December 1933. "Everything is going fine so far as you are concerned and I have nothing whatever to say. I would be pleasant though."[32]

Before Mumford embarked for Europe late in the spring of 1932 to further his research for *Technics and Civilization,* the first volume of *The Renewal of Life,* Ross managed to thrust an additional responsibility upon his critic's shoulders: the column "The Art Galleries."[33] This was another of the magazine's ongoing departments and one for which Mumford was already well-prepared, as he had been writing art criticism since the early 1920s. The new arrangement began in the fall, and it provided him with a more regular and generous source of income; between the two departments he produced almost a column every week at $75.00 per column, a considerable sum during the depression.[34] With "The Art Galleries" came the additional responsibility of contributing to the

"Goings-On About Town" department, the magazine's weekly listing of cultural events.35 Mumford would also occasionally submit a piece to the "Talk of the Town" department.

Given Mumford's past misgivings over committing too much of his time to journalism, it is not surprising that by the end of the first season he was ready to relinquish his expanded duties. In April 1933 he wrote to Ross: "Do you want to chuck your present art critic? By now you probably realize, as you didn't last spring, that *all* art critics are unsatisfactory, and only by changing them regularly can you even get the sensation momentarily that one is a little better than another."36 Ross responded in his characteristically brusque manner, ignoring the critic's plea. "Make your plans for next winter to include doing our work, for God's sake," he wrote Mumford a couple of days later. "I think you are a big success and I had intended to tell you so personally for weeks but have failed to meet you in the office."37

Despite occasional weak protests, Mumford continued to write "The Art Galleries" for the next four years, covering Manhattan's galleries and museums and, on occasion, shows that he encountered on his travels. Although this body of work falls largely outside of the present collection, it should be noted that Mumford's art criticism paralleled and complemented his architectural criticism. He could be considered progressive in his outlook (through his friendship with Alfred Stieglitz, Mumford became a staunch advocate of photography as a modern medium of expression), but as an outgrowth of his organicism, he favored figurative works over nonrepresentational experimentation.

A s an architecture critic, Mumford sought to relate to his readers how a truly well-planned, modern metropolis might appear and function, despite the economic realities imposed by the depression and the spatial limitations imposed by an existing city. His quasi-socialist outlook caused many architects and even enlightened clients to throw up their hands in despair. When he read that the New York City Housing Authority's First Houses were no better than the tenements they replaced ("The Sky Line: The New Housing," December 7, 1935), an exasperated commissioner complained to Ross, "The trouble with Mumford is, nobody can tell what he wants."38

Moreover, since Mumford's criticism was oriented toward the social and functional requirements of modern architecture, glossing over as unimportant the questions of style and ideology that racked the American profession during the 1930s, his views were especially infuriating to older architects. In one piece, Mumford criticized the neo-Georgian design of a new post office as hopelessly moribund ("The Sky Line: Fiftieth Anniversary— A Georgian Post Office," February 29, 1936). The critic's "dirty wise cracks" prompted New York architect Aymar Embury II to send Ross a fiery letter of complaint in March 1936 after first discussing the matter with Rea Irvin, the magazine's art director:

> I wonder if this sort of review is of any benefit to the *New Yorker*, and is not on the contrary rather a detriment. I would be the last to desire only laudatory reviews, nor do I even feel it desirable to have the critic pass over in silence things he does not like.... A little healthy scourging is a good thing for any profession, but it does seem very highly desirable to say a kind word once in a while if only for the heightening effect of contrast.39

Embury was not finished, for he added the following in a postscripted letter: "After I had dictated the letter herewith enclosed, my secretary said to me: 'Whenever I read Mumford's criticisms, I just boil. They are very offensive to me.' I have heard other people who are not architects say the same thing."40

After giving the matter some thought, Ross issued a stinging reply to Embury the following week:

> Speaking for myself, and not for Mumford, I sometimes realize that architecture is one of the few subjects I cannot detach myself from emotionally. The reason is a simple one: I don't have to go to a theatrical production if I don't want to, or a moving picture, or look at a painting, or, at worst, I can walk away from these things. But a building is there, and I've got to look at it, and realization of this sad fact frequently makes me indignant and downright bitter.... It was one of my ambitions when we started the *New Yorker* to, for God's sake!, do something about it, because nobody else seemed to be doing anything in a popular publication....
>
> The fact is that I have exulted in the frequent sternness of Mumford's articles, while realizing that they are among the sternest things we print. I recognize the constant possibility of our being unfair through the fact that an architect usually works under the limitations of an employer (such as a semi-literate who

wants a movie palace erected) but I think our readers are adult and understand that the results of an architect's work are rarely as he would have had them, given complete freedom.[41]

Privately, Ross reassured Mumford of his central importance to the magazine after the critic evidently offered to resign his post:

> We don't want any successor groomed; to hell with that. You're really just getting going and you're doing something of great importance, and no doubt about it. I know your pieces are read and taken seriously and they are providing all the leadership that Architecture of today is getting now (unless it's in professional magazines, which I don't read, of course) and it's your duty to go on.[42]

One result of Mumford's perceived negative outlook was that those who received positive notices from him were delighted all the more. Given his modernist sympathies, it is not surprising, for example, that he found much to admire in the new building of the Museum of Modern Art ("The Sky Line: Growing Pains—The New Museum," June 3, 1939). Nonetheless, Alfred H. Barr, Jr., the Museum's director, wrote Mumford to express his heartfelt thanks:

> I am sailing in a few hours but can't leave without writing you to tell you how much all of us here at the Museum appreciate your article on the building; not merely appreciate it because it says such agreeable things, but admire it for its remarkable understanding of our problems. Although naturally we are prejudiced, we think it one of the best pieces of architectural criticism published in an American magazine.[43]

An earlier review of another museum—the Cloisters in upper Manhattan—evidently caused a great deal of unfounded anxiety on the part of its staff ("The Sky Line: Pax in Urbe," May 21, 1938). Designed to house the extensive medieval collections of the Metropolitan Museum of Art, the Cloisters is an amalgam of several Romanesque and Gothic structures imported from Europe and joined by new construction. Rather than dismissing the design as a romantic pastiche, Mumford lauded it for providing an extraordinarily suitable context for the objects exhibited. In one of his most elegantly worded reviews, he skillfully juxtaposed the protective cloister gardens at the Museum's center with the brutality of the outside world. The sympathetic tenor of the review prompted James J. Rorimer, the Cloisters' curator, to express his gratitude:

I, and in fact all of us at the Museum, do indeed feel "Pax in Urbe" since your valued and telling article appeared in the *New Yorker*. Actually I walked the streets in Philadelphia until the early morning hours to obtain a copy to see what you had written. I told you all that was on my mind regarding your "interest" in The Cloisters, and I am recompensed in having placed my confidence in your judgement in spite of your original feelings about the undertaking.44

THROUGHOUT the 1930s, Mumford was extraordinarily active on projects outside the *New Yorker*. He continued writing for the *New Republic* and other magazines, and he researched and wrote the first two volumes of *The Renewal of Life*. Though the Regional Planning Association of America disbanded in 1933, he maintained an active interest in housing. With so many outside interests, one of them was bound to conflict with Mumford's duties as a *New Yorker* critic. The Museum of Modern Art's 1932 Modern Architecture: International Exhibition provided him with an early test, since he had been an advisor on the housing section of the show and had written the housing essay for the catalog.45 The show is considered to be a landmark event in architectural history for having introduced European architects such as Walter Gropius, Ludwig Mies van der Rohe, Le Corbusier, and J. J. P. Oud to the United States and for coining the label "International Style" to describe the Europeans' collective works, which bore admittedly striking similarities. Despite his association with the exhibition, Mumford reviewed it for the *New Yorker*, albeit somewhat sheepishly ("The Sky Line: Organic Architecture," February 27, 1932). To the dismay of the Museum and the exhibition's curators, Henry-Russell Hitchcock, Jr. and Philip Johnson, Mumford bestowed the greatest praise upon Frank Lloyd Wright at the expense of the European modernists who were being showcased. Mumford clearly did not follow a predictable or partisan path. Moreover, when the situation demanded it, he would not hesitate to criticize the work of personal friends such as Clarence Stein, formerly of the Regional Planning Association of America.

Toward the end of the decade a similar situation presented itself when Mumford was approached by the magazine to review the 1939 New York World's Fair, on whose planning committee he had once been a member. Ideological differences over the proposed housing section had caused him to resign from the committee, although he subsequently wrote the narrative for *The City,* a documentary film on housing produced by the American Institute of Planners that was screened at the fair.[46] In a letter to Ross from September 1936, Mumford explained his predicament:

> I am the last person in the world who should be assigned to the job; because if it turns out any good, it will partly be due to the fact that I planted the germ of the idea in the hostile soil of the Fair Committee; and if it turns out rotten, it will be because they rejected the idea—in any case, my comments would taste like either soft soap or sour grapes.[47]

As usual, however, Ross prevailed, and Mumford wrote a tempered preview of the fair ("The Sky Line: The World's Fair," May 8, 1937) and two negative reviews under a special heading ("The Sky Line In Flushing: West Is East," June 17, 1939; "The Sky Line in Flushing: Genuine Bootleg," July 29, 1939).

M UMFORD never really left his adolescent literary ambitions behind him, but except for an autobiographical novella published in *The Second American Caravan* (a 1928 yearbook for which he served as co-editor) they remained largely unfulfilled.[48] The idea of exploiting his childhood for literary material remained with him as he watched the landmarks and places of the early twentieth century being transformed beyond recognition during his adulthood. In the summer of 1933, while discussing a potential piece on Central Park with Don Wharton, an assistant to Ross, Mumford alluded to these nostalgic impulses, which could conceivably be tailored to fit "A New York Childhood," one of the magazine's occasional features. The piece on Central Park, Mumford wrote, "would also have the better part of a New York Childhood in it, too: one of my grandfathers was headwaiter at Delmonico's, and he used to spend the afternoon in the Park with me when I was a little boy, pointing out all the Rich People, whose houses and yachts he had had such a ripe backstairs view of."[49] The idea continued to simmer in Mumford's mind, and he drew liberally upon these memories when writing a tribute to Alfred Stieglitz that was published the following year.[50]

Finally in July 1934, prompted by meager summer savings and "overflow" from the Stieglitz piece, Mumford submitted to Wharton what was to become "A New York Childhood: Ta-Ra-Ra-Boom-De-Ay," the autobiographical sketch that opens the present collection.[51] Mumford was unsure of this uncharacteristic and rather sloppy first draft, and made this clear in a follow-up letter that he sent to Wharton in August:

> For heaven's sake don't keep the piece I wrote in the refrigerator: send it back & without waiting for your suggestions about cutting I'll put it in such a shape as to make an answer in September more easy. I should know better than to send out unfinished drafts: but at the moment my bank account had shriveled & I felt I had to do something about it.[52]

Mumford's piece caused a great stir in the magazine's editorial offices. In a memorandum to Katharine S. White, Wolcott Gibbs expressed his reservations: "It is difficult to judge this stuff because of the abominable form it's in, but to me it's definitely a quick job, not up to Mumford's standard at all. I think we've got most of the value if we take [the] Grandfather and let the rest go." Conversely, White expressed her support of Mumford's piece to Ross in a handwritten emendation to Gibbs's memorandum:

> I disagree with Gibbs & think this should be a N.Y. Childhood cut to a proper length. . . . I think he should be persuaded to make it his own childhood & sign it, but if he can't be, let him do it straight & sign another name. I think it is delightful, that it recreates a whole new background we've never had. . . . We've *never* had a memory of the *gayness* of the city before. . . . This has real literary quality & real historical value which our Childhood pieces seldom have.[53]

White emerged as the winner, and, after several months of editing and polishing, Mumford's piece was published in December 1934 over his initials. Its success emboldened him to submit a second sketch, "A New York Adolescence: Tennis, Quadratic Equations, and Love," which was published in December 1937 over his full name and which follows "A New York Childhood" at the front of the present collection. At turns lively, humorous, and poignant, both pieces effectively recapture the happiest moments of what must have been an often solitary youth, while providing a vivid account of metropolitan life at the turn of the twentieth century. Close on the heels of "A New York Adolescence," Mumford submitted "A New York Apprenticeship," a third sketch describing his early years as a journalist, but although Ross called the former "simply beautiful," he rejected the latter.[54] The unpleasant task of informing Mumford fell to Ross's assistant,

St. Clair McKelway. "I think the main objection to it is that it is so largely a piece about a writer's problems," McKelway wrote Mumford in February 1938, "and Ross' feeling has always been that most readers aren't interested in writers."55 Mumford did not pursue the matter further, but, never one to waste material, he borrowed from all three sketches when writing his autobiography many years later.

S IDEWALK CRITIC concludes where it begins, with a review of Rockefeller Center. On second inspection, Mumford found the project to be tolerably adequate if not completely successful ("The Sky Line: Rockefeller Center Revisited," May 4, 1940). He continued to write for the magazine until 1944, but his output trickled to a poem apiece in the two years leading up to that point, an indication that his career was entering a new phase. One reason for this change was that Mumford broke his residential bond with the city by moving his family to the upstate town of Amenia in 1936. This required that to view new buildings he commute back and forth from the countryside to the city, a tiring ninety-mile journey in each direction. A second was the international acclaim that he garnered with the 1938 publication of *The Culture of Cities*, the second volume of *The Renewal of Life*. A third was the political build-up to World War II; an ardent interventionist on the Allies' behalf, Mumford wrote two books and numerous articles articulating his position.56 The American response claimed the life of his son, Geddes, in 1944, ushering in a period of mourning that lasted for several years. When Mumford returned to "The Sky Line" in 1947, he consciously reoriented it away from New York and toward global currents in modern architecture.

Whether Mumford liked the early "Sky Lines" or not, they are among his most insightful writings, shedding critical light on New York City just as it was recovering from one building boom and about to enter another. Today, many of them have a great nostalgic appeal, especially in their ability to conjure up a place that has largely vanished. This is the city of Fiorello La Guardia, Berenice Abbott, and Alfred Lunt and Lynn Fontanne captured at a moment when Rockefeller Center, the Waldorf-Astoria, and Best & Company were new or recently remodeled. Other less building-specific "Sky Lines" are more enduring, for Mumford's demand that architecture respond to human need, harmonize with its surroundings, and reflect the honest aspirations of the civilization that built it knows no boundaries of time or place. With the support of a remarkable editor who was passionately interested in architecture, Mumford reached an audience more diverse than any critic who had preceded him in this field. *Sidewalk Critic* aims to extend this reach to a new generation of readers.

NOTES

1 On the life and work of Lewis Mumford, see his autobiography, *Sketches From Life: The Autobiography of Lewis Mumford, The Early Years* (New York: Dial Press, 1982) and his two memoirs, *Findings and Keepings: Analects for an Autobiography* (New York and London: Harcourt Brace Jovanovich, 1975) and *My Works and Days: A Personal Chronicle* (New York and London: Harcourt Brace Jovanovich, 1979). Donald L. Miller's *Lewis Mumford: A Life* (New York: Weidenfeld and Nicholson, 1989) is the only full-length biography of Mumford. On Mumford as an architectural critic, see Robert Wojtowicz, *Lewis Mumford and American Modernism: Eutopian Theories for Architecture and Urban Planning* (Cambridge, New York, and Melbourne: Cambridge University Press, 1996).

2 The four volumes that comprise Mumford's *The Renewal of Life* (New York: Harcourt, Brace and Company) are *Technics and Civilization* (1934), *The Culture of Cities* (1938), *The Condition of Man* (1944), and *The Conduct of Life* (1951).

3 Lewis Mumford, *The City in History, Its Origins, Its Transformations, and Its Prospects* (New York: Harcourt, Brace and Company, 1961). For this work he received the National Book Award for Non-Fiction in 1962.

4 Lewis Mumford, *From the Ground Up: Observations on Contemporary Architecture, Housing, Highway Building, and Civic Design* (New York: Harcourt, Brace and Company, 1956) and *The Highway and the City* (New York: Harcourt, Brace and World, 1963).

5 The most recent and thorough treatment of Geddes's life and work is Helen Meller's *Patrick Geddes: Social Evolutionist and City Planner* (London and New York: Routledge, 1990).

6 Ebenezer Howard, *Garden Cities of To-morrow* (London: Swan, Sonnenschein and Company, 1902).

7 Lewis Mumford, *The Story of Utopias* (New York: Boni and Liveright, 1922).

8 Lewis Mumford, *Sticks and Stones: A Study of American Architecture and Civilization* (New York: Boni and Liveright, 1924).

9 Lewis Mumford, *The Golden Day: A Study in American Experience and Culture* (New York: Boni and Liveright, 1926) and *Herman Melville* (New York: Harcourt, Brace and Company, 1929).

10 Lewis Mumford, *The Brown Decades: A Study of the Arts in America, 1865–1895* (New York: Harcourt, Brace and Company, 1931).

11 See Edward K. Spann, *Designing Modern America: The Regional Planning Association of America and Its Members* (Columbus: Ohio State University Press, 1996).

12 Mumford's papers have been deposited in the Special Collections of Van Pelt Library, University of Pennsylvania (hereafter known as Mumford Papers); the papers of the *New Yorker* are housed at the New York Public Library, Manuscripts and Archives Division (hereafter known as *New Yorker* Papers).

13 T-Square [George S. Chappell], "The Sky Line: Cheap Architecture—The Aeolian Building—Athletic Club Plans—New York Noises," *New Yorker* 2 (16 October 1926): 61–63.

14 T-Square, "The Sky Line: A Pat for the Tiger—Nautical—A Classical Touch," *New Yorker* 3 (11 February 1928): 65–66.

15 Lewis Mumford, "Notes on Modern Architecture," *New Republic* 66 (18 March 1931): 121.

16 Letter from Harold Ross to Lewis Mumford, 23 April 1931, *New Yorker* Papers, box 9. On Harold Ross's life and the early years of the *New Yorker,* see Thomas Kunkel, *Genius in Disguise: Harold Ross of* The New Yorker (New York: Random House, 1995).

17 Letter from Ross to Mumford, 5 May 1931, *New Yorker* Papers, box 9.

18 Letter from Mumford to Ross, 6 May 1931, *New Yorker* Papers, box 9.

19 Letter from Ross to Mumford, 7 May 1931, *New Yorker* Papers, box 9.

20 Letter from Mumford to Ross, 8 May 1931, *New Yorker* Papers, box 160.

21 Letter from Ross to Mumford, 13 May 1931, *New Yorker* Papers, box 160.

22 Letter from Mumford to Ross, 20 May 1931, *New Yorker* Papers, box 160.

23 Letter from Katharine S. White to Mumford, 29 May 1931, *New Yorker* Papers, box 160; unsigned memorandum with White's and Ross's handwritten emendations, "Notes on Radio City," n.d., *New Yorker* Papers, box 160; letter from Wolcott Gibbs to Mumford, 10 June 1931, Mumford Papers, folder 3580.

24 Mumford, *Sketches from Life,* 442.

25 Letter from Mumford to Gibbs, 11 June 1931, *New Yorker* Papers, box 160.

26 Letter from James M. Cain to Mumford, 16 October 1931, *New Yorker* Papers, box 160.

27 Letter from Mumford to Ross, 28 November 1931, *New Yorker* Papers, box 12.

28 Letter from Ross to Mumford, 30 November 1931, *New Yorker* Papers, box 12.

29 Letter from Ross to Mumford, 15 December 1931, *New Yorker* Papers, box 9.

30 Mumford, *Sketches from Life,* 442–443.

31 Letter from Ross to Mumford, 4 April 1932, Mumford Papers, folder 3580.

32 Letter from Ross to Mumford, 7 December 1933, *New Yorker* Papers, box 15.

33 Letter from Ross to Mumford, 2 April 1932, *New Yorker* Papers, box 187.

34 Letter from Ross to Mumford, 4 April 1932, Mumford Papers, folder 3580.

35 Letter from Ross to Mumford, 21 September 1932, Mumford Papers, folder 3580.

36 Letter from Mumford to Ross, 18 April 1933, *New Yorker* Papers, box 15.

37 Letter from Ross to Mumford, 20 April 1933, Mumford Papers, folder 3580.

38 Commissioner "Post" quoted in a letter from Ross to Mumford, 20 December 1935, Mumford Papers, folder 3580.

39 Letter from Aymar Embury II to Ross, 13 March 1936, Mumford Papers, folder 3581.

40 Postscripted letter from Embury to Ross, 13 March 1936, *New Yorker* Papers, box 259.

41 Letter from Ross to Embury, 20 March 1936, Mumford Papers, folder 3581.

42 Letter from Ross to Mumford, 26 March 1936, Mumford Papers, folder 3581.

43 Letter from Alfred H. Barr, Jr. to Mumford, 9 June 1939, Mumford Papers, folder 3461.

44 Letter from James J. Rorimer to Mumford, 26 May 1938, Mumford Papers, folder 3269.

45 Lewis Mumford, "Housing," in *Modern Architecture: International Exhibition* (New York: Museum of Modern Art, 1932), 179–192. On the exhibition and Mumford's involvement with it, see Terence Riley, *The International Style: Exhibition 15 and the Museum of Modern Art* (New York: Rizzoli, 1992).

46 Wojtowicz, *Lewis Mumford*, 142–144.

47 Letter from Mumford to Ross, 29 September 1936, *New Yorker* Papers, box 259.

48 Lewis Mumford, "The Little Testament of Bernard Martin Aet. 30," in Alfred Kreymborg, Lewis Mumford, and Paul Rosenfeld, eds., *The Second American Caravan: A Yearbook of American Literature* (New York: Macauley Company, 1928): 123–169.

49 Letter from Mumford to Don Wharton, 18 July 1933, *New Yorker* Papers, box 187.

50 Lewis Mumford, "The Metropolitan Milieu," in Waldo Frank, Lewis Mumford, Dorothy Norman, Paul Rosenfeld, and Harold Rugg, eds., *America and Alfred Stieglitz: A Collective Portrait* (Garden City, N.Y.: Doubleday, Doran and Company, 1934): 33–58.

51 Letter from Mumford to Wharton, 19 July 1934, *New Yorker* Papers, box 210.

52 Letter from Mumford to Wharton, 15 August 1934, *New Yorker* Papers, box 210.

53 Undated memorandum from Gibbs to White with handwritten emendations from White to Ross, *New Yorker* Papers, box 210.

54 Letter from Ross to Mumford, [22 July 1937], Mumford Papers, folder 3581.

55 Letter from St. Clair McKelway to Mumford, 24 February 1938, *New Yorker* Papers, box 302.

56 See, for example, Lewis Mumford, *Men Must Act* (New York: Harcourt, Brace and Company, 1939) and *Faith for Living* (New York: Harcourt, Brace and Company, 1940).

PROLOGUE

The two autobiographical sketches that follow are the only pieces in the collection that appear out of sequence. "A New York Childhood: Ta-Ra-Ra-Boom-De-Ay" was published in 1934 and "A New York Adolescence: Tennis, Quadratic Equations, and Love" three years later. Together they cover Mumford's life from about the age of five until the age of eighteen (c. 1900–13) when he was still a student at City College. The astonishing detail with which he recounts these years reveals that, even as a boy, he was unusually perceptive, scrutinizing his surroundings with the eyes of a budding critic.

A NEW YORK CHILDHOOD
TA~RA~RA~BOOM~DE~AY
DECEMBER 22, 1934

K ARL Marx characterized the class into which I was born as the
petty bourgeoisie. He didn't think much of it as a class, and neither do I; but that was the angle from which I saw New York. This
gave me a wider range than you or Marx might think. On one hand was the
Philadelphia uncle who retired from a young business with a comfortable
fortune, early in the nineties. At the other extreme was an uncle who
worked with his hands as a silversmith and once, somewhat reluctantly,
joined the union. Between was my more intimate world, which touched in
imagination, sometimes in vision, the fringe of High Life as it was lived for
the benefit of the readers of *Town Topics*. At second hand, I got a good
backstairs view of that life, for my grandfather, who introduced me to the
city, was headwaiter at Delmonico's during the nineties.

My ears opened to the New York that was singing "Ta-ra-ra-boom-de-
ay," the song the great nineteenth century died on. My infant ears also
heard the German words of "*Patsche, Patsche Kuchen, Bäcker hat gerufen*,"
and my Irish nurse sang to me about Casey, who danced with a strawberry
blonde while the band played on. She held me in her arms, in front of the
old Twenty-second Regiment armory at Broadway and Sixty-eighth Street,
while I cried in anguish or envy at the sight of the blue-clad soldiers, with
their red-lined capes, marching out to the Spanish-American War, prepared to fight everything but the dysentery and the ptomaines that awaited
them. The earliest visual memory that is not purely personal is the bill-
board painting of a graceful lady in flimsy garments, holding aloft an electric-light bulb, beneath the mysterious legend: "Wire to May to Wire." My
next impersonal memory is the sight of fat men with palm-leaf fans lounging in wicker chairs on the sidewalk in front of the old Astor House on a
summer night.

During my whole childhood we lived on the West Side. In the eighteen-
nineties, the district between Riverside Drive and Central Park West
showed every sign of becoming the fashionable part of the city. It was here

that the great new apartment houses, the darkly urbane Dakota and the San Remo, had been erected, and Seventy-second Street—now so sordid and shabby—was then very swell indeed. Riverside Drive was lined with roomy Richardsonian mansions, almost suburban in character, while a sudden consciousness of the Dutch element in Manhattan's history, probably abetted by the rise of the Roosevelts, was leading to some very pleasant trifling with the Dutch Renaissance in the new houses on West End Avenue. Broadway, till they began building the subway, was a grand avenue, lined with elms, big and little, and called by all good lower-class West Siders "the Bullavard." There was so little traffic then that bicycle-riders had the choice of Broadway itself or the finely gravelled bicycle path—not to be confused with the bridle path—which still runs, though most people have forgotten its original use, between the footpaths and the Drive on Riverside.

The gay, wicked world of fashion and sport hung with a sort of stale aura over my childhood; I boasted an aunt who crossed her legs, gingerly smoked Russian cigarettes, and occasionally was abandoned enough, after a cocktail or two, to expose her stockings fully three inches above the ankle. This world was, for me, secretly dominated by the masks and false faces that my grandfather, the headwaiter, would bring home after a celebration at Delmonico's, along with pâté de foie gras, boned turkey, and truffles; these masks were somehow of a piece with the writhing naked ladies and gentlemen that I beheld, at the timely age of four, on the walls of the saloon owned by John L. Sullivan's brother. There I shook hands with the great John L. himself. But I was more interested in the ladies and gentlemen painted in the style of Bouguereau than I was in Sullivan; maybe I suspected some sort of connection between them and the secretive, lemon-faced Wall Street brokers or the weather-beaten, healthy bookmakers who would dandle me on their laps at Asbury Park or Saratoga.

This New York of mine had outliers where the races were run: places called Sheepshead, Gravesend, Brighton Beach, Belmont Park, and in the summer it reached up to Saratoga Springs, still as lustrous in the early nineteen-hundreds as it had been directly after the Civil War. To match the brownstone fronts of the city, there were vast old-fashioned wooden hotels—the Brighton Beach, the United States, the Kensington, the old Fort William Henry at Lake George—with the coiled ropes by the bedroom windows which were to serve as fire-escapes for ladies who had been taught never to use their arms or to show their legs. And I still remember, with renewed grievance, the shuffleboard tables in the amuse-ment-rooms, tables which the grownups always unfairly persisted in monopolizing for themselves.

W E lived in a succession of brownstone houses and old-fashioned apartments, withdrawing to the latter only when the family fortunes dwindled, because, as my mother always used to explain, being in an apart-ment was not living, it was only existing. Most New Yorkers in that peri-od—the postwar shortage apparently broke the habit—preferred moving into a newly decorated place to having the painters and paperhangers in, unless they owned the house. And when one remembers the amount of bric-a-brac and drapery in the parlor alone, to say nothing of the gilt-framed prints—"Moonlight in Venice," "The Stolen Kiss," and of course Sir Luke Fildes's painting of the bewhiskered doctor at the bedside of the dying child—it is no wonder that people preferred to move. Moving was the only quick and tidy way of getting over the mess.

These brownstones were all pretty dreary houses. They were far too narrow and far too deep, and one room on each floor, called the music-room or the dressing-room or the storeroom, was always dark and airless. They had fireplaces that were not supposed to work, and a hot-air heating system that was supposed to work but didn't; also, they had speaking tubes between the floors which were neither private nor effective. Indeed, the only human and comfortable thing about them was the high stoop, where people could sit and cool off on a sweltering summer night; I can still recall with something that approaches tenderness riding on a push-wagon past the friendly groups that would sit on these stoops and drink beer or eat ice cream or sometimes break into song. But usually I think of those brown-stones in the gray November twilight, with the wind flickering the blue gas flame in the front hall when the door opened, and my associations are—Sherlock Holmes, Pimlico, the smell of roast-beef gravy, and Mme. Binner's corsets. Perhaps there is some connection.

Going to the race track, like going to the cemetery (the latter was a monthly or at least bimonthly excursion in my youth), was always a lark on account of the journey as well as the destination. Past Prospect Park, the houses gave way to open meadows and truck gardens, and the open Brooklyn trolleys, with their high steps, used to whizz through the placid countryside, with the wind bringing the delectable scent of cut grass or sea salt. Luncheons on the veranda of the Brighton Beach Hotel, with fried soft-shell crabs, whetted the appetite further for the excitement of the afternoon, the sight of one's favorite jockeys, Redfern and little Crimmins, and one's favorite horses—the great black Waterboy, who conquered at the long distances, and Sysonby, a small, low-lying Kentuckian that breezed through to a series of victories, only to end his career as a skeleton in the Museum of Natural History.

The visits to Woodlawn were not as exciting as those to the races, but they were very nice, too. Above MacCombs Dam Bridge, along Jerome Avenue, was also pure country, with the monument-makers and florists alternating, as one approached the cemetery, with the German roadhouses and beer gardens. The whole family would go on these excursions, with a sprinkling of aunts, uncles, and cousins. There would be remarks on how well the florist was keeping the grave-beds in order, on what sort of inscription my grandfather was to have, and on how—dear me!—the cemetery was filling up. After that there would be beer and sandwiches, perhaps sarsaparilla or ginger ale for the children, at one of the roadhouses, before starting home. At the age of four, I got my first lesson in the efficacy of abstract art at Woodlawn, for nothing that I had previously encountered in life struck such a deep note of horror in my soul as the draped urns on a pedestal that sometimes marked a grave. There was one near our family plot, and I learned never to look in that direction.

M Y grandfather, the headwaiter, was a gentleman of the old school, rigorous in his manners and easy in his morals. On the hottest summer evening he would never sit down to dinner in the bosom of his family without wearing a coat, nor would he come to table unless all the other males were equally clad. But he liked a broad story, as I know from the uneasy glances that were often cast at me, and from the number of times we children were helpfully ushered out of the room. In his time, he must have been a pretty gay dog—which is exactly what he looks like, with his black sideburns and his heavy, rakish eyebrows, in a little two-by-three photo-graph taken in the seventies. It was his custom to mix a large Manhattan cocktail for himself at ten-thirty every morning, but in his old age, at least, he was sober and moderate. He was no martinet; indeed, he had run out of Germany, where his father was a miller in the Black Forest, in order to escape the drill sergeant, and, like so many of the generation that came over between 1848 and 1870, he was a fine, upstanding man, with not a wrinkle of servility in him. Once, when he was the steward of a very wealthy club, the committee had come to him and explained that times were hard and that they would have to cut the salaries of all the employees, himself excepted. He answered stiffly that since he had the highest salary, they would please cut his pay first and take the largest amount from him, as he could afford it most easily. That shamed the committee into backing down on the whole business.

My grandfather retired voluntarily from Delmonico's at the age of sixty, with an income that not merely sufficed for his personal wants but enabled him to exercise little generosities, so that whenever he would call upon his old cronies, he would bring with him cigars or candy or cake. As a gentle-man of leisure, he would wear a cutaway coat in the afternoon, with a heavy gold watch chain spanning his lower vest pockets. When we walked in the seamier sections of the city, he would cover the chain up and never tell the time to inquiring strangers, for in the small-time gangsterdom of that peri-od, a gold watch chain or a watch was still considered good pickings.

Sometimes he would meet one of the waiters or the cooks in his circle, sauntering, like himself, in Central Park, and they would often be as rigor-ously dressed and as finely polished as he. I remember particularly the debonair Phillipini, then chef at Delmonico's, in a gray Prince Albert, with a gray hat to match his gray imperial, conversing with my grandfather in positively torrential French. Most of his friends, however, belonged to the cosmopolitanized Germans of New York, who had read Fenimore Cooper and George Sand in their youth, who liked freedom, and who had no illu-sions about Germany's greatness. While my grandfather sometimes conde-scended to take me to the Sängerbund Festival in Brooklyn after Christmas, with my Brooklyn cousin, he looked upon it as a joke and made fun of the sort of favors and candies they distributed to us. He liked the "Marseillaise" better than the "Die Wacht am Rhein," said *"Bonjour"* instead of *"Guten Tag,"* and preferred French food to German, although he had a weakness for green kern soup, *Hasenpfeffer*, and potato pancakes with applesauce.

My walks with my grandfather in Central Park were the background of my childhood. Central Park was not then the barren waste it became in the nineteen-twenties; the tall elms on the Mall were those that had been planted under Olmsted, and the paths in the Park were those that had been laid out by the authorities. We would stick close to the carriage drives on a fine spring afternoon, and watch the procession of open victorias, pulled by pairs of fat, chestnut geldings with docked black tails. He had served dinners and suppers in the houses of many of these people, and knew scores of them, at the very least, by sight. His attitude toward the rich was a sort of tolerant and kindly cynicism. My grandfather did not expect very much of these people, and was, therefore, never deeply disappointed in them, whereas my Brooklyn uncle, who used to be steward at the Harmonie Club, could never forgive the friendly banker who had unloaded some bad Interborough bonds on him when Uncle Frederick went to the banker for advice about placing his savings.

It was about 1905 that automobiles were becoming so common that crying "Get a horse!" didn't seem so funny any more. In fact, only a little later, one of my uncles, who manufactured cheap caramels with picture cards in the package, decided, on my advice, to introduce a series of automobile pictures, to follow those of the prize-fighters and the ball-players. The game of identifying automobiles started about 1908. Though there was pleasure in watching one's schoolmates eat the candy one's uncle had made, so to say, the caramels were not as satisfactory as the varicolored wafers with the taste of the gum on envelopes, or the black licorice shoestrings that most New York children used to eat—to say nothing of the papers of colored buttons that would melt in the mouth. I never tasted an all-day sucker, for some fiendish candy-store proprietor had circulated the rumor that if one took them out of the mouth, one got poisoned; and though boys often had to disgorge in the middle of a spelling lesson and still lived, I took that rumor seriously when I was young. There was a travelling waffle man who came around to our school in a high, white wagon about once a month. They were pale, oblong, flavorless waffles, at—I think—two cents each; but they were newly made and warm and dusted with powdered sugar, and his wagon would be mobbed. Among the other edibles that gladdened life were the sample packages of the new corn-flake breakfast foods. But none of these compared with the brilliant hard candies that Brummell's used to sell behind its glittering brass candy counters, next to Altman's, on Sixth Avenue. Across the street, at Siegel-Cooper's, was the great fountain with the gilded Statue of Liberty, where one could sit at tables and eat ices; but that extinct department store, like O'Neill's, like Adam's, like Ehrich's, was "low," and my sneaking pleasure in the fountain was never seconded by my mother.

Coney Island has become a little more elegant since the early nineteen-hundreds, but at that time Manhattan had its own Coney Islands. There was one up at Fort George, where there are now ramparts of apartment houses; it had a Ferris wheel and a rickety scenic railway, and tintype parlors galore; and there was another one, called Little Coney Island, between Broadway and Amsterdam Avenue, from 110th to 111th Streets. The latter had a dingy little wooden Mission House, to redeem the passing sinners, tucked away amid its peepshows and its shooting galleries, and perhaps they needed redemption. But it is not for its low character that I remember this part of New York, but for the rides on the miniature narrow-gauge railway that used to run under the 110th Street wall in Central Park.

L IKE every other West Side boy in my circle, from the age of ten onward, I frequented the vaudeville theatres on Saturdays and holidays, first at the old Colonial Theatre on Broadway at Sixty-second Street, then up at the Riviera at 96th Street and the Nemo at 110th Street. That was the great day of vaudeville, and the Colonial was part of our elementary education. I saw Vesta Victoria, and the swagger Vesta Tilley, and Anna Lloyd, and Pat Rooney and Marion Bent, and some of the best of the old-time monologists. I saw Eva Tanguay, too, when she rumpled her red hair and proclaimed that she was crazy. (Twenty years later, in a little four-a-day house in Pittsfield, I saw this same Eva, crying to an audience who had never known the thrill of her original abandon, "They say I'm crazy, but I don't care." It was pretty terrible, for the audience didn't understand, and they didn't care either.)

We would walk up Broadway after a vaudeville performance, on a cold December afternoon, humming "There was I, waiting at the church" or jauntily mimicking the debonair carriage of the latest magician, feeling very worldly, very cynical, and very full of quite juvenile anticipation of adventure, in which role one might be anything from a performer on the high trapeze to the Electrical Wizard who would supplant Edison. That feeling is probably the grip and high sign that bind in secret fraternity the West Side boys of my circle and generation. A lot of the things that puzzle our friends or mystify our wives or vex our mistresses could probably be explained in terms of our initiation in the vaudeville theatre. We are still seeking, in the stock market, the directors' meeting, the South African exploration, or the marriage bed, for the excitement of those Saturday afternoons.

The New York of my childhood slowly collapsed between 1905 and 1912. The Hughes anti-betting laws stopped the horse races; Schwarz's toy shop moved up from Twenty-third Street; the Singer Tower and the Woolworth Tower led that race upward which ended in the Empire State Building. Meanwhile Woodlawn was getting as crowded as the new subways; one needed a map, almost, to find one's way to the family grave. In 1912, the Kaiser turned down Lord Haldane's offer of peace, the Titanic crashed into an iceberg, and I smoked my first cigarette. That was the end of my New York childhood.

A NEW YORK ADOLESCENCE
TENNIS, QUADRATIC EQUATIONS, AND LOVE
DECEMBER 4, 1937

T OWARD the end of the first decade of the century, the horizons of New York visibly widened for me. My main activities ceased to be bounded by my neighborhood. Up to that time, one could be identified by the block one lived on. West Ninety-fourth Street boys were quite different in manner and social outlook and the ability to play one-old-cat from West Ninety-first Street boys, who were sissies, and we all would shrink into areaways or dive behind the portals of our apartment houses when the Ninety-eighth Street gang, tough, dirty, brutal, appeared on the scene. Occasionally friendships would break across block lines, but only rarely did they span a distance of more than a couple of blocks. It was like living in a walled town.

Adolescence and high school advanced together, although I don't think my voice broke or my legs became gangly till at least a year after I had left grammar school. When I was graduated from grammar school, we had sung a song at commencement about our eternal loyalty to dear old 166, but in our hearts we knew that in our part of the West Side one school was practically identical with another, whereas the high schools we had to choose from had names, not numbers, and each one had a collective character. Townsend Harris was almost collegiate in its standards, but, despite its playing fields on Convent Avenue, was terrible in sports. Commerce, at Sixty-fifth Street near Broadway, had a fine baseball team, and it turned out fellows who became bookkeepers, accountants, and male secretaries. De Witt Clinton, at Fifty-ninth Street near Tenth Avenue, was just literary, while Stuyvesant, which had a good basketball team and a new building, prepared people for engineering.

At the time the choice came to me, I was making clumsy models of airplanes on the lines of the Wright plane—models that would never fly in the air and would hardly even stay glued together in repose on my bedroom table. With the help of an old instrument-maker to whom Dr. Phillips, our family doctor, had introduced me, I had begun to rig up feeble little wireless sets with which I purposed to communicate with another ingenious lad in the next block, if either of us ever had the patience to master the Morse code. So I chose Stuyvesant. I think the good basketball team erased any lingering doubts I may have had about it.

Emerson used to say that the essence of a college education was having a room of one's own, with a fire, in a strange city. Going to high school on East Fifteenth Street, between Stuyvesant Square and First Avenue, gave me essentially the same sort of shock. In those days, the upper West Side had a fairly homogeneous population; there was the typical New York mixture of German and Irish stocks, interspersed with older branches of the American. Our fathers and mothers, at least, had usually been born in the United States, and in a class of forty boys, only eight or ten would be even identifiably Jewish, while the newer Russo-Polish migration was so sparsely represented that I can still remember the name of Malatzky, the bright, beady-eyed son of a glazier on Columbus Avenue.

Except for Broadway, which was very spottily built up until the opening of the subway in 1904 defined its new character, this part of the West Side had taken shape in the late eighties and nineties. The poorer classes lived on Amsterdam and Columbus Avenues: the cabmen and the clerks and the mechanics and the minor city employees. The rich lived in the big apartments on Central Park West or in the heavy, stone-encrusted mansions on Riverside Drive; between them, on the cross streets, and more sumptuously on West End Avenue, was the connecting tissue of the bourgeoisie, in brownstone rows whose dinginess was sometimes graced by some of the lighter-yellow, brick-and-limestone houses designed by Stanford White and his imitators. A boy growing up in such a neighborhood took middle-class comfort to be the dominant pattern of life, and except for an occasional twist of Irish, everyone spoke plain Manhattanese.

Suddenly I was thrown into a remote quarter of the city, and surrounded by a group of boys with foreign faces and uncouth, almost undecipherable accents and grubby, pushing manners: boys who ate strange food whose flavors pervaded their breath and seemed to hang about their clothes; boys whose aggressive vitality left me feeling like a sick goldfinch among a flock of greedy sparrows. One had to fend for oneself among people who had learned the art of survival in a far more difficult environment than I had come from, and in the lunch hour I would inevitably find myself near the tag end of the line that filed past the cafeteria counter, never capable of making decisions fast enough to get what I wanted before I was pushed beyond reach.

My school comrades were mostly the second generation of the great Russian and Polish Jewish immigration that had swept into the East Side after the assassination of Czar Alexander II. They had names like Moscowitz and Lefkowitz and Pinsky, and they had not merely learned in the settlement houses how to play circles round most of us in basketball or track sports, but they had an equally strenuous grip on the academic subjects. Indeed, most of them also excelled in the use of their hands, not having had so many of their manual opportunities shorn from them by solicitous parents and nursemaids. All in all, these boys were good stuff, but for one who had lived a more pallid existence, they were, during the first year, a little overwhelming.

My new schoolfellows brought the raw facts of life home to me with a rush. My own family knew the pinch of genteel poverty, but here was poverty on a grand scale, massive, extensive, blighting vast neighborhoods, altering the whole character of life, a poverty that, instead of shrinking submissively behind a false front, reached out into the city, creating its own forms, demanding, arguing, asserting, claiming its own, now busy with schemes for making money, now whispering the strange word Socialism as a key that would open the door. My political views were extremely conservative in those days; the rights of property seemed axiomatic; and I remember how shocked I was when I found out that one of my pals named Stamer, whose father was a Greenpoint cigarmaker of the old '48 German stock, was a Socialist. Stamer jarred my middle-class complacency with his scornful descriptions of what had hitherto seemed a reasonable and well-balanced world, and I was gradually unsettled in all my views, not so much through the strength of his arguments as through the obvious feebleness of my replies. Even a couple of teachers, quiet, upright men, were Socialists and would occasionally explain their views in class. I might have lived and died in my part of the upper West Side without realizing that neither the Democratic nor the Republican Party had ever recognized the Class Struggle.

Fourteenth Street, too, was something of an education for a provincial West Side boy. Tammany Hall still reigned in its dingy building near Third Avenue, embracing the old Tony Pastor's theatre, and almost across the way was Tom Sharkey's saloon, with a wide glass front, and the Dewey Theatre, painted white, where lurid posters of obese beauties, who did the belly dances that preceded strip tease, were spread before our gaze. "Don't do that dance I tell you Sadie, that ain't no business for a lady" was one of the popular songs of the period, and all of us knew, at least at second hand, how much farther Fourteenth Street went than Broadway's Sadie. My usual route to school was through Irving Place and along Fifteenth Street, because I discovered in my second year that a beautiful girl with austere white cheeks and black hair would pass me almost every morning on her way to the Quaker school at the corner of Stuyvesant Square. I can still see her graceful figure, in a blue serge dress, topped by a black hat with a jaunty feather, her poised, unhurried walk, and her slightly archaic inward smile, which was at once impenetrable and yet not indifferent, and I wonder now if I played anything of the part in her secret dream life that she did in mine.

When school was out, one would encounter in the same street, nearer Third Avenue, white-faced and heavily rouged prostitutes, no longer young, already on patrol. We knew what these ladies were, in a vague way; some of the boys, who lived on Forsythe or Chrystie Street, had even encountered them closer at hand in the halls of their own tenements; and we held a certain resentment against them because they were mainly responsible for the fact that we were not permitted to go out on the streets for lunch, but had to remain cooped in our building. The year after I was graduated, however, a new social ferment began to work in school. A group of boys rushed the teacher who was guarding the main door and broke for liberty during the lunch hour; this precipitated a school strike, and when the matter was settled the boys had won the right to eat outdoors. The squirrels in Stuyvesant Square benefited more by this arrangement, I am sure, than the painted ladies.

Often I preferred to spend my carfare on candy and walked home, usually with a couple of other lads. The path led diagonally across the city, sometimes up Broadway, sometimes around the open New York Central yards and across to Central Park. I watched the Public Library and the Grand Central Terminal during their building, and remember parts of Fifth Avenue below Fifty-ninth that were still lined with brownstone dwellings and plushy-looking mansions before which victorias and hansoms would stop, and the stages—as my mother still calls the buses—would roll by. Yet visually these walks remain dim, because so much of them, particularly when a sallow, evangelical boy named George Lush was along, was spent in talks about God and immortality and True Christianity. The openness of the midtown district then, its low buildings and the vast unbuilt spaces on Park Avenue, of course remain with me, for they were still visible when the Shelton was erected as late as 1924, but I dearly wish some heavenly stenographer would transcribe one of those theological debates for me. Both Lush and I were still pious lads. Could it be that we spent all those hours comparing the practices of the Baptists and the Episcopalians? Or were we battling with the Higher Criticism? I can't remember.

In grammar school, most of the male teachers were aged men, who had grown old in a profession they conducted with dignity untouched by inspiration—men who could remember the drafts riots, or the black-walled city that celebrated Lincoln's funeral. In high school, there were a lot of young teachers who brought into the place the contemporary flavor of Cornell, Chicago, or Wisconsin, as well as nearer universities, people who were stirred up over their subjects and who would break into their routine demonstrations in physics with hints of exciting scientific news that would not for a decade or more penetrate the textbooks—Einstein's first theory of relativity, or the electronic theory of matter, which made the old-fashioned doctrine of the indivisible atom look silly except as a convenience in writing chemical equations. Our principal, a sweet, portly man with a gray Vandyke beard and a bald head, was excited about science, too; he kept a class in physics for himself all through his principalship, and he would beam on us when he had made a good demonstration. Some of the more menial subjects in engineering, like mechanical drawing, seemed to attract routineers, but to make up for it, there were teachers in pattern-making or metal-turning who had worked with the Yale & Towne lock company or in the Baldwin Locomotive Works, and who were not tethered to the profession of teaching out of mere ineptitude for worldly tasks or for the sake of premature repose. As for the man who taught us forging, he was a German blacksmith of the old school, and his iron roses and scrolly leaves were our envy.

That a school so strenuously dedicated to science and the mechanical arts should have had a good English department was extremely fortunate for a lad whose mathematical aptitude waned shortly after he wrote his first love letter. The English teachers worked against odds, too, because the Board of Regents had chosen a lot of pretty stale literature for our edification, and it didn't help matters that, by some oversight, we had already gone through "The Lady of the Lake" and "Julius Caesar" in grammar school. But my teacher in freshman English, a rapt, brooding young man with a freckled face and a huge mop of carroty hair, encouraged a group of us to write a play, and from his lips I first heard the name of Bernard Shaw. That was what was important, as one looks back on it, in all the classes. Not the lesson itself, but the overflow—a hint, a pat on the shoulder, the confession of a secret ambition, a fragment of unposed life as someone had actually lived it.

I hated quadratic equations and I wasn't overly fond of geometry, but high school had none of the close-packed boredom that remains the chief impress of my earlier education. It was a big chunk of life to swallow, and maybe we were stretched a little too hard at study during a period when our bodies demanded a larger share of idleness and relaxation than we gave them. But there was no lack of intellectual stimulus in this new milieu. By the time we had visited foundries on the East River, practiced tennis on courts in Staten Island, travelling two hours for the sake of playing one, cheered baseball games in the Bronx, and dickered with one-horse job printers on John Street, we knew our way about the city and we knew a lot about what life had to offer ourselves and our fellows.

When I left high school, however, my ambitions had changed. I wanted to be a newspaperman as a first step toward becoming a novelist. Shep Friedman was then the city editor of the *Morning Telegraph*, and since he was a friend of the family, I kept on politely nagging him for a job for the next year or two. I would usually drop in around 6 P. M., before he had started the heavy business or the heavy drinking of the day, and although I was palpably a callow and ratty adolescent, he was always decent enough to drag me down to the corner bar for a friendly beer. After this he would give me a note of introduction to the most recent occupant of the *Evening Journal*'s city desk. Being idiotic as well as honorable, I never examined these notes. I suspect now that they said, "For God's sake dump this kid somewhere or drown him." At the end of six months I compromised with my ambitions and went on the *Evening Telegram* as copy boy for the lobster trick. My feelings were a little like those of a broken-down gentleman I once knew who was finally reduced to taking a job as dishwasher in a big hotel. But, he proudly explained to his friends, he was not an ordinary dishwasher; he washed only the dishes of the guests who were served privately in their rooms. It was understood that I was to become a cub reporter the first time someone moved up or out.

The job forced me to get up at 2:50 A. M., make my own breakfast, and catch a Sixth Avenue "L" to Herald Square. The back of our flat faced Columbus Avenue, and I could tell by leaning out the kitchen window and noting whether the passing train had green or white lights how much time I had left for finishing my cocoa. It made one feel slightly superior to be abroad in the city at that hour, before the milkman started on his rounds. The cold white flare of the arc lights intensified one's feeling of aloofness, and an occasional light in the bedroom of an otherwise darkened tenement house might even add a touch of mystery, hinting of someone in pain, someone quarrelling, someone dying or being born. But often I would be oblivious of the sleeping city because I was reading, with an indescribable priggish elation, a few pages in Plato or William James. Reading "A Pluralistic Universe" at 3:25 in the morning almost wiped away the humiliation of sweeping the floor and setting out the flimsy in the stale air of the city room half an hour later. If I happened to catch a train ten minutes earlier, I would encounter the last of the reporters, winding up their poker game in a corner of our common city room.

The *Telegram* was even in 1913 a pretty seedy sheet, but James Gordon Bennett was still alive, and some faint, ridiculous spark of his vindictive energy would cause an editor or a reporter suddenly to jump out of his skin. (Bennett was the same insolent devil who offered Stanley his old job on the *Herald* after he had found Livingstone and made himself famous.) At this time, the name Roosevelt was taboo; he could be referred to only as the Third Termer. Among other examples of Bennett's crotchets, there was an ice chest in one corner of the city room, which was duly filled with ice every day, supposedly because the Old Boy himself might suddenly appear and want ice for his champagne. Bennett's alpaca coat, too, hung on a hook in his private office, waiting. I rushed the beer and sandwiches and coffee while the night city editor was marking up the morning papers for the rewrite men. Even at that hour, the saloon on the northeast corner of Thirty-fifth Street would have a few stragglers in it. The rewrite men, who averaged around thirty-five dollars a week then—the night city editor got only fifty—used to tip me, too, even if I did read William James and sometimes do a stick or two of rewrite myself when one of the men got in late. If any small story broke in the neighborhood, I would be sent out to cover it, but a sewer explosion and a burning mattress were about all that came my way, and my pride suffered as my boredom grew, so I chucked the job after a couple of months. It was a cheap and harmless inoculation. I never looked for Life in newspaper offices any more, and thenceforward I read newspapers with a scorn and a skepticism born of intimacy. Had I not, when a freighter without a wireless sank near Halifax, seen a big front-page story manufactured in three-quarters of an hour out of a rewrite man's stinking clay pipe and his otherwise unaided imagination?

A LL this time, and for the next few years, I was studying at City College at night, from 7:30 to 10:20. In every way that was a remarkable experience, and one that only New York could have offered. Even New York could offer it only once, for the college I knew, with some five hundred students and a close, intimate life, disappeared—under mere pressure of congestion—within half a dozen years after its inception. It was one of those important experiments that the City College began before it went the way of other metropolitan institutions by succumbing to giantism. Dr. Stephen Duggan was the director and Dr. Frederick B. Robinson (he of umbrella memory) was then his assistant, an affable, clever man who was yet to disclose his remarkable talent for disingenuously setting a whole institution by the ears.

The students were mostly mature men, and they spoiled me for any other kind of undergraduate. One of them was a well-established maritime lawyer, with an argumentative Scotch tongue; another was a South

American consul; and there were doctors, brokers, accountants, engineers, as well as people almost as infirmly established as myself. Being under no obligations to regularity, I took my college education backward, skipping most of the freshman subjects and plunging into junior and senior cours-es in politics, philosophy, and English. In all the new plans for revising curricula that I have examined, not even Dr. Hutchins seems to have hit on this particular dodge, but perhaps it would work no worse for others than it did for me.

There is something amoeboid about the ordinary undergraduate, but we night students had a shape and a backbone and a definite point of view. Our discussions were battles, and though we often lived to change sides, there was nothing tentative or hesitating in our espousals; we did not suffer from the academic disease of evasive "open-mindedness." Our professors were men of character—men like Morris Cohen, who thought and taught out of a passion for things of the mind as pure as that of a Socrates or a Spinoza. There was Alfred Compton, a slim, sardonic gentleman with a touch of Robert Louis Stevenson about him. There was John Pickett Turner, a hand-some man with a massive dark head, a wart on his cheek, and shoulders of Platonic dimensions; he spoke with a Southern deliberation and enlivened his course on psychology with case histories drawn undisguised from his own life and marital experience. Even-handed and tolerant, he didn't quiver a hairbreadth when a sharp little Rumanian, Jallver, in the ethics class, declared that the *summum bonum* would be to die at the height of an orgasm in the arms of a beautiful woman. There was J. Salwyn Schapiro, one of the J. H. Robinson's brilliant disciples, who filled the air with epigrams and paradoxes, one of which seems even more startling in 1937 than it did in 1913—"The Constitution might be overthrown, but it could not be amend-ed." And then there was Earle Palmer, a little man with a drawn white face, hunched shoulders, and dark eyes that smoldered behind his glasses. He took us through Pancoast's anthology of poetry, living and enacting the poems, with an acrid humor in commentary that sprang out of passion rather than bitterness—a frail but ageless figure, half pixie, half demon, with the sudden dark touch of one who had not lightly triumphed over ter-ror and wrath and pain. My Harvard friends have overfilled me with tales about their famous Copey, but none of them has ever made me feel the least regretful that I missed the histrionic Harvard professor. One touch of Palmer's ruthless sincerity was at least half a college education.

The Trustees of City College had chosen a grand site for their new buildings when the college moved up from Twenty-third Street, and the architecture had a powerful effect when one climbed the hill past the Hebrew Orphan Asylum through the deepening October twilight and saw the college buildings, in their dark stone masses and white terra-cotta quoins and moldings, rising like a collection of crystals out of the formless rocks on the crest. Below, the plain of Harlem spread, a vapor of light beneath the twinkle and flood of a large beer sign. In the afterglow, or on a dark night, these buildings could awaken nostalgic memory as easily as those of Brasenose or Magdalen. Often we would accompany one of our professors to his home, along Convent Avenue or Broadway, or sometimes a group of us, heady with the discussions started in the classroom, would stalk down Riverside Drive, matching outrageous puns, arguing about free will and determinism, bursting into irrelevant song. It had the intimacy that only a small college can give, plus the variety and intensity of stimulus that come in a great city.

T HE other part of my adolescence, particularly in the earlier years, centred chiefly around the old tennis courts in Central Park on the south side of the transverse at Ninety-sixth Street. The courts were then covered with grass, and the most popular court, half-denuded by constant playing, was called the dirt court. An aged keeper, with a gray beard spattered with tobacco juice, had charge of the marking of the courts and the stowing away of the nets. He was probably one of those Civil War pensioners who were still favored on the public payrolls, and we called him "Captain," but he had a vile temper and carried on an uncivil war of his own with most of the people who played there. He was often drunk, and the white lines he marked with his sprinkler showed no disposition to follow the straight and narrow path, but this crusty character gave the place a certain flavor which contrasts with the colorless, antiseptic courtesy of today. We couldn't start playing till the Captain raised the flag on the flagpole.

It was a queer gang that hung around the courts in those days—a few newspaper reporters on the *American* and the *Press*; a theatrical agent

whom we called Ted; a little hunchback with no visible occupation, whom
we called Dirty Ferdie; a few semi-professional loafers who used to play
for stakes; and a handful of young women who were usually attached to the
older men, ancients who might be at least thirty years old, as well as a few
boys of my own age who took tennis very seriously. Day after day through
the muggy summer we would lounge around on the hill behind the dirt
court, and play, and lounge, and play again till we could scarcely drag our
feet around the court. This was a complete, self-contained world; even on
a rainy day, we would come over to the courts with our racquets, sprawl-
ing on benches beneath the trees toward the reservoir, speculating on the
weather. When the males were alone, the conversation would often
descend to basement level, and I would go home with new words I could-
n't find in the ten-volume Century Dictionary, sometimes with lickerish
hints about aspects of life I hadn't the faintest clue to till I studied abnor-
mal psychology. On the whole, perhaps it was a good thing we played so
much tennis.

I don't know if I can convey the precise flavor of the city that one
inhaled on those Central Park courts in my day. It was perhaps closest to
what one feels on a clean, sunny beach onto which the ocean periodically
washes stale watermelon rinds, mildewed oranges, and discarded paper
boxes. There was nothing particular in my immediate life to make me look
naturally for meanness or sordidness or dishonesty, but constant hints of
these things seeped in from the world around me. By the time I was fifteen,
I had acquired a layer of protective cynicism that would have honored the
proverbial cub reporter, and my tennis coach in high school, an excellent
English teacher named Quimby, once said in perfectly justifiable horror,
"You talk like a disillusioned man of sixty." Yet with all my early knowing-
ness, I went through the first experience of being in love at fifteen—with
Sybil, a girl I met at the tennis courts—as if all my life had been spent
among the innocents of Arcadia. The other day I attended a singing festival given by the girls in one of our municipal colleges, a charming mass of
hussies whose dance routines would have done credit to Broadway. In the
very alluring performance they put on, in the songs they had made up, I
detected the same combination of virginity and cynicism, of chastity and
shamelessness—the curious patina of hardness that forms over youth in the

big city. They were exquisitely young and fresh, yet already they were a little cheapened, a little soiled.

My own girl was one of those ruthless beauties who are never at ease unless they put five or six men simultaneously in a state of torture. With one, she danced for tango prizes in the footsteps of Irene Castle; with another, she swam; with another, she went to football games. She had us all, in fact, pretty well specialized and subordinated, and it was usually for one of the older lads that she reserved her emotional complications. If I began earlier and remained on the scene longer than any of her other young admirers, it was because I served as a sort of fixed spar to mark the height of the incoming or the ebbing tide. Every once in a while she would cling to me to get her bearings. My specialty was playing tennis on the courts near Morningside Park, a few blocks from her apartment, at six in the morning, before she started her day as artist's model. It was perhaps the only time in my life, except in the Navy, that I visibly profited by my gift of waking up easily.

I can't pretend that there was anything very typical of New York in this relationship. The closest it came to taking on the color of the city was one hot summer night, on a street swarming with children and inundated by a hurdy-gurdy thumping out "Cavalleria Rusticana," when I told her I wanted to marry her. She was very self-possessed about that. She sent me round the corner for some ice cream, which the dealers then used to heap up in flimsy paper boxes, and then she took me up to the roof of her apartment house, a flight higher than the elevator went, so that we could talk matters over while we dipped, turn and turn, into the ice-cream box. The thick summer sky flared to the east with the lights of Harlem, and on this high roof one had a sense of separation from the rest of the world one usually doesn't achieve in Nature at a level lower than five thousand feet. But nobody ever succeeded in making love convincingly when his hands were all sticky from ice cream. Perhaps Sybil knew that when she complained about the heat. On her telling me what good friends we would always be—pals, in fact—I abruptly left her, and went down onto the steamy pavement, on which big raindrops were beginning to spatter, feeling dramatically solemn. The same tune—probably from the same hand organ—was still clanging in the distance. And I was already sketching in my mind the first act of a play to be called "Love on Morningside Heights."

1931~32

Mumford took over "The Sky Line" as the worst effects of the depression were being felt in New York City and across the United States. Except for Rockefeller Center and an assortment of public works, virtually no new construction was under way; earlier projects such as the Empire State Building were completed but under-leased. Mayor James Walker led a city with swollen relief rolls and a jobless rate approaching one-quarter of the population. In June 1931, Mumford wrote his first piece for the magazine, assessing the plans for Rockefeller Center. His first "Sky Lines," critiques of the George Washington Bridge and New York Hospital, appeared later that fall. A review of the Museum of Modern Art's Modern Architecture: International Exhibition and several omnibus pieces were published in the spring of 1932.

FROZEN MUSIC OR SOLIDIFIED STATIC?
REFLECTIONS ON RADIO CITY
JUNE 20, 1931

WHEN the plans for Radio City were first announced a healthy reaction expressed itself: no one liked them. Half the reasons for not liking them were, perhaps, as indefensible as the plans and buildings themselves; but the point is that everyone had a sense that a great opportunity had been lost. There was nothing surprising about Radio City except the fact that it looked exactly like the helter-skelter, hit-or-miss constructions that make up the rest of the city. But for the fact that the three biggest office buildings on the site were grouped around a tiny plaza, there was small evidence of any underlying unity of conception. Park Avenue, before 1925, was more unified.

WHAT was wrong? Let us begin at the beginning. The architects started with three almost empty blocks, running from Forty-eighth Street to Fifty-first Street. On the Sixth Avenue side they touch the unkempt fringe of the theatre district; in Fifth Avenue they face Saks and St. Patrick's. The name Radio City derives from the fact that, at an early stage in the project, someone had the notion of dedicating this site to radio broadcasting, and with the prospect of television not very distant, had conceived of putting vaudeville theatres and the Metropolitan Opera House on the same site.

Three buildings were dedicated on the original plans to administration offices for various amusement industries; two sites were planned for theatres; one was tentatively allotted to the opera house; one building—on the original model an oval structure between Forty-ninth and Fiftieth Streets in Fifth Avenue—was to house a bank, shops, and showrooms; two forty-five-story buildings, in Forty-eighth and Fifty-first Streets respectively, and a large building between Fiftieth and Fifty-first Streets in Fifth Avenue, were to serve as offices, too; later it was announced that one of these skyscrapers might serve as a parking garage. This left one large unassigned site in the middle of the northernmost block.

Is it all clear? I have forgotten to say that the ground area is approximately the equivalent of ten Graybar Building sites or thirteen Chrysler Building sites. This is another way of saying that the site of Radio City is larger than Madison Square Park, and that this is the first time that any such tract has been cleared away in the middle of the city for development as unit. The architects who are handling this job are: Reinhard & Hofmeister, Corbett, Harrison & MacMurray, and Hood & Fouilhoux.

In the first glow of publicity one got the impression that Mr. John D. Rockefeller, Jr., who had leased this huge tract from Columbia University, had started out to do a handsome thing for the city. When the tomatoes and catcalls that greeted the project became visible and audible, a second barrage of publicity was laid down, to show that Mr. Rockefeller intended nothing of the kind. Mr. Rockefeller was a practical man; his architects were practical men; from first to last, the grand idea was in the hands of practical men. They all had a duty to the great university which transcended any minor public interests they might wish to promote; namely, they must do nothing which would prevent a large increase of land values during the term of the lease. "The importance of these income-producing considerations," Mr. L. A. Reinhard has admirably observed, "cannot be stressed too much." They account for the masterful clot of congestion that the architects have produced.

In other words, Radio City is to be no different in character from any other part of the city. If that had been made clear at the beginning, public expectation might have been dulled, and public disappointment might not have been so keen. I use the subjunctive mode advisedly. There was something in those three free blocks, without building lines, without serious encumbrances, that stirred the imagination. Given the possibility of treating those blocks as a unit, people willfully, unfairly, unreasonably thought that they could expect a touch or two of public spirit from Mr. Rockefeller or from whoever is finally responsible for the development. To give a chance to sound planning, to show that intelligence and public interest are not ultimately a great financial handicap, to do these things even if the last million were not wrung out of ground values—was that expecting too much? Of course it was. There were a dozen obstacles to any such reasonable result. Let us consider a few of them.

F IRST of all there is Mr. Rockefeller himself. He is a rich man, and there must be a special choir of angels who see that rich men do not acquire any illusions of omnipotence when they are in the act of assembling large city building sites. Mr. Rockefeller's particular thorn was the church on the corner of Fifth Avenue and Forty-eighth Street. It was doubtless very good for his soul that the Church of St. Nicholas should be as firm as the Rock of St. Peter; but it would be a handicap to the best architects in the world to have the most important corner of their project taken out of the picture. In point of fact, the whole Avenue frontage from Forty-eighth Street to Forty-ninth Street will remain in other hands; and the sting of this is not lessened by the recent building of an excellent period reproduction— Modernique, 1925—on the Forty-ninth Street corner. That was a bad start.

Our great patron has apparently another unfortunate defect, which he shares with perhaps the majority of his fellow-citizens: he likes the wrong kind of architecture. In the first announcements about Radio City it was pointed out that Mr. Rockefeller, after a winter out in Egypt, had suggest- ed an Egyptian style of architecture for the steel-framed skyscrapers which the practical men assigned to the site. One wonders that someone did not think immediately of the Pyramids, and discover that their setback exactly met the restrictions of the zoning law. No one thought of a Pyramid or tried to render it, to suit modern urban conditions, as a Babylonian zikkurat; but that didn't help matters much. Mr. Rockefeller, it will be recalled, wishes generously to replace the Barnard Cloisters, the most perfect museum in the city, with a "genuine" Gothic building—something like the Riverside Church, one has every reason to fear. Alas! that his taste in architecture is not to be compared with his father's taste in university presidents or direc- tors of medical research!

R EAL-ESTATE experts, salesmen, radio executives, and miscellaneous roxies dictated the number and kind and height of buildings that would be immediately profitable, according to their usual short-sighted and somewhat superstitious canons, in Radio City: there was nothing left for the architects and Mr. Rockefeller except the trimmings. Under pressure of public opinion, the architects went into retirement after the announcement of the first tentative scheme, for the purpose, one supposes, of doing over the trimmings. I hope Mr. Rockefeller will be suited in the end, and I am sure that he will. Whether the result be called Egyptian or Classic or Modern will not matter very much. The question has nothing essentially to do with architecture; for architecture is concerned with the order and disposition of the whole—and that had been settled a long time before, when it was decided that the project was to be merely practical.

Are the practical men practical? That is another question. The practical men are probably no more practical than the modern architects are modern. Here was a grand chance for Mr. Harvey Wiley Corbett to embody his almost religious belief that the skyscraper of the future would house a variety of functions under its lofty roof; here was a chance for Mr. Raymond Hood to put one tall building in the midst of an open square, as he has frequently advocated; neither of these dreams came off. Instead, there are three super-skyscrapers and a pocket handkerchief of open space called a plaza. This creation of congestion was, as the architects have repeatedly pointed out, deliberate. When they add, as Mr. Reinhard has done, that while "traffic is an unsolved problem in New York, it was, however, given much thought in the planning of this group" one can find only an ironic humor in the statement. Having piled more buildings on this site than could be accommodated by a dozen streets of the normal width—New York was designed, in 1811, for buildings from four to six stories high— they have eased the congestion of crosstown traffic by widening two of the streets...fifteen feet!

THE practical men, whose astuteness consists in picking up and assembling small parcels of land, and piling them with towers more topless than Ilion's, are really not to be trusted with a large plot of ground. There is not an office building in the city, according to the best business and architectural advice I have been able to gather, that is anything except an extravagance and a non-negotiable jewel when it pushes beyond the fortieth story; the losses may be written off as advertisement, or, with the large margin of safety under which these investments are made, they may be covered up by the general success of the building, but still the upper stories are an extravagance. Of all possible forms of office building, the tower is the most wasteful of elevator space in proportion to floor coverage. Let us not speak of the benefits of vertical transportation; under our present building code it is limited to the dizzy rate of less than nine miles per hour, and when one allows for stops and waits it compares pretty unfavorably with the lamest forms of horizontal transportation. The architects who have put forth vertical transportation as a remedy for street congestion—which in turn is caused by this very overcrowding of the land—are only having their little joke.

In other words, the tall skyscraper is the businessman's toy, his plaything, his gewgaw; in an expansive mood, he calls it alternately a temple or a cathedral, and he looks upon the romantic altitudinous disorder of a modern city with the same blissful feeling that the Victorian industrialist had for his factory chimneys, belching forth soot and foul gases. The skyscraper makes him feel prosperous even when he is losing money on it. In the interests of congestion, the businessman is willing to make the streets impassable, lose thousands of dollars a day in lost motion and delay, waste millions in building more subways to promote more congestion, and in general to put up with any and every sort of nuisance, so long as he can feed his inflated romantic dream.

The tallest building in Radio City is to be sixty-eight stories high and to have more floor space than the Empire State Building. When the crosstown traffic permanently blocks the downtown traffic in our main avenues, as happens so frequently, although temporarily, already, and when queues form at the subway stations at five o'clock to permit entrance, or when—as ominously threatens now—we begin to reckon the costs of this financial inflation, the practical man may finally come down to earth. At present he is still in Cloudcuckooland. It was by the canons of Cloudcuckooland that Radio City was designed.

I N criticizing the projected development of Radio City I am not taking sides with those who wished to turn it into a Place de l'Opéra. That might have been fun; but it is perhaps even more important that someone with a little financial margin should play with the idea of a really practical layout for shops, offices, restaurants, theatres, once the need for paying attention to awkward and cramped lot sizes and conflicting property interests was eliminated. Buildings proportioned to the traffic space available, buildings with exits that did not get congested, buildings that were properly oriented and would give daylight and fresh air to the denizens who now work in their stuffy interiors and would provide plenty of roof space for noonday recreation—what would these look like?

With such questions in view, the solution might have been a shallow continuous palisade of ten-story buildings around the perimeter of the whole tract, shutting out the incongruous jangle of buildings that are already in Forty-eighth Street and that presently will be everywhere. Within would be a large quiet tract: here might have been the auditoriums, the theatres, the stores, the shops, and, one hopes, the easily accessible roof-gardens and restaurants. What a relief after the razzle-dazzle of height: what a relief not by any chance to have one's meal spoiled by the sight of the latest golden pinnacle or Gothic crown!

I am not proposing this as a solution. Half a dozen other rational solutions present themselves; such as, for example, rows of office buildings properly oriented north and south, with private streets between, affording entrances to the theatres and shops that would space these tiers of commercial buildings: that would be another kind of order. All I wish to do is to indicate the difference between the fundamental architectural and civic problem that Radio City might have attacked, and the financial criteria that actually dictated the present designs. The great dictum that form must follow function is a sound one only if the architect has a share in criticizing and determining the functions he serves.

If we are all a little huffed about Radio City it is not, certainly, because the architectural conception is modern, but rather because it is very old-fashioned. We cannot join with the architects in accepting the conditions that Mr. Rockefeller and his advisers laid down. The proper answer to this is that we expected something better. We could pay no higher compliment to Mr. Rockefeller than to protest against his curious picture of himself as a private citizen, and to refuse to accept a plan that leads nowhere except back again into the chaos from which we should like to emerge. If Radio City, as now forecast, is the best that could be done, there is not the faintest reason for anyone to attempt to assemble a big site. Chaos does not have to be planned.

T HE George Washington Bridge now marks high water in current architecture. This statement is something of a paradox, for the bridge is sheer engineering, and such architectural treatment as has been planned for the bridge proper would probably only take away from its present beauty. Fortunately, the tradition of anonymity, which has died out in architecture, still clings to engineering and the allied arts. How many people know that this bridge was designed and built by Mr. Othmar Ammann for the Port of New York Authority.

The new bridge was opened a century after John A. Roebling, the founder of the organization that erected it, came to America. The Niagara Bridge, the Brooklyn Bridge, and the Philadelphia-Camden Bridge are some of the landmarks that give a sense of the steady progression that has taken place in the technique of bridge-building. The George Washington Bridge is now the best around the waters of New York, and that is no mean praise; for the oldest of them all, the High Bridge, before the army engineers butchered it to facilitate navigation, was the finest monument in stone created before the Civil War, and old John Roebling's Brooklyn Bridge is perhaps the most satisfactory example of American art in the nineteenth century.

O NE could hardly have guessed from the first designs how good the new bridge would be. Originally the very element that gives the towers such interest and unifies the vertical and horizontal elements—namely, the steelwork itself—was to be hidden behind a facing of stone, designed by Mr. Cass Gilbert. Happily for the aesthetic success of the bridge, the stonework would cost more than two million dollars, and this part of the program was suspended. Let us hope that the lack of funds will last long enough to abolish in everyone's mind the notion that the steel should be encased.

The critical point in the design of a suspension bridge is the relationship of the cables and the piers. While Roebling apparently solved this problem in the original Niagara Railroad Suspension Bridge, which was demolished in the eighties, none of the later bridges followed this solution. Even the Brooklyn Bridge fell down at this point: the heavy masonry cornice spoiled the line of the cables and gave no indication of their continuous passage across the vertical support. As far as the eye could gather, each end of the cable might have been embedded separately in the pier. In the Manhattan Bridge, the big globes atop the piers were irrelevant and worthless; in the Williamsburg Bridge, the cage-effect spoiled the flow of the cables.

M R. Ammann's solution of this problem is excellent. The cables are carried on the cradle over the tower in full view: for once one sees a suspension bridge aesthetically as well as mechanically in a state of suspension. And that is the whole point—the point that our bridge-builders have, with every good and honorable intention, so steadily missed. The square-shouldered towers are plainly there to carry the weight; in masonry these towers would look more bulky, but they could not possibly seem more sturdy and firm-set. At no other point in the design does one have the faintest feeling of weight: the cables draping themselves in a catenary curve—the curve made by a chain hanging between two fixed points—seem doubly delicate in contrast with the broad steel trusses of the towers.

The span itself forms another delicate line, almost tangent to the arc of the cables. Contrast this with the clumsy Peekskill Bridge: the smaller structure gives a far greater impression of weight, load, effort. In the new bridge one notices the weight the cables carry as little as one notices the speed of a high-powered car on a smooth concrete road: the very quality of effortlessness is part of the aesthetic effect. Here is that resolution of conflicting impulses in an harmonious order, which Messrs. Ogden and Richards, in "The Foundations of Aesthetics," have sought to show is the very soul and body of any aesthetic achievement. And how much this nonchalance, this sense of fluent ease, is due to the fact that the line of the cables is unbroken. Result: the profile from the river is perfect.

S INCE the approach to the bridge is still unfinished, one need say nothing about its present unsatisfactory state: the abrupt change from the ramp to the tower on the Manhattan side now creates a sharp right angle which cries for some transitional buttress. The towers themselves straddle the bridge in such a fashion as to bring the cables on either side of the inner arch; the head-on effect is therefore not quite as happy as in the different design of the Brooklyn Bridge. But all in all the structure is a delight to the eye: a piece of harmonious and imaginative engineering, the like of which is not yet to be found in any of our skyscrapers.

THE Starrett Lehigh Building is another victory for engineering. It is a multiple factory building that goes from Eleventh to Thirteenth Avenue in Twenty-sixth and Twenty-seventh Streets; the architects are Cory & Cory. Here a cantilevered front has been used, not as a cliché of modernism, but as a means of achieving a maximum amount of daylight and unbroken floor space for work requiring direct lighting. The aesthetic result is very happy indeed. The contrast between the long, continuous red-brick bands and the green-framed windows, with sapphire reflections or depths, is as sound a use of color as one can see about the city. The north side of the structure is genuinely exciting: here the requirements of the building code have created a setback of the otherwise unbroken upper windows, and the curved passage has been very ably handled.

Across the way from the Starrett Lehigh Building is an admirable old warehouse of the eighties, with solid brick walls, grudgingly punctuated with windows: the contrast between the two structures points not merely to different functions, but to an essential difference between the old architecture, with its emphasis on the wall, and the new architecture, with its interest in the opening. There is one weak point in the newer building: in what is apparently a section for administrative offices on the south side, the rhythm of the building is broken: the windows are narrow and high, and the vertical effect is heightened by feeble tabs of ornament on the uppermost walls. Even granting the difference in purpose between the factory section and the offices, there was no reason for breaking the horizontal accent—still less for spoiling the noble severity of the façade. Had the interest that went into this ornament been spent in marshalling into an effective design the rabble of water tanks on the top of the factory building, the effort would have been better spent. But the notion that ornament is architecture and that vertical lines are sacred to office buildings somehow dies hard.

THE SKY LINE
THE MODERN HOSPITAL
DECEMBER 12, 1931

THE view of the towers of Manhattan from the Queensboro Bridge now rivals that from the Brooklyn Bridge. Indeed, with the building of giant structures near the lower waterfront, the masses no longer rise so eloquently as they did when Front Street was regular and low, and the Woolworth Tower was the last and highest peak of the range that started at the Battery. But the truth is that accidental picturesqueness is a bad formula for city development: for accidents quickly pass, and cannot be recovered—except by accident. At present, the finest pile of unpremeditated beauty stretches through the Forties; yet the most impressive element in the panorama from the bridge is one that is least dependent upon mere chance. I mean the group of monumental structures which form the new Cornell Medical Centre.

VIEWED from above Welfare Island, or approached along Avenue A, this Medical Centre is equally effective; whatever one *thinks* about the architecture, the immediate effect is indisputably exhilarating. Sheer white walls; tall glass bays jutting out from the central mass; uninterrupted vertical openings, forming in appearance but not in fact a solid glass wall—coming upon these buildings from the sordid streets around the bridge, dominated by the gasworks, is like leaving a dirty third-class railway carriage and suddenly beholding the ice-fields and the summit of a glacier. The central building seems even higher than it actually is, by reason of the lines of lower buildings, regimented in the foreground on the river and on Avenue A. Here one has a chance to see again how important a uniform building height and a well-scaled repeating unit are to any massive architectural effect. Many of our New York architects are so used to working within cramped building lines, so much of their ability consists in squeezing out from an inadequate site the last square foot of rentable space, so much are they accustomed to regard building as a form of competitive advertisement, that they have no conception of how to deal with a unified whole. Is it altogether an accident that the architects of the Cornell Medical Centre are a Boston firm: Coolidge, Shipley, Bulfinch & Abbott?

This whole group of buildings is so nearly good that one resents the blemishes one detects on nearer view. Why on earth, for example, did the architects terminate their vertical window panels with pointed arches? This strikes one like a touch of Wardour Street English in the midst of a straightforward piece of modern prose. The attempts at expressive ornament, in the form of a sunburst wall pattern, spoil the calm surfaces of the walls themselves; never was gilt so badly wasted on a lily. These touches are all the more disappointing because the essential ornament has been handled so well: the white façades, for example, are not a dead white; they are a living white composed of four different shades of brick. Fine bands of stone neatly mark the rooflines. Though few people will stop to examine the infinite preciosity of pattern in the bricks, it must have given both the architects and the bricklayers a great deal of satisfaction; there is nothing better in the city.

But the crowning mistake of the superficial design is the termination of the central mass. Following Mr. Raymond Hood's sensible precedent in the Daily News Building, the architects made no attempt to "finish it off": the wall comes to an end without visible punctuation marks. But the upper part is broken by a series of tall, narrow, ogive windows with deep reveals. This gives the effect of masonry construction, and the building has a curiously top-heavy look; for the beauty of the lower part of the building is due to the fact that the architects have zealously contrived to give the impression of great lightness and airiness. This effect of lightness might have been increased at the top by the more extensive use of glass; but even if, for interior reasons, this were not desirable, every possible means should have been taken to reduce the apparent solidity of the wall.

So much for one's first impressions. When the Centre is opened in the fall of 1932, it will be worth another inspection from the inside out. Meanwhile, one thing is certain: if the interior is as good as the exterior, an attack of appendicitis in the Cornell Medical Centre will be more endurable than an attack of boredom in Radio City.

AFTER looking repeatedly at the great mass of limestone at No. 1 Wall Street, with its air of expensive solidity, I feel like congratulating Messrs. Voorhees, Gmelin & Walker on quite another kind of building: their small Institute for the Crippled and Disabled on the corner of Twenty-third Street and First Avenue. This plain, simple, elegant, workmanlike building, with its generous window spaces and its fine command of standard materials and units, is the nicest refutation I know of all the studied artfulness and costly fancywork that went into the Irving Trust Company Building. No. 1 Wall Street is a work of the untrammelled imagination: it is not factual, *sachlich*, economic, or functional, and I can fancy that the designers took great pleasure in all the leeway they had—although from my standpoint it was just so much rope to hang themselves with. By creating a scalloped façade of concave stone, the architects succeeded in making a steel-frame building with a curtain wall look like a solid pile of stone; but why? Chaste though that exterior is, it is mere swank, and unconvincing swank at that. The Irving Trust Company Building is only a more refined and subtle version of the notion that modern domestic life can be happily encased in Ye Olde Tudor Manor House—and if we believe this, where are we?

In building the little Institute, the architects were probably confined and harassed at every point by limitations of funds and by special medical requirements in the program; but the result is a sincere and straightforward achievement, done entirely in harmony with the needs and essential beliefs of modern life, a happy contribution to that new "vernacular of the machine" which has begun to appear. The fact is that the untrammelled imagination is never to be trusted with a building; what Goethe said once of literature applies equally to architecture: it is by his restrictions that the master first discloses himself. I remember congratulating an architect once upon a little church I like to look at every time I ride on the Harlem Division of the New York Central. "Yes," he answered, "that turned out very well; for once we weren't handicapped by having too much money to spend."

THE SKY LINE

THE other day a learned critic informed me that the window panels of the Cornell Medical Centre, whose brickwork and white monumentality I had praised, were deliberately modelled after the Palace of the Popes. This fully explains the feeling of intellectual dissatisfaction which went along with the direct sensory appeal of these structures, particularly at a distance: for architecture is more than a series of tricks worked on the eye in the open air, and if a building doesn't bear thinking about, its foundations are shaky. How much of the Cornell Medical Centre will stand detailed rational criticism? I wonder. Why do these buildings run predominantly, not north and south, but east and west, thus leaving a good part of the interior without direct sunlight at any time of the day? Why do the glass bays, which look magnificently open, have so little actual window space? I might have kept these questions under my belt until I had examined the interior and had opportunity to compare the internal functions with the external design; but the suspicion that the Palace of the Popes had as much to do with the façades as the actual hospital requirements spoils one's appetite a little. Perhaps this is just a big whitewashed brother to the new library at Yale—a ghastly thought. I have changed my mind, at all events, about enjoying an illness here. One might ask for a bath and find oneself in a baptismal font.

THE city has been blossoming cantilevered fronts this past year, some good, some bad, some real, some faked. For the benefit of the completely uninitiated, I should perhaps explain the mysterious word "cantilever." Usually the floors are supported at the outer wall by columns; but it is possible to support them by means of what is in effect a bracket—the upright member being in this case anywhere from two to twelve feet in back of the window. This permits an unbroken horizontal window, and a maximum amount of light on the space between the window and the first columns. At times, this mode of construction is uneconomical and senseless; sometimes it is not suited to the actual function of the room; but at other times it is useful and elegant. When used by a duffer to give a building a "modern" look, the cantilevered front must, of course, be dismissed as unworthy decoration.

One of the most adroit and handsome examples of good cantilever construction is the little shop building that Thompson & Churchill have designed for the northwest corner of Fifty-seventh Street and Lexington Avenue; it is now finished. Here the whole exterior wall is hung from the sixth story, an ingenious method of construction that was worked out by the coöperating engineer, Mr. Charles Mayer. The windows alternate horizontally with bands of cream tile, whose upper border of green is repeated throughout the top band. All the materials are drawn from regular stock patterns; the individuality of the building is due to the skill of the designer, Mr. Henry Churchill, in assembling and appropriately relating these standardized parts. The elements of this little building have been thought through and, on the whole, very effectively expressed.

Objection to this form of construction comes from those who cling to a vertical theory of design, derived from masonry construction, in which the outer wall actually bore a good part of the load and became solider and thicker as it approached the ground. But the notion that the human eye demands such evidence of support is absurd. One must be morbid on the subject of empathy to feel that a cantilevered structure *looks* as if it would collapse. After all, a tree is a system of cantilevers, and the eye does not demand that the outermost branches be held up by posts.

So far, indeed, have we renounced the desire for visible means of structural support that the architects of the new building across the way, the Firm of Ely Jacques Kahn, have actually concealed the columns on the ground floor behind mirrors, which give a maximum of invisibility. This building, too, is worth more than a passing glance: the windows, designed in large panels that include two floors, give the effect of a single unit through the use of black glass spandrels; as a result, the design seems more open than it actually is. Whatever decorative interest the façade possesses is due to the rust-colored shades and to the play of the vertical lines of the steel window frames against the horizontal lines of the brick. To see how far 1931 edged away from picture-book romanticism, one should compare this building with the apartment house on the southwest corner of Fifty-seventh Street and Seventh Avenue: the external designs are closely parallel, but the expression is entirely different. At least the medieval iron lace has disappeared.

T HIS same firm has designed still another building, the Commerce Building at 155 East Forty-fourth Street, in a fashion that must call forth praise, not perhaps so much for what is done, but for all the things that have happily been left undone or have been eliminated. The shape of the Commerce Building is undistinguished: its setbacks seem plainly determined by the building regulations. The windows are undistinguished, too: they are a simple repetitive unit in a brick wall. It is just an office building, capable of being divided into a maximum number of cubicles. That is not much? In plan or in expression, I grant that it is not much, but in spirit the Commerce Building seems to me to tower miles above its competitors. First of all, it is an office building, not a cathedral, an advertising symbol, a monument to prosperity, an unusable landing place for illusory dirigibles, or a pathological symptom of somebody's repressed desires. The lobby does not remind one of the nave of Winchester Cathedral or the foyer of the Roxy: its polished stone walls and its low glass ceiling merely mark it as a place where one may get in and out of elevators. It is scarcely fair to call undistinguished a building where the elements that have been left to the discretion of the architect have been carried through so handsomely. (Consider the imposing three-story entrance, which actually does not slice off more than three or four feet of usable depth.) But as a matter of fact, to call a business building undistinguished should be high praise: what we need is less individual fireworks and noise, and more quiet honesty, decency, and urbanity; more clever economy and less bombast and futile expense. The skyscraper as a form has encouraged every species of romantic extravagance; but the day of reckoning is now here, and such a return to sobriety as the Commerce Building indicates in its decorative aspects is a welcome sign.

ORE than a generation ago, Samuel Butler set people talking about "unconscious humor." Perhaps the most interesting buildings in New York at present come under the head of unconscious architecture. There are plenty of recent examples: When the scaffolding was still up around the mooring mast of the Empire State tower it was far better in design than the structure that was finally revealed. An even handsomer example of unconscious work existed when the steeple of the Collegiate Church of St. Nicholas, at Fifth Avenue and Forty-eighth Street, was being repaired and was enveloped in spidery metal rods.

For the moment, our unconscious architecture has gone Surréaliste: indecent and extravagant, like the dreams a dutiful patient prepares for a psychoanalyst. The printmakers have long been aware of the nightmarish chimney that leans against the downtown site of the Queensboro Bridge; but just above the Bridge, on a wide expanse of waterfront, is an old crenellated tower, the last survival of the brewery that once sprawled over this scene. With a prancing white horse in the foreground, it would be sublime. Need I mention, too, the old stone mansion that nestles amid the Gargantuan gas tanks in the same neighborhood?

THE latest piece of Surréaliste architecture is the Roosevelt Memorial, at Central Park West and Seventy-ninth Street: a few heavy, half-built limestone columns and broken Classic openings, set in between the pink granite of the new wings of the Museum of Natural History. This Classic monument, so painfully, so grotesquely inappropriate, so defiantly out of the picture of the Museum itself, will never look better than it does now. Today one can swallow it as sheer ghastly fantasy, but when it is completed it will be only pompous bad taste.

The Memorial causes one to grit one's teeth all the more because the Museum is one of the best pieces of Victorian architecture that the country can boast. Designed in 1867 by Calvert Vaux, in a manner one may still perhaps call Romanesque, it is as strong and straightforward a structure as anything that the country produced then, outside the work of H. H. Richardson; on the whole, it is better than most of his own early buildings. Not merely is the Museum far superior architecturally to the Natural History Museum in South Kensington, London, built by Alfred Waterhouse at about the same time, in the same sort of dreary elegant middle-class neighborhood; but it is good in its own right, and the architects who designed the additions did well, I think, to respect the original design and even the original choice of stone. Nothing short of positive genius would have justified a complete departure. All the more odious, then, is this new foreign lump, the Roosevelt Memorial. In a year it will be finished, and then it will not even be funny.

S OME buildings defy criticism by their almost miraculous mixture of good and bad elements, as difficult to sort as a thousand grains of light and dark sand. I find that this is true of the new Waldorf-Astoria (Schultze & Weaver, architects), a building I have been trying to come to terms with for months. In almost everything that concerns taste, the Waldorf seems either feeble or vulgar. The aluminum pepper and salt-shakers at the top; the shaky, tinny-sounding middle rail that helps one ascend the staircases; the dull limestone lower façade which becomes an equally dull brick wall— all these things stimulate nothing better than a polite sneer. On the other hand, the commodious entrance for vehicles on the street level seems very fine; even the ornamental green tiles do not spoil either the general effect or the plan. I have a similar admiration for the way that the space is broken up on the main floor, which is both a continuous corridor and a series of rooms, each varying in size and shape and height with the function it performs. The plan and disposition of this floor, which involves both that above and that below, seem to me adroit. But the ornamental effects are mediocre and aimless; even the sense of luxury is not very convincing. Modernism, revivalism, eclecticism, and plain gimcrackery have all had their hand in producing the Waldorf. Nothing is decisive and clear; perhaps that is the capital defect.

THE Exhibition of Modern Architecture at the Museum of Modern Art should not be missed. The best buildings in New York at the moment are the models and photographs that Mr. Philip Johnson has arranged with such clarity and intelligence on its walls.

A faintly official connection with the Exhibition prevents me from saying in any but very chaste terms how good I think the show is; a slightly closer relationship to the section on Housing seals my lips even more tightly in this department. But at least I may say that nothing like it has appeared in America before. If the buildings were bad, the photographs would surely be interesting; if the photographs were dull, their arrangement would still be admirable. Actually, they are remarkably good: the exhibition and the exhibited honor each other with similar virtues.

Here are the leaders of modern architecture: Frank Lloyd Wright, Le Corbusier, Gropius, Oud, van der Rohe; here is the work of its most important community planners: Otto Haesler, Ernst May, Henry Wright, Clarence S. Stein. The selection is rigorous, but the effect is just. Modern architecture can well afford to stand or fall by these examples.

THIS exhibition will, I trust, scandalize those who have taken seriously the notion that the skyscrapers produced by the New York City setback ordinances and the reckless gambling of our bankers were the chief boast of modern architecture. Far from dominating the exhibition, the skyscraper has scarcely a corner for itself. Even here, the model for a series of low-rental apartment houses by Howe & Lescaze is much more convincing as pure architecture than their Philadelphia skyscraper.

The most handsome objects in the show happen to be country houses designed on the grand scale: Frank Lloyd Wright's model for a house on the mesa in Colorado; the photographs of his Tulsa house for R. L. Jones; Miës van der Rohe's Tugendhat house in Brno, Czechoslovakia; and J. J. P. Oud's preliminary model for a country house in North Carolina. In these houses one beholds the virtues that had crept into architecture through the backdoor in the design of factories, grain elevators, bridges, power dams, subway stations. Our conventional architects have sought assiduously to conceal these virtues in their designs for houses and university buildings; but in these new country houses they are intellectually grasped, humanly embodied, architecturally expressed. Why should one seek archaic methods of escape from forms which so obviously lend themselves to use and enjoyment?

I NCIDENTALLY, the show is a great triumph for Mr. Frank Lloyd Wright. If the modern movement began anywhere, it began in Chicago in the eighties; if any one person has carried it forward consistently during the past forty years, beyond the point where Richardson and Sullivan established it, Wright is that man. Here his work stands face to face with the buildings of those Europeans and Americans who consciously or unconsciously have come under his influence, absorbing it or reacting against it.

None of the usual labels applies to Mr. Wright's work. He likes to describe himself as a romantic and an individualist; but his Jones house is severe, systematic, classic. One could conceive a whole city on the same terms. By contrast with it, Le Corbusier's Savoye house is sheer romantic expressionism, an oil-and-water mixture of fantasy and mechanics. Mr. Wright's work is not so far away from the best European architecture as he imagines—or as they perhaps do. His new buildings have lost the ornamental exuberance of the Midway Gardens and the Imperial Hotel: they are more in the line of his earlier houses. Meanwhile, the Europeans have moved nearer to Wright: passing from dogma to building, they have lost a little of their faith in ferro-concrete as an absolute; they have acquired some of Wright's love for natural materials, his interest in the site and the landscape, his feeling for the region.

W HILE there is perhaps something a little disproportionate in the space and attention given to the country house, this selection serves to emphasize two important things about modern architecture. First, it is not confined to one particular kind of building. It seeks with Louis Sullivan a rule so broad as to admit of no exceptions. Again, modern design, while based on the aesthetic principle of economy, and while peculiarly adapted to translate into aesthetic terms the minimal requirements of housing, for instance, is not restricted to the lowest common denominator. The same aesthetic works with equal effectiveness in creating an environment of comfort, largesse, even unrestricted luxury. (Compare van der Rohe's Stuttgart apartments with his Lange house at Krefeld.)

In discussing the forms of architecture which integrate both the practical and the ideal elements in modern civilization, I prefer Mr. Wright's term, "organic," to the more current adjectives, "modern" or "international;" and this organic architecture is not merely a matter of using new materials and techniques or of conceiving new forms for their effective employment; it is a matter of relating air, sunlight, space, gardens, outlook, social intercourse, economic activity, in such a fashion as to form a concrete whole.

A piece of jerry-builder's slum in Queens or a Manhattan skyscraper may have ten times as many mechanical knicknacks and utilities as Oud's handsome and so far unexcelled Hook of Holland houses; but the latter work is organic and real, while the American buildings, with all their affectations of modernity, are chaotic and incomplete. In short, modern architecture, in its organic sense, is a way of feeling, seeing, acting, living. Through modern architecture, certain common desires and methods have clarified themselves and have taken on concrete form throughout Western civilization. That fact is plain in this exhibition. It is as important as any of the buildings. Nothing like this fundamental unity has existed since the Middle Ages.

THE SKY LINE
A SURVIVOR OF THE BROWN DECADES~DE MORTUIS
WHAT MIGHT HAVE BEEN~MARCH 19, 1932

THE new exercises in period modernism along Central Park West cause one's eyes to linger with extra pleasure on the Dakota Apartments, one of the few survivors of the more spacious manners of the Brown Decades. In the course of fifty years or so, the Dakota has really worn very well: a solid, commodious, respectable building. I daresay its high ceilings take a pretty heavy toll in housekeeping and domestic service—the hangings are almost twice as long and the moldings twice as high as in the ordinary apartments of today—but will our half-baked "modern" apartment houses that are now springing up along the Park look half as real and convincing fifty years from now?

I will answer that question. Absolutely not! The "modernism" of these buildings is merely a thin veneer: banked corner windows that light long, narrow rooms; occasional terraces fitfully disposed about the upper parts of the structure; massive brick enclosures of water tanks. Even the relatively plain façades do not authenticate these structures. The most hopeful feature about a great many of the new apartment houses is the increasing breadth of the windows. The fear of sunlight and air, which we quaintly think confined to the French, is beginning to disappear among the well-to-do, who have so often been content with dark, back-to-back houses and apartments which differed only in price, space, and internal cleanliness from our worst slums. But these apartments are far from being solid and useful examples of modern architecture, and they do not give a hint of what a good architect could do were he able to work on land of reasonable price and on plots large enough to permit effective planning. In all essentials the Dakota is as close to organic architecture as its most up-to-date neighbor: that is, they are both about fifty years away from the real thing.

IF I said anything about the current show of the Architectural League of New York this year, it could not be anything but good: *de mortuis nil nisi bonum*. Empty draughting-rooms and empty pocketbooks enlist one's sympathies; but one would feel more warmly responsive to the plight of the architects did the Architectural League show not also present the spectacle of empty heads. In similar lean years, the architects of Europe clarified their social problems and worked out with imagination and logic the basis of a new architecture. Experimental thinking in architecture is now being done in some of the architectural periodicals; but there was hardly a breath of it in the League's show.

Mr. Joseph Urban's handsomely hung show at the Architectural League's clubhouse was much more interesting: his design for the Palace of the Soviets in Moscow was surely more effective than that which mysteriously took first place, and his study for a beach-front hotel, with a maximum of privacy for every room, was excellent. As for the housing projects done at his kindly behest by the unemployed draughtsmen, the quality was remarkably good when one considers that the competition was hastily improvised. Mr. Urban and the draughtsmen set a good example to their confreres.

THE Childs restaurants have been undergoing renovations again; but all their improvements only make me wish someone had been a little more conscious of what the original Childs restaurants were capable of becoming. Those spacious, hard, white-tiled interiors were the beginning of a real machine-form; I take pleasure in remembering that I pointed this out over ten years ago, before Le Corbusier had printed a word on the subject. Here were sound primitive elements, capable of development.

Unfortunately, this basis was abandoned in an effort to achieve refinement cheaply, by the application of historical ornament, by wholesale archaism, or by modernistic interpretations even more dreadful than the archeology of "Olde English"—if that be possible. The new restaurant in the R.C.A. Building is an example of the last failing, although by no means the worst. The stairs to the balcony are buttressed on one side by plastically designed telephone booths, as appropriate as pressed papier-mâché elephants. Above is a mural which contributes decibels of painted noise to the interior. The green ceiling downstairs impends even lower because of its color and the indirect system of lighting. There has been an agony of effort to make the little restaurant impressive and individual and modern; but except for the charming magical doors to the kitchen, the total effect is pre-cisely that: an agony of effort.

T HE Childs restaurant at Fifty-seventh Street and Fifth Avenue is another story. The interior was always spacious, and space itself is not only a luxury but a pleasure in New York; but it was a little dreary. It has been made over by Steffens & Gustafson into a fairly elegant and attrac-tive room whose strength has been frittered away by an unfortunate accep-tance of the conventional literary symbols for elegance: gilt fasces, blue vases, crystal electroliers, Napoleonic trinkets. But the body of the room is good: space made emphatic by pale-ivory walls, dark-brown chairs and tables, a claret-colored carpet that sweeps through the middle of the restau-rant and up the staircase, with its fine black railing. That is all, or almost all; and it would be quite enough without the trinkets.

But when the decorative element is so subdued, every part of the room must count; above all, the occupants. When the restaurant was reopened, the uniform of the waitresses was black and white; now it has been changed to a vapid buff and blue, and an essential part of the decoration has been lost, some of the smartness has gone. Plainly, the whole restaurant could and should have been carried through in direct contemporary terms. Counting out literary allusions, all the ingredients of the original Childs chain were here: spaciousness, directness, purity. I am willing to back these qualities to win against acres of Waldorf-Astoria and Alice Foote MacDougall.

R ECENTLY, the New York chapter of the American Institute of Architects bestowed its annual awards for the best New York apartment houses.

The Medal of Honor for a city apartment house went to Vincent Astor's 120 East End Avenue, designed by Mr. Charles A. Platt. I have often heard conservative English critics ask how a man of impeccable taste like Mr. Platt proceeds with a big apartment house. Here is one answer: a steel frame, treated by a marmoreal and monumental classic formula; chaste, reserved, devoid of ornament except in the delicate iron guards on some of the rectangular sash windows, and except again for the five horizontal cornices that arbitrarily break the vertical grouping of the windows. The taste is excellent; the architectural conception, deficient.

Why does this building deserve a medal? The committee chose it "for excellence of plan and harmony between exterior design and interior arrangement." While these are plausible reasons, I am a little mystified by their application. The great virtue of the harmony of interior and exterior lies in the fact that the windows do not accidentally appear in awkward corners of the room. This feat would strike one a little more massively were it not for the fact that the architect of the very next apartment house in East End Avenue, bound by no classic formula, has practiced the far more effective trick of extending the window the full width of the room—and opening up maximum view of the river.

The virtues of 120 East End Avenue are perhaps real, but they are negative; its vices are positive. Like most of the upper-class apartment houses built in New York during the past decade, it was conceived without the least apparent regard for rational standards of light, air, exposure, outlook. The building occupies a good sixty-eight per cent of its lot; it is hemmed in by other tall apartment houses, present and prospective. No one can blame the architect for the cramped site and the city's lax provisions for sunlight and open spaces. (Under the Multiple Dwellings Act a corner apartment house may cover ninety per cent of the lot up to the first set-back; so with respect to *legal* requirements the plan is a model of restraint.) But I cannot see that a program which disregards standards that are now accepted as minimal for the lower income groups deserves any sort of prize or commendation whatever.

The architects' committee was indeed a little uneasy about this over-crowding of the land; but in palliation it took refuge in the fact that Carl Schurz Park, hard by, could provide the necessary light and air. Light and air for what? For one side of the building. Obviously, the sound doctrine that every house must provide, as part of its original cost and equipment, the open spaces needed for amenity and decency has a good long way to go, particularly in upper-class housing. In the matter of housing, one must surely reverse the popular song: "What's good enough for Rocky is good enough for me." Mr. Vincent Astor's standards would not do for the Amalgamated Clothing Workers.

FORTUNATELY, the Medal of Honor for large-scale planning went to the Phipps garden apartments in Long Island City, designed by Mr. Clarence S. Stein. This apartment group shows what can be done in the way of commodious planning when the unit of design is no longer a few building lots on the regulation street layout, but two whole blocks thrown together. These apartment units consist of buildings two rooms deep around the perimeter of an entire tract, four hundred and sixty feet by two hundred and sixty; at the centre and at each end are six-story elevator buildings which project into the interior court; the rest are four stories high. Only forty-three per cent of the plot is used. The enormous inner court is landscaped with trees and shrubs that have plenty of sunlight for growth; here Mrs. Marjorie S. Cautley has done an excellent job.

The Phipps garden apartments are, to date, the best example of large-scale planning in the city for any income group whatever. Architecturally, the building is full of interesting beginnings: the fire-escapes are particu-larly good and the open balconies in some of the units make one wish for their extensive use throughout the development. Unfortunately, while the orange brick and the green trim are excellent in color, the design has few special virtues of its own to complete the communal plan itself. The ornamental brick relief around the upper façade and the brick arches, blind and open, spoil the most positive point in the whole design: the handsome fire-escapes. The architect used this horizontal fire-escape motive only for part of the parapet in the central unit; but the building would have gained enormously if the brickwork had been kept entirely subordinate to it, and if emphasis had been placed rather on a more interesting window-unit than the old-fashioned double-hung window.

Architecturally, the Phipps garden apartments not only fall short of the possibilities of the fine communal plan, they also fall short of Mr. Stein's other work in Sunnyside Gardens. Where the prime elements have been handled so competently and straightforwardly, one regrets all the more the weakness in the façade. Had Mr. Stein carried through the exterior design with the rigor and logic and imagination he applies to the design of art museums, these apartments would have been in every province the outstanding event of the year.

ONE can say little about the Honorable Mentions. Mr. Andrew Thomas received one for a feeble city apartment house with a little, conglomerate Romanesque court; whereas he really deserved credit for the apartment houses he designed in Tarrytown, in which he recovered most of the original simplicity of his early model tenements, augmented by a more generous open space. The architects' committee liked River House for its silhouette, and the white-brick apartment house at First Avenue and Fifty-seventh Street because of its top-heavy, pseudo-modern balconies. The choices might have been worse; but the reasons might have been better. For my part, I would store the gold medals away indefinitely and melt them all together in honor of the first building to be organically and imaginatively carried through from the ground plan and the garden up to the roof.

THE making-over of the old houses in Eighth Street for the Whitney Museum raises again all the nice problems associated with additions and rehabilitations: Shall the architect preserve the original shell, shall he merely use the old building as a scaffolding and redesign the façade as completely as necessary, or shall he depart from the design but try to retain the spirit? These houses were not fine enough to tempt Messrs. Noel and Miller, the architects who reconstructed them, into any archeological fidelity to the originals. For this, one must be grateful. But they kept the conventional window openings and painted the exterior a good dull orange and panelled the lower stories with aluminum-finished moldings. Without these panels, the effect would have been fairly respectable; and in a city where traditions disappear more rapidly than the foam on beer, and where there is so little respect for the common street façade, I have no objections to such a mild obeisance to tradition.

The interior is a different matter; and had it been handled more decisively, the exterior would have been a different matter, too. Mr. Bruce Buttfield, the designer, has treated the halls and most of the galleries in a sort of fussy modernistic interpretation of old American: the spread-eagle wallpaper and the lighting fixtures at the entrance are a little irritating. The only room that comes off fairly well by itself is the sculpture gallery with its whitish-blue brick interior. Here the lavender-gray floor and pedestals combine on a sunny day with the reflected reds that come through the high skylight to give a whole paletteful of shimmering colors: an impressionistic contrast to the sculpture itself. Indeed, the effect is so charming that it belittles most of the statues, and perhaps one should say in extenuation that the designer had possibly not counted on the iridescent effects produced by the outside walls.

S TILL, the Whitney Museum should have been better; Mr. Alfred Stieglitz had shown the way. By taking the floor of an office building, accepting its generous light, providing a clear neutral background, he created in An American Place a gallery in which pictures could be seen in their real values and their true colors. To have achieved anything like this, the architects would have had, no doubt, to reconstruct completely the entire façade; this might have been cruel to the old buildings, but it would have been kinder to the pictures. Since the Whitney Museum failed to use this opportunity, one must take what comfort one can from the fact that its rakish little departures are at least a cut above the dull Georgian literacy of the new Museum of the City of New York.

P SYCHOLOGICALLY speaking, the aesthetics of skyscrapers have long passed the point of diminishing returns; there is nothing to say about a new skyscraper tower except that it is another skyscraper tower. Ten years ago, Sixty Wall Tower might have occasioned a considerable amount of comment; its sixty-seven stories and its 125-foot mast would have seen to that. But what can one add now except that, coming at the end of the boom, its upper floors will probably retain their sunlight and view a little longer than would have been true in the past; and since this is so, the failure of the architects to make the fullest use of this opportunity, by following Mr. Hood's example in the McGraw-Hill Building or that of Messrs. Howe and Lescaze in their Philadelphia bank, is all the more deplorable? There are escalators for six floors and double-decked elevators and a special ventilating system; but these mechanical devices are nowhere matched, so far as I can see, in the design itself. Aesthetically speaking, the cantilevered metal front of the little building by Shreve, Lamb & Harmon in Madison Avenue, between Forty-first and Forty-second Streets, is much more important: it points at least obliquely toward the future, whereas the new tower is little more than a sad, admonitory finger, reminding us of the past.

T HE Foltis-Fischer restaurant at Third Avenue and Forty-second Street is interesting for two reasons: It comes within shooting distance of being a good building; and its designer is Mr. Hector Hamilton, who recently won the first prize for his design for the Palace of the Soviets in Moscow. The Soviet award is enough to justify Mr. Diego Rivera's unkind remarks about the academic Struldbrugs who apparently now have a stranglehold on official Russian art: his Palace was designed according to the tamest and most bourgeois American formula, including the accentuation of the vertical. As far as one can compare them, the Foltis-Fischer restaurant is really a little better than that: its expansive glass windows and its straightforward concrete façade just lack the virtue of being carried through to the end. But the interior has more than one stupid modernistic mistake, including lights inset in the ceiling like gigantic diamond kites.

The mathematical equation which is responsible for this error is: the Machine Age equals jazz equals triangles equals modernism. The equation has only one serious defect: it means nothing. Despite this fact, Mr. Hamilton's work here is closer to a consistent workable contemporary restaurant devoted primarily to food than any other I can think of. Gertner's new restaurant, by Mr. L. M. Lebhar, at Broadway and Forty-seventh Street, at present takes the palm for a purely advertising façade. The best window before this was probably that of Schulte, the optician, in Fifth Avenue; but for sheer display, Gertner's, with its yellow and red and blue glass panels, is a touch more effective; and it stands out amid the shoddiness and shabbiness of Broadway, probably the most slatternly street in the world, not excepting Tottenham Court Road.

1932~33

This was the worst phase of the depression, with the city tee-
tering on the brink of bankruptcy. Mayor Walker was forced
from office and was replaced temporarily by Joseph McKee
and for the remainder of the term by John O'Brien. "Hoover-
ville," a vast homeless encampment of makeshift shacks that
arose in Central Park, was emblematic of the despair that
engulfed the city. Curiously, Mumford's tone remained light,
in this, his first full season as "The Sky Line" and "The Art
Galleries" columnist, if for no other reason than that he
believed that the lull in the real-estate market might allow for
some post-boom reflection. With the inauguration of former
New York State Governor Franklin D. Roosevelt as President
of the United States and the enactment of reform legislation
during the "Hundred Days," the mood of the nation and the
city began to lift. The completion of the theaters at Rockefeller Center provided Mumford with some new material to
discuss at the beginning of the new year; the concealment of
Diego Rivera's mural, *Man at the Crossroads*, in the lobby of
the RCA Building yielded another opportunity for wry reflection in the spring.

THE SKY LINE
GAS TANKS AND TOWERS—THE NEW ARCHITECT
OCTOBER 22, 1932

O NE comes back to the sky line of New York from Europe with a new sharpness of vision. What stays in one's memory from the whole assortment of modern buildings that range from Fleet Street in London to the furthermost suburb of Vienna is not a new kind of picture but a fresh way of doing things: the value of light; the orientation toward the sun; the elimination of drudgery; the necessity for trees and gardens right up to the very doors of the factory and the school and even, in Rotterdam, of the new office building. In short, what is positive in the new architecture in Europe is not a change of taste alone but a new sense of living: a sense of space and clarity and order.

With all this in mind, one leans over the rail and greets the long fore-shore of Long Island on a sunny afternoon, with the first skyscraper hotel jutting up at a point which a gentleman from the Bronx vociferously iden-tifies as Forty-second Street, but which is possibly Long Beach. One has a sense immediately of how the skyscraper might be properly used: to accen-tuate the clean and lonely qualities of a place; the direct opposite of its pre-sent function: to foster and reap a financial harvest from congestion. (It is in the first fashion that F. L. Wright, in America, and Wijdeveld, the Dutch architect, have proposed to use the high building.)

M ILES to the left of the beach hotel looms a gas tank; that is good, too. There is nothing wrong with the American gas tank except its lack of scale and the fact that it is usually surrounded by dingy tenements in which people are supposed to live. Set off by itself, insulated from human companionship, the gas tank is not noxious; aesthetically, it is a serene object, and with a girdle of poplars around it at a distance of two hundred feet the tank would be a stunning monument. Some day, perhaps, when American civilization can afford a luxury or two, we will play a little with such possibilities. Even the little stuccoed houses in the foreground of Brooklyn are not without possibilities of charm; the color is surprisingly

good, though the designs are childish. Finally, one becomes aware of
Manhattan itself in the distance, a shimmering silvery-blue mass, moun-
tainous and buoyant, like a bundle of Zeppelins set on end; and, though one
sees it now for the hundredth time, one feels like a little boy witnessing a
skyrocket ascend, one wants to greet it with a cheer. As architecture, New
York ought to be in fact what it seems so surely at a distance: the most exhilarating embodiment of modern form. Unfortunately, it is not. As one walks
through the streets of the city once more, amid such a mass of new and
almost new buildings, one has a fresh sense of shame over all this misap-
plied energy and wasted magnificence.

ONE of the fortunate results of the depression is that New York architects will at last have a little time to think over what they have been
doing; they may even have a chance to visit and inspect, with whatever mingled feelings of triumph and nausea the occasion may demand, the buildings that were designed in their offices during the past ten years. Not for
nothing did the story go the rounds a few years ago about Mr. X, the senior
partner of one of the famous architectural firms, who on a ferryboat one
day, coming back to the city with a party of clients, roundly denounced the
betrayal of the sacred cause of architecture in one particularly bad new skyscraper on the horizon—only to discover that the building had been done
by his own office a year or so before.

Another of the good results of the depression is that for the next ten
years New York architects will not be called upon by any sane investors or
bankers to repeat the sort of thing they have been doing. Once the architects get accustomed to a regimen of plain living, they may even have a try
at high thinking, too. Looking at what has been done architecturally in
Holland and Germany and Switzerland and Scandinavia, they will realize
that, with all their illusions of being both successful and up-to-date, they
have been essentially dragging along at the tail of the procession. For the
new task of architecture in New York—and for this purpose New York *is*
America—is housing; and here only a handful of architects, bravely cap-
tained by Mr. Robert D. Kohn, have the faintest notion of what the shooting is about.

A N interesting clue to what lies before us was to be found in the recent special exhibition at the Architectural League of "Hillside Group Housing." The drawings and models prompted me to the same sort of cheer that the first outlines of Manhattan stimulate; but, unlike our picturesque mass of skyscrapers, they stood a more intimate inspection. The thinking and the work were done by a group of young architects, busy all summer in an improvised *atelier* in the country under Mr. Henry Wright, the town-planner of Radburn. The fact that the exhibition concluded with a caricature of itself entitled "Hillside Housing for the South Seas" was not the least of its virtues—for the one fatal absence in propaganda for modern architecture has been a sense of humor.

From the very problem that this group chose, one has a foretaste of the quality of their achievement. Their aim was to design "adequate shelter in a desirable environment," and they took as the focus of their scheme not an abstract house but a group of houses on a hillside in the northeastern climatic zone. Hillside housing, despite the fact that hillsides represent cheap marginal land around our big cities, would ordinarily be the most expensive type possible; but by utilizing every new possibility in plan, in layout, in heating, and the supply of utilities, the designers have shown how all the handicaps of a hillside site can be turned into handsome opportunities. This work has both imaginative rigor and scientific accuracy; outlook, open spaces, isolation, economy, and comeliness are all determined in principle before they are worked out in detail.

As a result, the architecture itself achieves its variety and unity by meeting the problem in one of the four possible ways that have been worked out for the appropriate slope and exposure; it is modern not because it has copied certain superficial tags of European or American architects but because it has worked upward from the basic conditions to the outward form. This group housing uses the site economically, achieves excellent interior plans, takes maximum advantage of view and sunlight and wind, and out of all these elements creates an ordered whole. The usable roof space, as worked out in these plans, seems to me better than was achieved in Neubühl, near Zürich, on a similar hillside tract—one of the very finest examples in Europe. Indeed, one has the feeling that once American architecture is started on the path Mr. Wright and his collaborators have mapped out, it will go further than the contemporary movement in Europe, which already shows signs of being bogged a little by the practice of turning expedients into dogmas and accidents into principles. (Le Corbusier's first house on stilts was a real attempt to meet a peculiar problem of a cramped site; when he copied himself in the house at Poissy, he turned it into a stylistic trick which would be hard to justify in rhyme or reason.)

THE important thing about "Hillside Group Housing" is that it does not stand alone; it is an example of a fundamental reorientation of thought which American architecture is now undergoing at the hands of the younger architects just coming out of college, in collaboration with the sympathetic and vital leaders of the older group. With half a chance, it will alter the sky line of New York during the next generation; for whatever other virtues the skyscrapers of the past may boast, surely no one will ever be able to claim for that architecture again that it was either safe or sound.

A RCHITECTURE is cropping up today in the least expected places. Who would have guessed that two of the latest buildings to puzzle and entertain the eye would be laundries?

One of them is that of the Knickerbocker Laundry. Long Island commuters who sit on the right-hand side going into the city can see it when they are sliding past Sunnyside. This is a white building, with two wings in front that thrust inward at a slight angle into a massive squat tower with a large clock; the white masonry of the central mass is repeated at the ends, each of the piles terminating in a series of stony billows—a snow-palace plasticity. The triple bank of horizontal windows in the front is well handled: the wall itself is cantilevered and the effect of all this sunlight and air is admirable. But the building (designed by Mr. Irving M. Fenichel) suffers as a whole from a vice that is so characteristic of American architecture that I must invent a special name for it: the vice of misplaced monumentality.

The truth is, this monumental front gives both too much and too little. The curving balustrade that leads up to the entrance, and the stone-covered masses themselves, divert the eye from the genuine possibilities of the building as a whole; while the abrupt change from stone to brick on the sides is unworthy of a structure that has three dimensions. Although the details of the building have been carried out with great care, down to the design of the sidewalk, in contrasting strips of gray concrete, the unity and clarity of the structure have been sacrificed to a monumental front. This is in effect an overcompensation for the crude factory building of the past, which neglected the effect upon the eye completely—only, one does not improve the appearance of a laundry by treating it as if it were a town hall.

T HE Cashman Laundry, at Gerard Avenue and 140th Street in the Bronx, by R. G. & Walter Cory, has similar virtues and similar defects. In both buildings the windows have been decisively treated; in both the natural rhythm is broken by a chunk of masonry in the middle. But the

Messrs. Cory had already made this mistake in the Starrett Lehigh Building on the West Side, which I mentioned last winter, so I am less willing to forgive them for repeating it in the present building.

T HE steady progress of subway design is one of the reassuring aspects of modern architecture; certainly, the new Eighth Avenue subway is a step in advance of anything else that has been done so far. The stations are not, perhaps, as positively handsome as those that the late Professor Alfred Grenander designed for the Berliner Nord-Süd-Bahn, for Grenander used resources in color that the present designers, perhaps wisely, left unexplored, but the white-tiled walls and the strong black numerals closely repeated the whole length of the stations form an interior that will show less signs of age and decay and outmoding than any other one might think of.

Even the cars are a little in advance of the admirable B.-M. T. design; and the temporary absence of advertisements in either the station platforms or the cars gives one a feeling of quiet and repose I had not experienced in public travel since the Grand Central Terminal was opened and was being used only by people who were catching or leaving trains—or who had just discovered the Oyster Bar. When one stops to think about it, our subways have usually been much better than our sky line. This is true not merely of New York but of Paris, London, Berlin, Boston, Philadelphia; and I am afraid there is some ominous moral in it—either that we must build buildings without windows or go around without eyes.

I NLAND Freight Terminal No. 1 is a distinct letdown after the Port Authority's superb achievements in the George Washington Bridge. A professor I know, who lives in the wing of a certain dreadful museum, is often asked by people who visit his apartment for the first time what sort of pictures are in the building, and he always answers: "Very big pictures." That is all I can say about the Port Authority building: it is a very big building. The economic idea back of this terminal was certainly much more positive than the architectural execution; perhaps the building would have been a little more impressive if it could have ended at the point where the zoning-law setbacks begin.

THE ART GALLERIES
THE ROCKEFELLER COLLECTION
JANUARY 7, 1933

P ROBABLY the most-visited art galleries during the next few weeks will be the two new theatres in Rockefeller Center. It will be the first large-scale vulgar tryout of modern art—or so much of modern art as has survived the virtuous glare of Mr. Rothafel. Fortunately for the sensitive public—there were people who became publicly ill when the Armory show introduced Matisse and Marcel Duchamp to this country twenty years ago—fortunately, the modern has been watered down with the anemic-academic and the classic-banal.

But the real wonder is that the murals are not worse. The program laid down for the artists in Rockefeller Center by Hartley Burr Alexander, sometime professor of philosophy at the University of Nebraska, was an amazing piece of unctuous drivel, to speak about it only in the kindliest terms. To the honor of American painters, a handful managed to evade Mr. Alexander's influence and Mr. Rothafel's influence and do very creditable work. The sculptors had a tougher time of it. Robert Laurent's handsome goose girl was still to be seen when I visited the Music Hall; but the other statues had been placed, according to rumor, in the theatre's hospital, and for all I know may have died there; at all events, no one seemed to know what had become of them. As for the goose girl, whose aluminum form looked particularly well in the reflected light of golden mirrors, she was attacked, I believe, for reasons that will be clear only to the more learned readers of *Broadway Brevities*. The fate of the goose girl is perhaps a new justification of abstract art; Mr. Noguchi's abstract form has apparently not awakened lewd thoughts in anyone's mind.

L ET us consider the paintings in the great International Music Hall first. The big mistake here is that the most conspicuous mural, that over the main staircase, is a grandiose piece of empty painting, called "The Fountain of Youth," by Ezra Winter. Its chief virtue is the fact that, like wallpaper, it blends somewhat with the golden light of the mirrors; and one's eye is fortunately held by the abstract pattern of musical instruments in Miss Ruth Reeves' carpet. If the wall had been carpeted and the floor had been painted, the result would have been quite as good; perhaps better, for one would then have been spared the shock of creating high-tension currents which one discharges against the brass rails of the stairs.

The main lounge below contains Louis Bouché's murals on the subject of the Theatre. Donald Deskey, the designer, has apparently endeavored to make this lounge dark and quiet and soothing; but the effect of the clever lighting fixtures is to throw Mr. Bouché's reticent murals into even greater obscurity, and I was unable to form any just estimate of them as pictures. Stuart Davis' abstract mural, "Men Without Women," in the men's smoking-room is, however, both a surprise and a pleasure. It shows the true destination of such abstract designs as Davis has been painting: what is their weakness as easel pictures becomes a real element of strength on the wall. The discovery of Davis' potentialities as a mural painter is one of the outstanding facts of the whole experiment.

Witold Gordon's "History of Cosmetics" in the women's lounge is, if you please, pretty; but, like his decorative map in the men's lounge on the first mezzanine, this must be classed as negative decoration. I prefer the plain wall, and for sheer gaiety and glitter and dash, Mr. Deskey's women's lounge on the first mezzanine, with no mural decorations whatever, except the necessary mirrors and chairs, came off much better. Yasuo Kuniyoshi's huge flowers in the women's powder-room are a different matter: they are not merely very charming, but they make the room. Though his palette is not so sombre as usual and therefore in a sense not so positively his own, his walls, which curve to meet the ceiling, do not attempt to recede: the motif is "ladies-powdering-their-faces-among-Kuniyoshi's-lush-and-charming-and-possibly-symbolic-flowers." This is not merely better painting than Mr. Gordon's: it is, from my point of view, a sounder theory of modern mural painting. One school emphasizes the wall, the other the painting.

Henry Billings' abstract and slightly Surréaliste "Lion Among the Ruins" is good, firm painting; it needs every bit of its firmness to stand up against the somewhat too positive brown-and-white background. Here Buk Ulreich's cubistic interpretation of the Wild West falls down: the room was more positive than the picture, which needed bolder color to avoid being swallowed by the dark-brown frame.

T HE murals in the RKO Roxy Theatre are much less important. Perhaps the best of them is a photographic mural of airplanes by Edward Steichen: the part that shows a fleet of white planes in the sky is particularly good, and one appreciates the clear, direct statement with doubled force because one has to go past a sweet and dreadful painting by Arthur Crisp before one reaches it. Hugo Gellert's interpretation of the proletariat of the world rising out a of a manhole and ascending to the Soviet Heaven is excellent as a literary conception; but it lacks space for execution and is little more than a sketch for the mural that might have been painted. I think Mr. Rothafel's attention should be called to it. Does it elevate public taste to show potential patrons of his theatre ascending *from* a manhole—and *to* a red Soviet star? The only equivalents of Gellert's painting I can think of off-hand are the Aztec idols the Indian workman used to hide under the altars of the Christian churches in Mexico.

T HERE are, I think, two large morals to be drawn from these murals— or is it vice versa? The first is that a good clean wall is better than a third-rate mural: the word "mural" is no guarantee whatever of aesthetic effectiveness, or even of human interest. The second is that non-academic painters like Davis and Kuniyoshi have a much sounder conception of the place of the mural in modern architecture than the old-style practitioners of the art. Plainly, these new murals represent neither the enthronement of American art nor its complete debauchment. They stand midway between Mr. Nelson Rockefeller's hopes and Mr. Thomas Craven's fears. As a whole, they might have been worse. In the midst of a Crisp Winter, it is encouraging to find even a few signs of spring.

S O many foolish things have been said and written about the melancholy pile known as Rockefeller Center that one approaches the new theatres there with the feeling that the auditoriums are probably composed of hanging gardens faced with Indiana limestone in a modified Egyptian style, surrounded on each side by smaller balconies forty-six stories high, with a microphone and television screen attached to every seat. But the deed is better than the word. The fact is that both the International Music Hall and the RKO Roxy are so far above the Hollywood-Grauman-Paramount-Albee tradition that it is scarcely fair to couple them in the same breath.

I would indeed be a pretty ungrateful critic to say less of these theatres; for, ten years ago, I observed in the *Freeman* that some day an architect would be bold enough to design the electric sign and metallic awning as the chief decorative motif of a theatre's façade; and in both theatres the architects have done this. The lettering of the signs seems to me unsatisfactory in its proportions, and the RKO emblem is definitely bad; but at least Reinhard & Hofmeister, the architects, did not at first design a Greek temple and then wake up and find to their great surprise that it was necessary to cut into the front with an awning and an electric sign. Moreover, when the Paramount Theatre was opened, I urged that in such theatres colored lights should be used instead of architectural ornament; and lo! in both new theatres colored lights are at work.

T HE Music Hall is the more positive and dashing piece of architecture. From the moment one enters the lobby, with its panelled circles of lights, one has the feeling that the atmosphere of the place will be gay; and on the whole it is, although the very gayest spot happens to be Donald Deskey's dizzily mirrored women's powder-room—from which half the human race is barred. There is a touch of the new Waldorf in the refined golds and browns that pervade the theatre; and this seems to me regrettable. Was it the unconscious effect of the *Zeitgeist?* The whole Music Hall seems to have been "built around" Mr. Winter's golden mural, whereas brighter, purer colors not merely would have been more jolly but might have made the golden mural impossible. In the other theatre, designed by Eugene Schoen, the effect is even more sombre. On the other hand, Mr. Schoen used a strong blue for one of his walls, and this worked so well one wishes the note had been struck more often.

All the elements, good and indifferent, in the Music Hall are out-weighed by the excellence of the auditorium itself. The ceiling descends like a telescoped portion of an eggshell to the semicircular opening of the stage itself; and the panels through which the lights are cast follow this movement down to the stage. Every line pulls one's eye toward the stage. The effect is stunning. Mr. Rothafel has been given credit for this form of theatre; but the truth is that it was used before in what has hitherto been the best auditorium in the country, the Hill Auditorium at Ann Arbor, designed by Ernest Wilby for Albert Kahn. Although to talk of intimacy in a theatre of this size is nonsense, the sight lines from the most distant seats are perfect, and the architects, by creating an illusion of nearness to the stage, have overcome one's natural impulse to commit suicide by stumbling on a step of the top balcony.

THE auditorium of the RKO Roxy is quite differently conceived. For one thing, it harbors a monumental electrolier suspended from an equally vast plaque decorated with gigantic figures: a somewhat distracting element. Moreover, the proscenium opening breaks the smooth curve of the walls, and, since there was no need for the stage to touch the ceiling, it would have created a more unified effect to lower the top and carry some of the wall around.

In sum, both these theatres are at least halfway to a firm and consistent modern architecture; and the auditorium of the Music Hall is more than halfway: it is very nearly there. Plainly, in Rockefeller Center, the worst is yet to come.

I N the days when buildings were syphoned up into the skies scarcely five minutes after a charcoal sketch had been rendered by Mr. Hugh Ferriss, the annual show of the Architectural League of New York resembled the city outside: it was a jungle. There was too much to see and too little reason for seeing it. But if these empty years have not yet taught the architect how to face the tasks of the future, they have at all events shown him how to put the best face possible upon the surviving pretensions of the past. The exhibition arranged at the Fine Arts Building by Mr. Joseph Urban and his associates is such a superb piece of showmanship that one readily forgets how few of the buildings or the works of art have any significance. The choice of materials, the scheme of presentation (namely, lowering the ceiling and utilizing adroitly the space between the floor and the usual first line of drawings and photographs), the emphasis and concentration of the whole show, are admirable.

A s usual, the main exhibit is devoted to architecture and the crafts. Here, apart from the Cornell Medical Center, the best things are Gilmore Clarke's landscape designs for Westchester County Parks and Charles Downing Lay's design for the Marine Park in Brooklyn. In the Medical Center itself, by Coolidge, Shepley, Bulfinch & Abbott, the individual room units, the kitchens, the operating-rooms, and the library, are far superior to those portions of the building upon which the seductions of traditional architecture have been practiced. The Westchester County Office Building, by Morris & O'Connor, while spoiled for modern taste by its classic allusions, points nevertheless to a new order in office building: it is shallow, limited in height, and has no setbacks; I recommend it cheerfully to those Russell Sage Regional Planners who as late as 1931 simply could not imagine a shallow office building without setbacks. Delano & Aldrich's buildings for the Yale Divinity School at New Haven, though they lean heavily on Mr. Jefferson's university at Charlottesville, show the possibilities of small units in school design.

In photographs, perhaps the most interesting piece of eclectic architecture is the Church of Our Lady of Mount Carmel, in Brooklyn, by French, Hume, and Lefante; while the most hopeful piece of modern design is James Timpson's proposed developments for a United States Naval Air Base at Pensacola, Florida.

T HE second section, devoted to the arts of the theatre, must be passed over at this time. The third is an exhibition of modern housing in America and Europe displayed by means of handsomely mounted photographs and charts arranged in repeating units. This exhibit, conceived on different lines and for different purposes from the main portion, was mainly the work of Mr. Clarence S. Stein and Miss Catherine Bauer; and if I may, as a member of the committee, have any public opinion about it, it is as handsome as it is educative. Here are more realistic indications of the architecture of the future than in any of the country houses or belated skyscrapers in the main gallery. Furthermore, the European housing gives perhaps a better indication of the modern architectural whole—including playgrounds and gardens—than do isolated department stores, country houses, or other showpieces. Mr. Philip Johnson's excellent work in the International Exhibition last year, and in his recent admirable documentation of the architecture of the Brown Decades in Chicago at the Museum of Modern Art, has set a new standard of presentation. It increases the work of the exhibitor, but it lightens that of the spectator. Until the architects have the opportunity to build more houses, they could do worse than set their unemployed fellows to preparing more good exhibitions.

Cornell Medical Centre
"Coming upon these buildings from the sordid streets around the bridge, dominated by the gasworks, is like leaving a dirty third-class railway carriage and suddenly beholding the ice-fields and
the summit of a glacier." —from "The Modern Hospital," December 12, 1931

WPA Photograph, Federal Writers Project

George Washington Bridge
"The cables are carried on the cradle over the tower in full view: for once one sees a suspension bridge aesthetically as well as mechanically in a state of suspension." —from "Bridges and Buildings," November 21, 1931

WPA Photograph, Federal Writers Project

Roosevelt Memorial of the American Museum of Natural History
"This Classic monument [is] so painfully, so grotesquely inappropriate, so defiantly out of the picture of the Museum itself." —from "Unconscious Architecture," February 13, 1932

Waldorf-Astoria Hotel
"The aluminum pepper and salt-shakers at the top;...the dull limestone lower façade which becomes an equally dull brick wall—all these things stimulate nothing better than a polite sneer."
—from "Unconscious Architecture," February 13, 1932

Midtown Manhattan

"The skyscraper period is fast coming to an end, and the skyscraper, as we knew it during the past fifty years, has now pretty well reached the peak of its development. . . . As a result of the architects' building classic colossi and Gothic pinnacles and Byzantine battlements till their scrapbooks were

exhausted, they are now back once more to the essential form, cleaned and clarified."
—from "Skyscrapers and Tenements," June 3, 1933

WPA Photograph, Federal Writers Project

Foley Square; left to right: Board of Health Building, New York State Building, New York County Courthouse, and Federal Court Building
"[The buildings] are supposed to form a new civic centre, but one could scarcely guess it from the way they are placed." —from "Concerning Foley Square," October 13, 1934

Schwartz

Bryant Park
"The worst [weakness] probably is the fact that the park is planned on a false axis, with a grand entrance up a flight of steps from Sixth Avenue, and with a fountain on the terrace.... The plan does not encourage circulation." —from "The New Bryant Park," December 1, 1934

Central Park
"It says something for Mr. Moses' reconstructions that he has introduced so many popular touches—including the neat little children's playgrounds that now skirt the park—without utterly destroying the original atmosphere." —from "Parks and Playgrounds," October 24, 1936

West Side Highway
"East Side, West Side, all around the town, Mr. Moses' improvements are creating the framework of a new city." —from "Bridges and Beaches," July 17, 1937

Triborough Bridge
"The designers [of the bridge] so despised the whole notion of walking that they have not even had the grace or the good manners to provide benches, where one might rest and take in the view."
—from "Bridges and Beaches," July 17, 1937

O NE of the healthy things about modern art is that in the act of temporarily covering up some of the tedious stretches of the past it has opened up forgotten landscapes. The resurrection of El Greco and the discovery of the Congo idols are familiar stories; but the work of the Mexican artists Rivera, Orozco, and Charlot has brought to light another "usable past"—that which flourished in the Western Hemisphere. The exhibition of the American sources of modern art happens to be one of the most impressive and exciting that the Museum of Modern Art has put on.

Here is an Aztec figure of a Maize Goddess that reminds one of Egypt; there is a stone Totonac disc with a head that looks as if it had come from an early Greek vase; in another place is a lintel in low relief that would have honored the Assyrians. And here are cultures that run the whole gamut from naïveté to sophistication, and from the pure joy in life of the Peruvian potteries and textiles to the mystical brutality of the Aztecs. In short, here is a very great art indeed, but except for the Peruvian textiles at the Metropolitan, one will look for it in vain within the walls of our art museums, for the major specimens all come from the museums of anthropology and natural history, and they might have rested there in dusty silence but for the fine passionate interest of the Post-Impressionists. Chalk up another victory for the modern movement, and place this on top of the latest funeral oration over its death.

T HE Modern Museum has underlined the point of the exhibition by showing modern pictures by various artists who have come under the influence of these early American forms. In the case of the Mexicans, that influence is an entirely natural one, but if we are not to drown in a wave of Mayan and Aztec adaptations, the absorption of these foreign cultures will have to be as subtle and inward as it is in the paintings of Weber and Weston—coloring the plastic imagination, rather than supplying ready-made symbols. In a sense, one hopes that the influence of this ancient art, particularly that of the more or less parvenu Aztecs, will remain superficial. While there is perhaps a parallel between their religious rites and the more exquisite forms of butchery in modern gangsterdom, the melancholy fact is that the Aztecs were at their best in art when they were at their worst in life: perhaps one of the most serene things in the exhibition is the sculptured god Xipe Totec dressed in the flayed, dripping hide of his human ceremonial victim. All in all, this is a rare opportunity in the United States to see, side by side, so many different aspects of our ancient art, culture, feeling, thought, emotion. It is something to realize how much we can claim from the Peruvians besides quinine and lima beans and llamas' wool.

I DID not see Ben Shahn's paintings of the Sacco-Vanzetti case. From the praises of them I have heard, I should imagine they were superior to the series on the Mooney case he is showing at the Downtown Gallery— although so eminent a critic as Diego Rivera says the contrary. Plainly, the new work is sincere and emphatic: with an appearance of archaic naïveté, Shahn simplifies the background, removes the impedimenta of realism, and presents the dramatic essence of the subject. But where was the drama of Tom Mooney—the drama of a man railroaded to prison by means of perjury and kept there by a mixture of poltroonery and vindictiveness? There was a promise of this drama in the "Apotheosis;" but for the most part these pictures of the lawyers for the defence, of Mr. Bourke Cockran, of Mooney and his warden, went around rather than into the subject. And as for the three pictures of the slick gentleman who was once Mayor of New York— or was it Coney Island?—they occupy far too large a place in the show, and they leave one in a little doubt as to what the artist's intention was. In dealing with the Mayor of Monte Carlo—or was it New York?—Shahn was far too kind, and he wasted three good rounds of ammunition aiming at—or saluting—someone who was scarcely good enough to be a target. In sum, one welcomes Shahn's social intention and his method; but the pictures themselves fail to be as plain-speaking and inescapable and haunting as the facts behind them. In the name of art, one has a right to demand more effective propaganda.

THE main hall of the R.C.A. Building in Rockefeller Center is now dedicated, as the author of "Eimi" would say, to artless unmurals. Rivera's work, when I last inspected it, was coyly hidden, except for the two narrow panels that turn the corner, by a wood-and-paper screen and by a few private shock troops in debonair uniform. José Maria Sert's murals did not have to be hidden, since they occupy walls which permit only sidelong glances at the paintings themselves and since the work itself is as innocuous as the black-and-white illustrations that used to grace the pages of *Scribner's* in the early nineties.

Sert is an illustrator with a flair for simple rhythmic contrasts in motion and form; the murals are supposed to represent the emancipation of mankind from the brute conditions of slavery and mechanism, but one needs printed information to discover what they are all about, for the forms themselves are meaningless, as meaningless, if not as stilted, as the usual Prix de Rome essay. ("Mankind Conquering War" shows chiefly a few urchins having fun on the barrel of a cannon.) When Turner found one of his sunsets throwing a neighboring landscape by Constable out of key, he temporarily toned down his colors; but if Rivera had had any reason to practice such gallantry with Sert, he would have had to erase his entire fresco: one is vigorous and significant painting and the other is so much wallpaper. The guardians of Rockefeller Center have wisely chosen to hide the painting and to display the wallpaper. One says "wisely" because the unity of the building was threatened by Rivera's painting—an imaginative work which would have redeemed its colossal and unfaltering inanity. One remembers how the Indian craftsmen who helped build the great churches of Mexico used to bury one of their favorite idols under the altars of their Spanish conquerors; and one wonders if Rivera should not have made it a condition of his painting that the work should be hidden behind a sheath of fine marble, to rest there in ironic splendor until the day of reckoning.

THE SKY LINE
SKYSCRAPERS AND TENEMENTS
JUNE 3, 1933

THE skyscraper period is fast coming to an end, and the skyscraper, as we knew it during the past fifty years, has now pretty well reached the peak of its development. By a turn of the wheel, we are back at the point where we started; no sensible person would say that our present buildings are fundamentally better than the old Monadnock Building in Chicago, but as a result of the architects' building classic colossi and Gothic pinnacles and Byzantine battlements till their scrapbooks were exhausted, they are now back once more to the essential form, cleaned and clarified. Behold the building of the Insurance Company of North America, at 99 John Street, designed by Shreve, Lamb & Harmon.

In no sense of disparagement, one may say that this building combines the best points of the Empire State Building and the News Building. It is a much more resolute design than the first, for there is no *art moderne* mooring mast and no meaningless rosettes to terminate the verticals, framed in chromium-coated steel, as in the Empire State; but the windows are arranged in alternation with the piers, as in the News Building; the black spandrels have no ornament except vertical lines, which provide small shafts of highlight on the topmost rows. The twelve lower floors are mechanically ventilated. There are five minor setbacks in the twenty-eight stories, and the corners of the lower stories are chamfered.

The beautiful directness of the structure is lost in the fussy treatment of the entrance hall, where the staring black-and-white whirl of marble, though bad in itself, has the slight merit of completely obliterating the murals. But the building as a whole is both honest and handsome: there is nothing left to be done in the design of business buildings but repeat this fundamental pattern—nothing, that is, until one completely revises the underlying program of the design.

T HE next move is to recognize the skyscraper as a blind alley and an insupportable luxury and to begin all over again on a new line. This means planning long, shallow buildings—under ten stories—in multiple rows; eliminating the partly unused and therefore extravagant express elevator shafts; providing daylight and natural ventilation for every worker and as much direct sunlight as is tolerable; turning the roofs into noon-hour recreation spaces and providing for pedestrian movement and for shops at the street level on the *inner* sides of the buildings. Such structures would retain the advantages of vertical circulation without wasting space in corridors and needless elevator banks, and they would create an entirely new problem of design for the architect whose ingenuity is now exhausted in filling out an arbitrary lot shape and keeping within an equally arbitrary "zoning envelope." I expect to see someone get hold of a whole city block and try this sort of design presently; what stands in the way of the experiment is the fact that the practical real-estate man believes with a holy and unshakable faith that the returns from a building increase directly with the amount of unusable and unrentable space in it, and that a building which would be badly designed if it were only six stories high will cover him with profit and glory if he multiplies the original error by ten.

I F anything proves that Manhattan has traditions, as hoary and fast as the unwritten laws of a Pall Mall club, the achievements of model-tenement-house competitions would prove it. The first model tenement in the eighteen-fifties had so many dark, unventilated rooms in it that within a few years it became a reeking slum, inhabited only by thieves and prostitutes. The noble tenement-house competition of 1879 provided the prize design of the dumb-bell flat, in which each bedroom was a corridor as well, and in which the rooms on the airshaft were all fortified against breezes and sunlight—to compensate for which one could always, on a summer evening, see the lady downstairs taking a bath. The tenement-house competition that preceded the so-called model law of 1901 encouraged the standardized semi-slums which dominate the Bronx today: examples of spurious order and decency, human dreariness and decay. Now comes the Phelps-Stokes Fund competition again. If the competitors keep to the terms of the competition, they must either produce another slum plan or boost the rents above the generous ten dollars a month which the judges have allotted. But what can one expect from a Fund which warns the architects that "it would be unwise to *insist* upon conditions more ideal than those which usually pertain in [*sic*] the housing of the rich"? Have we sunk *that* low?

T HE very best new shop front I have seen is that of Courmettes & Schneider near Fifty-seventh Street on Lexington Avenue. When architectural criticism becomes really subtle and expert, it will perhaps be able to explain why the shops of opticians and photographers are usually so much better than those of any other business. Is it due to the fact that they themselves work in glass and metal and are ready to meet halfway the architect who knows how to use these materials? This front is simplicity itself: black glass, gray metal, metallic letters separated from their background for indirect lighting in silhouette. There is no attempt, as in the excellent display fronts of the Schulte shops, at startling advertisement; but every time I pass this shop on a bus, I find my head turning around automatically for another look at it. The architect is Eugene Schoen.

1933~34

This season witnessed the shake-up of New York City politics, with the crushing of the old Tammany Hall machine and the election of Mayor Fiorello La Guardia, who pushed through a municipal version of the "Hundred Days" in early 1934. One of La Guardia's most significant cabinet appointments was Robert Moses, who, as commissioner of parks, began rebuilding the city's infrastructure. A major highlight of "The Sky Line" was Mumford's review of Rockefeller Center in December 1933, by then about half-completed.

T HE suffocated knots of traffic on Fifth Avenue have made passage almost as slow once more as in the best days of 1928, so let us look at the new shop windows while we wait. There have been a number of changes these last six months.

The greatest departure in shop fronts, like so many other excellent things in modern architecture, had its origin on Third Avenue. I refer to the small window, big enough to display only two or three articles at most, now sometimes created by blackening up the vast expanse of plate glass in such a fashion as to give the redecorated shop the appearance of a black ship's side, with an open porthole. This innovation first took place in the McAn shoestores, at least fifteen years ago, if my memory serves me. By now, the McAn window has become an expanse of glass once more, but the old shop front was one of the most effective in the city, saving the scalloped metal edging and the absurd script of the name itself.

W ELL, this excellent fashion has now seized Fifth Avenue. The theory is that instead of being dazzled by a gross of stockings or a battlefield of shoes, you behold at a rapid glance one or two; your attention is concentrated, your appreciation heightened. The theory probably is sound, at least for small articles; but the blackened glass windows are not, to my notion, very successful; the change seems too palpably a makeshift, and in a row of exhibits, as at Saks-Fifth Avenue, the effect is a little too obvious. Perhaps the most intelligent application of this style is in the new Pinet shop near Fifty-seventh Street. Here the glass window remains transparent throughout, but a wood-and-metal frame surrounds the showcase itself, and a grill of metal unifies the whole window without blocking off all the light. The all-metal frame of Marcus & Company, the jewelers, at Fifty-third Street is a little less interesting in itself, but that is atoned for by the dramatic exhibition of the precious stones themselves. The point about these little windows is that they are really model stages, and they can legitimately take advantage of color and lighting effects which would be pretty terrible if the scale were larger. For big windows, however, those which Kiesler and Archipenko did in successive years for Saks still seem to me the most exciting; unfortunately, perhaps, Fifth Avenue has heard about the Neo-Romantic reaction, and Cubism is no longer "modern"— for Fifth Avenue.

The most elegant example of this Romantic reaction is the window Mr. Lee Simonson has done for the Dorothy Gray shop. A white Venus gazes into a mirror held by a white Cupid; and if either of them should slip, he or she would fall down the glossy sides of a white grotto that occupies the greater part of the window on the street level. Mr. Simonson had a very difficult job; not merely was it important to symbolize beauty but it was necessary to fit the decoration into a preexisting frame, and to unify the upper and lower window without attempting to erase the dividing line of the floor. This white statuary with a blue ground certainly attracts the eye, but I should hate to see the precedent imitated. The next person who tried it would probably achieve the effect of the living statues at the circus; as it is, one scans Venus a little severely to see if one can detect the white tights.

A T Sixty-fourth Street and Madison Avenue, a rather large Colonial house, two stories high, with a gable roof and dormers has reared its head. The front is an impeccable and quite defunct Georgian; it differs from most of the residences in the neighborhood because the door is open between nine and three, and because one observes that one's host has stationed a functionary with a revolver in his holster in the hall, as was the custom in the good old days of breeches and cocked hats. Who is one's host? It is the Bank of the Manhattan Company. The whole business is very puzzling. This tender effort to make a bank look like a private home—the adding machines are stowed out of sight in a corner of the second story— recalls the days when ladies did not know the difference between a checkbook and a passbook and when an effort was made to keep the dear things from getting flustered by giving them a special room. (In those days, there were ladies' entrances in saloons, too, but *that* was to keep the men from getting flustered.)

Here is a whole building designed, apparently, to glorify the Daughters of the American Revolution. There is even a fine attic equipped with rows and rows of ladderback and Windsor chairs—have you ever sat through a two-hour meeting in a ladderback chair, lady?—in which neighborhood meetings might be held if anyone could think of a reason for holding them. Since I do not believe in the resurrection of the eighteenth century, or in the attempt to make Park Avenue community-conscious, or in the revival of autarchy, or even in the refining influence of good taste upon the safety of bonds and mortgages, I cannot think of anything about the building to praise except the back stairs, which are just stairs, and the blue carpet, which is a nice blue. Yes. One thing more is good. The bank has adopted the English type of open counter for its tellers, instead of the American cage that admirably protects the tellers against everything except tear gas and sawed-off shotguns. Has it ever occurred to any architect that the best protection for money not in the vaults would be a complete glass front, which would make it impossible for anyone to stage a holdup without the whole world knowing about it? Columns and heavy masonry fronts look safe, but glass would *be* safe. Since bankers are weird enough to imagine a completely equipped Georgian house as their home, might they not in a moment of inspiration picture the advantages of a good goldfish bowl?

ROCKEFELLER Center has now reached a convenient halfway point in its construction. The mice have labored, and they have brought forth their mountain. Like most of the things that were conceived during the last days of the boom, the central building is very big. And when one has said this, one has said almost everything. Shall we leave it at that—or shall we dwell on the holes and the little scratchy tooth marks the mice have left in their cheese?

The best time to see the Center is at night. Under artificial lighting, in a slight haze, the group of buildings that now make up the Center looks like one of Hugh Ferriss' visions of the City of the Future. At night one can forget that every touch of ornament is bad with an almost juvenile badness; one can forget that the only interior painting to which the Center can point with pride is primly hidden by an improvised wall; one can forget that the broad face of the main building, running from east to west, and seventy stories high, permanently cuts off sunlight from a large swath of buildings to the north; one can forget that the buildings will constitute a planned chaos not to be distinguished objectively from the unplanned chaos around them.

Here, at night, is what Ferriss meant: something large, exciting, romantic. A mountain or an ash heap of the same size would do the trick almost as well if the lights were cleverly arranged; for architectural design, far from being revealed by the lighting, is rather mercifully hidden or veiled in the strong contrasts of light and dark. Again life has imitated art; for these drawings of Ferriss, with their emphasis on mass, combining bulk and power with the soft romantic edge one can achieve only in charcoal, were the pinnacle which the Big Boys steadily sought to reach. To get the effect at its best, one must see it from a point close to the low buildings on Fifth Avenue; for by itself the main building, from the distance, is a graceless hulk and will never be anything better until it is hidden.

Comes the dawn and the headache. Looking at it soberly by daylight, what does one find? First, a gigantic slab of a building, flying a red flag, with a series of irregular step-ups on each side which destroy the unity of the face without making it any more interesting. Seeing its thin edge between the British and the French buildings, the thinness becomes a little ridiculous in proportion to the height; head on, it looks like the scrawniest of towers. In the Daily News Building, the irregularity of the step-up was successfully used as a help to the design, and in the Empire State Building, the dignity of the unbroken shaft gives it—until the dreadful mooring mast is reached—the same grand effect that the Washington Monument has; but here one has monotony without strength and irregularity without any dynamic force.

For practical purposes, the long, narrow ground plan of the RCA Building is superior to the usual tower form; but unfortunately this superiority is lost by reason of the excessive amount of space that must be wasted on express transportation. At a third of the present height, the RCA Building would probably be a rational unit. Indeed, a series of such units, properly related, would have knocked the eye out of any existing office building. But the design of such a centre would have required intelligence and business imagination of an order that was not very common in the Dizzy Decade.

T HE ornamental features are no less painful than its more utilitarian efforts. The approach from Fifth Avenue is by way of a series of fountains that leads downward between the two smaller buildings, and opens onto a sunken plaza, which is backed by a grand basin, above which rises the frame of the main entrance. Who could put a monumental entrance beneath seventy stories that would not look a little silly, no matter how colossal its scale? The most sensible thing to do would have been to leave out the sculpture and use the present discreet panel of glass to tell the whole story. Unfortunately, this honest solution would have interfered with a curiously misbegotten desire to "encourage art," all of which has only added to the muddle and the grief. I cannot find a word of even faint praise for any of the sculptural or graphic decoration now visible on any of the buildings. From the little golden figures over the entrance of the British Empire Building to the Lachaise sculptures on the Sixth Avenue side, which one can see, indeed, only from the south end of the "L" station, the sister arts of architecture have turned out to be pretty weak ladies indeed; the work of the most distinguished artists, like Lachaise, by some fatal curse of the fairy godmother comes to as little as that of the most minor artists. Perhaps the clearest example of botching is the grand basin itself: the little figures, bad in scale, inept in conception, tawdry in their golden visibility, spoil the really fine smooth mass of the granite itself. The courage to have let "art" and "decoration" go hang would have added to the modest strength of these buildings.

But the architects were soft when they should have been hard, and they were hardboiled when they should have been little gentlemen. They chose to use a crumbly surfaced limestone with the saw marks left, which will absorb soot and stain irregularly; their hanging gardens give the effect, from the street, of inverted mustaches; and the ornament that terminates their verticals is mere jitters. On the other hand, their refined little buildings, so conservatively nothing at all in their style, have a raw battery of lamps on top which is even less assimilated in the design than the ventilators on top of the theatres. As for the interior, it is not within miles of the positive standard of beauty achieved by Howe & Lescaze in their Philadelphia savings-bank building; and perhaps the only enjoyable touch is the use of blue Venetian blinds, which take away a little from the drabness of the façade.

ARCHITECTURALLY, in short, Rockefeller Center is much ado about nothing. It lacks the distinction, the strength, the confidence of good architecture just because it lacks any solidity of purpose and sincerity of intention. On the one hand, the projectors have eaten into a colossal fortune with a series of bad guesses, blind stabs, and grandiose inanities; on the other, they have trimmed and played for a decent mediocrity. And the whole effect of the Center is mediocrity—seen through a magnifying glass.

A s I have probably said before, the great change that has come over the city during the past year is that, in the upper reaches of the air, nothing has changed. It is close to bed rock that the real upheavals have taken place. On Madison Avenue between Fifty-ninth and Sixtieth Streets, for instance, a two-story building has now replaced a seven-story building. It is a horizontally designed structure, with rounded corners, cantilevered floor construction to give clear window space, and windows that were meant by the architect to give both light and ventilation. Most of its positive virtues have been quietly exterminated by the occupants of the upper floor. By using four or five varieties of window curtain, they have done their best to make the building look like a Victorian parlor that has had its face lifted. By using every height and type of lettering to announce their presence, they have robbed the exterior of a legitimate source of decoration. All that is left of the architect's original intention is the blue enamelled sheets and the metal window frames and borders that give the building its special character.

The color is all right: about the tone and intensity of a shadow on a white surface in full sunlight. Unfortunately, the sheeting itself seems here, as in the Midtown Bus Terminal on Forty-fourth Street just east of Broadway, to be a little too thin: the wavy surface makes for a feeling of uncertainty and a lack of mechanical rigidity. Compare it with a similar building at Lexington and Sixty-first Street: paradoxically, the travertine stone on the latter face seems more in the spirit of the construction. So, for that matter, seem the glazed black bricks that are used at the side of the Fifty-ninth Street building. This may appear to be a little matter, but since modern architecture cannot conceal its mistakes behind stone foliage or the Five Orders, it is just in such little matters that choice must be perfect. As for the interiors of this building, the most conspicuous to date are the lunchroom and the motion-picture theatre. The latter is mediocre. The lunchroom, if one can overcome the indigestible lettering of the advertising slogan—and if one can also forget the slogan—is well done, but for the architect's introduction of a colossal panel of flowers. These flowers are not decoration: they are just dehydrated garbage.

A DISTINGUISHED German architectural critic, Dr. W. C. Behrendt, remarked the other day that the one place where vital architectural design seemed to be common in New York was in the cheaper lunchrooms and restaurants. He is right. The design is sometimes so decent that it can even overcome such names as that of the Trufood Restaurant, on Forty-fourth Street, just east of Broadway. I recommend that little job, on purely aesthetic grounds, for the following reasons. Glass brick is used very intelligently as a frame for the transparent window. The color of the brick is carried into the interior walls in a lighter tone of green, and that is a welcome relief from the blaring poster colors of sandwich-shop modernism. The unvarnished wood of the woodwork and the indirect-lighting fixtures are both admirable, and, finally, the ancient bent-wood chair has been redesigned and improved. If the tables had only carried through the color scheme, with green-glass tops, the effect would have been stunning. As it is, the whole thing is a modest triumph, from which much more expensive places could learn a lesson. (I hope the food is a modest triumph, too.) The architect was Mr. V. St. George.

WHILE we are dealing with minor examples of comeliness, let us look at the Pennsylvania Drug Company's store at the corner of Fifty-first Street and Sixth Avenue. It is a big and bright and cheerful place. The bigness is emphasized by the open treatment of the windows, the brightness by the now happily fashionable moon lamps, and the cheerfulness by a fairly intelligent use of color. One would probably have to give this the palm as the best shop of the year so far were it not for the fact that the drug company's window displays very carefully conceal the interior and cut off half the light. Plainly, the notion that miscellaneous exhibitions of drugs, lotions, flatirons, and toys are attractive to the human eye dies hard among druggists. Because the superstition is such a fast one, I would even compromise with it to the extent of giving a big shop like this one little window, arranged no higher than the eye level, in which the bargains of the day would be on exhibition. If the shopkeeper liked that sort of thing, he could change the display every hour. But the drama of a well-arranged shop, the thing that lures people in, is what is inside: the shelves, the counters, the goods, the people. It is a sheer waste of plate glass to conceal this drama with the dreary banality of displays.

A NYONE who wishes to have an opinion as to what the rational development of New York *may* be should look at the series of plans made by an able group of architects and community planners, lately on view at the New School for Social Research. (It will probably appear in other parts of the city presently.) Messrs. Aronovici, Churchill, Lescaze, Mayer, and Wright have taken a waste area on the Astoria waterfront and shown how it could be planned for living. The ABC of such planning consists in wiping out expensive streets designed for nonexistent traffic and converting them into parks and playgrounds, and in readjusting the block schemes and the housing layouts so as to secure sunlight and take advantage of views across the parks and river. Once you have learned the ABC's, they seem so obvious that the wonder is we have built anything else.

But this is almost the only set of plans I have seen during the past year—and heaven knows there have been bushels of them—that applies systematically the principles of modern city development to a local area. Many of the plans that have been offered for slum clearance and city design look as if their authors had acquired most of their knowledge from the Chicago Fair of 1893 and combined it with powerful lessons in congestion derived from the more respectable-looking Berlin slums of the nineties. And the joke of the matter is that the new plans for Astoria do not represent an advance in cost; they are merely an advance in intelligence and art.

1934~35

By 1934, money from Washington began to revive New York's economy, chiefly through the creation of large public works throughout the city. The list of these works that Mumford reviewed that season is impressive: an incinerator uptown, two courthouses downtown, a revamped Bryant Park in midtown, and a zoo in Central Park. A different conception of the modern city was unveiled at Rockefeller Center in the spring of 1935: a model of Broadacre City by Frank Lloyd Wright, which Mumford judged favorably.

W HEN the Mayor of New York dedicated the new incinerator at 215th Street and Ninth Avenue a little while ago, he said plainly that he didn't like it. Perhaps he was justified in his opinion of it as a piece of sanitary engineering, but when he went on to say that it looked ungainly and unsightly, and that it reminded him of Sing Sing, one wondered what he really wanted. Did he want it dressed up to look like the Municipal Building, or dressed down to look more like an incinerator? I hope it was the latter, for the Mayor's whole reputation as an architectural critic rests upon this decision.

The incinerator is *unsitely* enough; indeed, it is probably as misplaced as such a building could be. It lies on the lowland near the Harlem River, and its chimneys breathe their smoke into the face of University Heights, aided by the prevailing north and west winds. On a square two-story base sits a setback third story with a different window arrangement; the proportions are not bad. Three huge chimneys of pale, buff brick—inaccurately and unjustly called "drab" in the newspaper reports—rise from the front of the building, which is done in the same sort of brick, with limestone trimmings. The architects have given the chimneys a "base" by carrying the wall of the two-story structure around them: a mask of brick with three arched recesses and two arched openings. These form a triumphal entrance to nothing whatever, since the rubbish wagons swing around the side.

T HE elements of such a building are simple; and, as I have often remarked, such elements always daunt architects brought up on traditional precepts, who do not realize that simple elements can also be dramatic. Most of the trouble with this incinerator is that the architects, contrary to the Mayor's impression, did try very hard to keep it from looking like Sing Sing. But the only means they knew for doing this was "ornament." Hence they introduced dreary bands of hashed limestone and equally dreary pilasters, to emphasize elements which should have been kept clean so that the mass would remain unified. Since it was impossible to hide the chimneys completely, the architects smugly concealed the base of these three noble columns.

Granting that this type of incinerator is a public nuisance, what could have been done to redeem it for the eye? The answer is simple: concentrate on the chimneys. Utilize the rondure of the chimneys themselves to play off against the cubical mass of the building; expose the base of these great stacks by following their curves, departing from this, perhaps, only to reverse the curves in joining the building. The romantic school of modern Amsterdam architects, brought up among the brick windmills of Holland, have shown how to use curving brick walls in just such a play of cube and cylinder. Indeed, despite what the architects have done to make the building look commonplace, the clean buff chimneys against a blue sky look fine; and they are none the worse because a good-sized elm tree just in front of them gives scale to their colossal proportions. That tree should be preserved at any cost. I predict that this elm and the chimneys will appear in more than one lithograph presently, and that His Honor will like the effect, too, when he sees it in a picture.

PERHAPS the most interesting recent example of renovation is the house Mr. William Lescaze has designed for Mr. and Mrs. William Lescaze on East Forty-eighth Street, between Second and Third Avenues. This is a remarkable block anyhow. Fifteen years or so ago, it was the best example of large-scale remodelling the city could show, for someone had the happy notion of doing over groups of brownstones on Forty-eighth and Forty-ninth Streets in a sort of mild Bloomsbury Georgian manner, and throwing the nasty back yards into a handsome common garden. This turned a blighted area into an attractive spot before the parents of Sutton Place had even met. Now Mr. Lescaze has pioneered in the remodelling of a single unit, only seventeen feet in width, and shown what can be done within these drastic limits. Necessarily the virtues of such a design must be those of detail, rather than of plan, particularly since Mr. Lescaze has incorporated into the basement his architectural drafting-room and thus taken away part of the old-time service quarters.

The outside is white stucco. The high stoop to the domestic quarters is protected against rain by a flat louver; against the solid side of the stoop, the number, 211, can be seen at a good distance, to the joy of taxi-drivers and other motorists on rainy nights. (Plain numbers and visible signs, by the way, are one of the real contributions of modern architecture. Howe & Lescaze set an excellent precedent in their Philadelphia bank.) A ribbon window, enclosing the servant's bedroom and the kitchen, runs around the front; there is a steel service casement for accepting packages, and a peep-hole for inspecting visitors—which shows what life has come to in the fourth decade of the twentieth century in New York. Within, instead of let-ting the balustrade return on itself, as was always the practice when wood was used, the architect has economized on space by using a solid slab, admirable alike for looks and saving of labor in dusting. The windows of the two upper stories are really walls of hollow glass tile.

T HE principal departures in the design are in the use of these glass tiles, and in the rational employment of air-conditioning. Air-condi-tioning is not a cure for all the ills of humanity, but it is a very useful agent in making possible the renovation of the old-fashioned New York brown-stone. The curse of such houses was the wasteful dark interior space; thanks to air-conditioning, Mr. Lescaze was able to turn this space into daz-zling white bathrooms on the second, or bedroom, floor. In the front bed-room, instead of using air-conditioning, he has inserted two casement win-dows in the glass walls. These glass tiles seem to work admirably. They break up the images on the outside, including the sun's, and give complete privacy while providing a maximum amount of light. The ribbon windows in the rear, on the upper floors, follow the outward curve of the west end of the rooms, thereby not merely adding to their apparent space but opening a better view on the gardens to the east, an ingenious deviation probably well worth the extra expense. Add to all this a dining-room that opens on a one-story terrace which covers most of what was once the back yard—a terrace with a water-lily pool, and even a young birch tree—while at the top is a library and social room that occupies the entire floor. All in all, Mr. Lescaze has done a very useful piece of individual pioneering. I should not be surprised if his ingenious treatment of plot and site started a wave of renovation in the old brownstones.

Before the wave breaks, I have a suggestion to make to those who can afford to take it seriously. This is to buy *two* narrow brownstones and throw them together, eliminating one stairs and hall, and using the space thus gained to make rooms of a commodious shape and size. By gaining space in the width, one need make the house only two rooms deep. This would avoid the necessity for air-conditioning, and give even the bathrooms direct air and light. The result would be far better than those expensive houses off Fifth and Park Avenues, built over the entire lot, and called palatial only by those who have neither analyzed their plans nor tried to live in them. When one thinks of their airless back rooms, untouched by daylight, whose hangings are always drawn in order to keep the occupants from staring at the blank wall ten feet away, one wonders that more murders are not committed there. Or perhaps that's the reason so many murders are committed there.

D O not be scared away by the alliterative title, "Rameses to Rocke-feller," from reading the best popular history of architecture that has appeared since Viollet-le-Duc's defunct classic, "The Habita-tions of Man in All Ages." The author, Mr. Charles Harris Whitaker, was the editor of the *Journal of the American Institute of Architects* from 1913 to 1927, and his old department, "Shadows and Straws," was one of the fea-tures that made the *Journal* known widely outside the profession. He not merely knows architecture, understands craftsmanship, and hates humbug; he is a writer of distinction. "Rameses to Rockefeller" is not a Baedeker of architecture; neither is it a work of exhaustive factual scholarship: its value derives as much from Mr. Whitaker's personality as from the material with which he deals. His charm, eloquence, discernment, and freedom from pedantry make him a much more useful guide than Dr. Dryasdust. No one is better aware than Mr. Whitaker of the more sinister aspects of architec-ture. He dwells in detail on the mournful way in which the life of the liv-ing creature dwindles and shrinks precisely at the moment that its shell becomes more magnificent. This sort of criticism should be good medicine for architects, too—particularly if they meditate long upon the urbane Voltairean irony of the last two chapters.

M R. Whitaker's reflections upon the new triangle in Washington are a useful prelude to the buildings we are going to look at now: they are products of the same kind of systematized aesthetic unintelligence. The scene is Foley Square, if you know where that is. It is bounded on the south by McKim, Mead & White's Municipal Building, chiefly useful because it provides a good frame through which to look at the Woolworth tower, and the north end, if I remember the old maps right, is somewhere near the lower boundary of the Collect Pond. (None of the architecture that has been spread over this scene, from the original Egyptian Tombs onward, has ever justified filling up the old Collect Pond. It should have been kept as a memorial to John Fitch, whose steamboat chugged over its waters long before Robert Fulton hired a publicity man. It would still be a useful place in which to throw retiring police commissioners.)

The two new buildings that are going up here are only half-finished, but one may as well look at them now as at any other time. Like the proverbial egg, you don't have to finish them to find out how bad they are. The supreme example of pretentiousness, mediocrity, bad design, and fake grandeur is the new Federal Court Building, whose tower now heaves upward on Centre Street. It is by the late Cass Gilbert. His one partial success was the Woolworth Building—marred by archaic jitters, yet somehow slightly poetic. He will probably go down in history as one of the worst monumental architects America has produced. That is saying something in a country that contains, among other dead colossi, the Lincoln Memorial and the Rockefeller Church on Riverside Drive.

The lower part of the Federal Court Building contains, I should imagine from the elevation, the bulging chambers devoted to justice. From the centre of this rises an office building with a pyramidal top. The material of these buildings is granite, and with the small windows and heavy walls and demi-Grecian ornament, the deceased architect has done his best to make the steel-framed building look like a natural offspring of the blowsy monument beneath it. It is the sort of design that might have occurred to an early-nineteenth-century architect if he had suddenly been asked to solve this new problem with no further help than he could get from current plates and engravings; but what might have been a pardonable blunder in 1834 is nothing short of a major crime in 1934. These two unlovely and unrelated forms, the court house and the office building, remind one of the way in which the skyscraping Boston Custom House was plumped on the decent little building beneath it, an error no one should ever have repeated.

As for the Court Building proper, you can tell in an instant that it is a temple devoted to august matters—either a bank, or an insurance company, or a hall of justice. You can tell because it is fronted with a Macedonian phalanx of preposterous—and also preposterously expensive—classic columns. To create such a dingy and oppressive design, an architect must, in addition to a lot of negative qualifications, have a great deal of money to spend. Merely removing the columns from the front of this building would probably have lowered the income tax and helped balance the national budget. Unfortunately, it is not much of a relief to turn from this architectural spectacle to the other monuments of Foley Square. They are supposed to form a new civic centre, but one could scarcely guess it from the way they are placed.

O ver Mr. Guy Lowell's melancholy County Court House, charity should draw a veil; not the least of its sins is that it is coyly turned southward, as if to do honor to some nonexistent axis or terminal point. If it honestly fronted the square before it, something might have been done to whip these buildings into shape, no matter what their failings as individual units. As often happens in schemes like this, the whole "monumental" effect was planned without control over the fourth side of the square. Hence one of the slabs of land remaining on this side will shortly be adorned with a shop building; there are also a tall office building and the blank walls of another building as resting spots for the eye when one leaves the court houses. The city might at least have planted a good stiff row of poplars to blot out these unseemly buildings, but even the planting of the square is wrong. The tiny park is broken up into irregular spaces, bounded by iron fences, and the trees are planted in a semi-naturalistic fashion. Here is a case where formal banks of trees would have helped to pull together these badly related buildings. The new setup in Bryant Park is an example of the sort of treatment that Foley Square needs.

I should like to report that the new Health Building of the municipality, now being finished, on Worth Street, the north side of this centre, is a happy exception to these dreary examples. But the truth is that it is not as good as its neighbor, the New York State Office Building. There are the usual columns between the window bays, the usual deep reveals, the usual eagles, the usual plaques, the usual band of names, beginning in this case with Moses and suddenly jumping to Jenner. Architecturally, however, it gives no signs of health. All the elements of which it is composed are the leftovers of past banquets; by right they ought to be hauled up to the municipality's new incinerator.

I T will probably take me years to stop shuddering retrospectively over the attempt to revive Victorian decoration that took place at an Industrial Art Exhibition in the Metropolitan Museum a few years ago. Fortunately, the designers and manufacturers have a shorter memory. They have swung into production of modern pieces with a will once more; unfortunately, half of them are as far as ever from realizing what the shooting is about.

Except in details, the exhibition now at the Metropolitan Museum is marking time. There has been no substantial advance over the forms that were on view five years ago. But in the central hall of the present show, Mr. Arthur Loomis Harmon has gone one step further in presentation: one looks through real windows into the rooms of the house he has set up, and establishes the relationship between the outside and the inside at a glance— a very good lesson for those who have not grasped the continuity of interior and exterior in modern design. The effect of the natural lighting, coming from the far windows, is likewise pleasant.

T HERE are various reasons for the slowing up of modern design. In part it may be due to a healthy distrust of mere novelty. One would give more weight to this motive, however, if the designers were steadily refining the essential forms. The fact is that manufacturers are loath to recognize the skill and competence involved in turning out a design almost exactly like last year's model, only a little better; yet it is exactly that sort of thing that improved the motorcar. Nor are furniture makers any more eager than motorcar manufacturers to sponsor a design that breaks radically with an established line. The most useful departure that the last few years have shown is upholstered-chair units that can be built up into couches. This is a small matter, perhaps, but it indicates the right direction.

Fundamental improvements are difficult when the chief thought of the designer is how to make a thing look luxurious and expensive to people who have no appreciation of the costliness of good craftsmanship and good materials. Take the matter of dining-room tables. The great need in a dining-room table, from the standpoint of the diners, is to eliminate the legs. This is not achieved in the present show by Mr. Donald Deskey's design of U-shaped bands of metal on a flat base, nor is it achieved by Mr. Walter D. Teague's elegant notion of making the legs out of glass cylinders.

A real step in the elimination of the Leg Evil is indicated by Messrs. Simonson and Loewy in their Designer's Office and Studio. They centre the support and anchor the table in the floor. (A similar device in a dining-table would remove all doubts at dinners as to whose leg was touching yours.) Incidentally, in the same office the designers have neatly combined an adjustable lighting standard with the table support, and they have shown how to take the chromium curse off metal-work by using a gun-metal finish. That is real modern design—simple, direct, unpretentious, genuine. For contrast, note the cumbersome games table on the porch of the exhibition house, combined into a single inflexible unit for no reason at all except to avoid the obvious.

What is lacking in this exhibition is at least one modest room, composed of run-of-the-mill products, such as Mr. Philip Johnson recently showed at the Museum of Modern Art. That would be an object lesson in the grand fact that with the machine, beauty does not hinge upon expense. In its present form, the exhibition hardly differs seriously enough from that of a good department store to warrant the Metropolitan's special efforts.

THE first appearance of order in Bryant Park was bound to make one feel glad. Think of those long, dreary years when it looked as if someone had struck oil there, and those other dreary years when it seemed as if Mr. Sol Bloom were promoting the Better Homes Movement with a genuine Early American house for only $8,ooo (estimated). I wish I hadn't spent part of an afternoon looking at the new park carefully. For the only thing that stands up well is the designer's original hunch that a city square should not be treated like a *jardin anglais*.

The most pleasant part of the design is the formal banking of trees at the sides of the park, and the broad expanse of grass in the middle. Nothing could be more restful than that lush expanse of grass. The use of different shades of green, ranging from the light green of the plane tree through the ivy ground-cover and the dark green of the Japanese-yew border (if that's what it is), in the central space is likewise happy. But how much of the grass does one see from a bench? The only really good view is from the "L" station. For the pedestrian, the view is stupidly spoilt by a stone balustrade. And what a balustrade! The architect looked at the solid Carrère & Hastings model on the east side of the park and thinned his own design out into something that must be described as a stone railing. The result is an eyesore and an affront. Here was just the place to obviate the need for a railing by sinking the whole central green, a feat that should have been easy, since the level of the park was raised.

As for the other weaknesses in the design, the worst probably is the fact that the park is planned on a false axis, with a grand entrance up a flight of steps from Sixth Avenue, and with a fountain on the terrace. The total effect is that the part of the landscape that needs most seriously to be blotted out by a solid wall of trees—namely, the solemn beauties of the Elevated and Forty-first Street—is instead revealed, perhaps as dingy a piece of urban architecture as was ever used to close a vista. (I am not forgetting the horrible effect of the Museum of Natural History from Seventy-ninth Street). This plaza on the west end crowds the green up against the stone steps at the east end and makes the wide stairs themselves seem senseless.

I suppose it is silly to complain that the walks look too narrow for comfortable circulation, because the plan does not encourage circulation. The grand effect of the design is to invite one to slump on a backless bench and look through a toothless balustrade at a piece of green one mustn't walk on and cannot see. If I stayed on one of those benches long enough, I'd be prepared to lead an uprising on the part of the unemployed for the purpose of tearing down the balustrade and providing the benches with backs. Now that the architect has had his fun, let's throw the design into the wastebasket and begin all over again. Perhaps one could even persuade the next architect to fasten a little attention on the rear of the Library, its best façade. Better, at all events, than Sixth Avenue and Forty-first Street.

MR. Moses, the magician, waved his wand a year ago over the old menagerie in Central Park. Presto! those dreary wooden buildings vanished. Today, in their place, is a cluster of gray slate roofs and leaden ventilator cupolas and red brick walls. This mass looks extremely nice from the Park wall at Sixty-first Street, and if you want to get the best effect of the new zoo, you should prop yourself up against the wall and not go a step farther.

Roughly, there are three ways of designing a zoo. You can do it from the standpoint of the animals, and try to make them feel at home. The first attempt to give the animals a break was in the Hagenbeck Zoo at Hamburg, now moth-eaten and funny with its *art nouveau* rocks, but only a generation old. The last word in this kind of planning is Whipsnade, near London. The second way, which is proper enough for the midst of a crowded city, is to arrange the animals in such a manner as to amuse the visitors. In practice, this means domesticating the animals and encouraging them to be showoffs; also, it means concentrating attention heavily on such natural actors as the bears and the monkeys. To do this, the more important cages and runs must be made in bays, so that there will be visibility from three sides, without too much neck-stretching and stepping on toes. And it means changing the type of bars to offer as much visibility as will go with safety. But there is still a third method of designing the zoo: to forget about the needs of the animals and the visitors, and to centre all the attention upon the buildings, considered purely as masses in a formal architectural scheme. It was in this fashion, apparently, that the Central Park Zoo was created.

As a mere eyeful of architecture, there is something to be said for these buildings. They are not, thank heaven, Georgian, as some of the newspapers have called them; they are, rather, conceived in the sort of free vernacular that was being done in England in the nineties, and that was used by Mears in the Edinburgh zoo. As with the older British architects, Mr.

Aymar Embury II, the designer of the zoo, is at his best in the craftsman-like handling of traditional materials. The brickwork is excellent, and if he had only thrown out such clichés as round arches and limestone diapers and stuccoed gable ends, the effect would have been both straightforward and fresh. The buff-tiled interiors are good, too, as far as materials go; Mr. Embury very sensibly did not attempt to paint artificial landscapes on the walls of the cages. The restaurant interior, which carries out the same general scheme, is light and pleasant. In external decoration, the effect is not so happy: the silvered wooden doors, the extravagant sentry boxes at the entrance, the artful cages in the central plaza, and above all the dreadful wishy-washy painted friezes on the stuccoed clerestory of the two flat-roofed buildings show to what silly lengths "architect's architecture" will go when it muffs its real opportunities.

Mark you, the real opportunities were there. Why should the houses not have been specially designed for the more extensive use of both living animals and plants for decoration? Mr. Embury's large windows were a step in this direction, of which he did not take full advantage. Why should more tropical plants not have been used in such well-heated places as the monkey houses and the bird house? Placed between the cages and glass walls outside, they might have served for both exterior and interior decoration. Why should trees not have been used outdoors, instead of leaving the whole story to be told in brick and stone and third-rate painted decoration?

IF the zoo is at its best in the use of materials, it is at its worst in the general layout. It was designed as a series of connected buildings, joined by covered passages, around a large sunken garden. The proportions of this whole were more or less dictated by the central mass—the old Arsenal. Here the architect had a happy inspiration. By scraping the mud-colored paint off the Arsenal and making a few minor alterations, he recreated a handsome building. So far, good. Unfortunately, instead of converting the two lower floors into refreshment-rooms, and thus doubly justifying the preservation of the Arsenal, he built a large central mass opposite it and made that the restaurant. Doing this, he broke the zoo up into two unrelated parts in such a way as to nullify the functional advantage of the connecting passageways. The result is to diminish the space that could be devoted to outdoor runs and cages, and the outdoor quarters are cramped. If the aim of a zoo is to feed the maximum amount of business to the refreshment house, the design is eminently successful. Even here a grand opportunity was passed up, for though there is an elevated terrace outside this house, the building is designed for indoor use alone.

THIS failure calls attention to the fact that the whole emphasis of the design is indoors. Instead of shading the paths in the plaza with banks of trees, the area is left open, to become a perfect bake oven in the summertime, when it is heavily used. The pool for seals in the middle is quite good, but there is no place where one can sit down and have a view of what is going on in the zoo as a whole. The old open-air birdcage, with its pelicans and pigeons, is gone, and another popular feature, the run with the barnyard animals, is gone, too. Had the architect been thinking of the animals and the people, and not of a Beaux-Arts *esquisse,* the open cages would have been in close connection with this central space—if, indeed, such a space would have been retained at all in a well-conceived design. The final misdemeanor of this siteless and functionless planning is the covering up of the rocky background of the bears' dens, and the absurd failure here to do away with bars. This is matched only by the fact that one of the pleasantest outcrops of rock in the Park, where the bed of iris is most beautiful in June, is mashed up between a pony concession and the new buildings on the right as one enters from the south.

If you want to know my score on the zoo as a whole, here it is, on the basis of ten as a perfect mark and seven as a passing grade: Materials and workmanship, 9; visual effect, 7; structure, 6; decoration, 5; function, 4; site-planning and layout, 3. In Mr. Embury's defence, however, one should add that the whole project was, according to report, done in sixteen days. The result is just what one might expect with such a rush job: a stage set worked up to please the client, and perhaps, incidentally, the architect. Whereas in a good zoo one would scarcely notice the buildings, in the Central Park zoo one can scarcely notice anything else. Surely architecture, like patriotism, is not enough.

THE age of remodelling is now in full swing. Shall we anticipate history and call it the age of remuddling? The nicest things that the city can show as a result of these efforts are the little pocket handkerchiefs of playgrounds that Mr. Moses and his collaborators have been scattering over the city. They would be even nicer if Mr. Moses' taste in architecture, though decent, were not tainted with the suburbanism of the twenties. He has dogmatically, I understand, refused to countenance "modern architecture." He might learn something from Mr. M. of Italy, whose most valiant efforts have not been able to cope with two powerful contemporary forces—birth control and architecture. Even he has accepted in architecture the idiom of our own day. A vacation in Zurich, if someone would put him up at Neubühl, would do Mr. Moses a lot of good. The rest houses and shelters in Manhattan would be the better for it, too.

To come so close to achieving positive form in building, and then to have our estimable public servants draw back, is enough to drive us all to drink. So let us take a sober look at the bars and cocktail lounges that have been tunneled out of our hotels. How are the adult playgrounds?

Most of our drinking places, for better or worse, stem from two other traditions: the English pub and the American saloon on one side, and the purely feminine rendezvous for dancing and flirting on the other. The American saloon was always an overrated institution, frowsty and garish and uncomfortable, so all that it has done for the architect is to provide him with an open bar, which, unless judiciously curbed, cramps every other part of the room. Most of the architectural elements derive directly from the pub: dull light, dark wood, smoke-laden air. These features have been carried out, again and again, in what is, after all, the most satisfactory type of drinking place for men: the smoking-room of a good steamship.

Perhaps the best recent example in this tradition is the Roosevelt bar. The background is a veneer of warm brown wood; the chairs and the wall divan are covered in red leather. (Incidentally, it's important to use nonabsorbent materials in coverings and hangings; otherwise the smells of time-soured liquor and smoke defy the best system of ventilation.) In the dim light, the carpet seems a deep purplish maroon. Except for the patterned hangings and the few bangles of ornament on the lighting fixtures, the whole effect is quiet and straightforward. No glare. Nothing to distract one's attention from drink or talk. (When will all architects learn that if one wanted to be reminded of their presence constantly, one would send them a personal invitation to join the party?)

The general effect of the Roosevelt bar (designed by Milliken & Bevin) is that which was achieved by the Café Wien in Frankfurt am Main a few years earlier. The feeling is traditional, but the means are the direct vernacular of our own day. In addition to its warm restfulness, what makes the Roosevelt bar so good is the scale and disposition of the room. It is on two levels, and in the warmer weather, when the street door was open, there was a pretty little drama of people passing in and out, below the eye level of the upper section. Also, whether there are three people in the place or fifty, the scale remains correct. Contrast this with gigantic halls for dining and drinking, like the Flying Trapeze, in which three people are as lost as a pea in a hippopotamus's mouth. Most of the bars and lounges in hotels have, fortunately, not been threatened with too much space; hence their scale remains human and comfortable.

As for the cocktail lounge, the feminine touch has been a little overdone. Architecturally speaking, most of these places are the equivalent of an Alexander, and I can think of nothing worse to say about either the imagination or the handiwork of man. Personally, if I must choose, I prefer plain plastered walls and decorated ladies to decorated walls and plastered ladies. But even here there are exceptions. By far the best of the lounges—within my provincial tourist's knowledge of such places—is that of the Crillon. For consistent modern decoration, it is even better than the Roosevelt bar, because the whole thing has been carried through without any weak or false touches. Light pine boards cover the walls part way up, variations in their natural color lighten the surface, while the wainscot is bound to the rest of the room by fine lines of white and blue that separate the boards. My one criticism is that the room could have been made to seem wider by setting the boards and lines horizontally. The carpet is blue, the table tops black, the covers of the divans are a blue-and-white check, while those of the chairs are a yellow-and-white check. The Venetian blinds are white, and the high windows and ceiling give spaciousness to what is actually a small, intimate interior. The designer, Winold Reiss, happily didn't think it was necessary to have the wall painted with undressed little choirboys at play to make you realize that neither laughing nor drinking was forbidden on the premises. Nor did he think that it was necessary to make the room so exciting that you would get drunk at the first smell of a Martini. Moreover, the Crillon demonstrates what the more vital modern architects, like Wright and Oud, always knew: that architecture designed for our present style of living does not need to seek its exponents and admirers among the color-blind.

COMPARED to these two cafés, all the other places I have sampled are either pretty nondescript or downright jittery. Sometimes the drama of space is misconceived, as in the men's bar at the Waldorf, where the central point in the room, emphasized by an outburst of decoration, is the cashier's desk. Sometimes, as in the Chatham, with its turquoise-top tables and doors, with its black-and-white floor, with its mirrors bepaint with skyscrapers, and its over-bright neo-Napoleonic air, it establishes for the whole round of the day the very special atmosphere of late evening. Which makes one wonder why some good decorator should not manage his colors and lights in such a fashion as to vary the mood from the quiet of daylight to the color of the cocktail hour, and from that to the more formal brilliance of after-theatre drinking. It could be done. Some day a good stage designer will be called in to do it.

THE Industrial Arts Exposition at Rockefeller Center was opened by a beam of light, a talk by Mayor La Guardia, and a protest against the National Art Alliance by the group of designers who boycotted the show. Since the last included most of the people—with the exception of Mr. Nathan Horwitt—who are doing good or even passable work, you can draw your own conclusions about the exhibition. You will suspect that the marbleizers have been busy making burlesque versions of marble in glossy plastics and synthetics. Right. You may even guess that the radio cabinets still have that fine nutty flavor the sherry importers boast about. Right again. The real reason for going to the show is a large scale model and diagrams by Frank Lloyd Wright of the new type of decongested city that the motorcar and the autogiro have made technically possible.

The central model of Broadacre City is an effective piece of work, done entirely in wood, with even the trees reduced to cubical blocks. Here is something that has been lacking in Mr. Wright's individual projects for wealthy patrons—the conception of a whole community. Wright is a man of the open country, and the basis of his city is private cultivated land, with public forests and parks adding to the communal beauty. In this community, Wright carries the tradition of romantic isolation and reunion with the soil to its conclusion by having as the basis a minimum of five acres of land for every family. Each house has a workshop and a garden. Arterial motor traffic is united with the railroad system, the autogiro is used to solve the problems of landing fields, and the schools and residential areas are separated from the traffic arteries, as at Radburn. Here and there tall buildings rise as single units in the landscape. The massing of woods and gardens and fields is in great rectangles, but where the river and the topography alter the situation, the variation on the main pattern is boldly accepted. There is no axis, fake or otherwise; there is no attempt to make any one set of buildings the centre. The "city," four miles square, functions as an organic whole.

Broadacre City, as Wright has conceived it, is both a generous dream and a rational plan, and in both respects it adds valuable elements that have been left out of a great many current projects for the replanning of our cities and countrysides. Whatever Wright touches he vitalizes; consider the design for his suspension bridge, and consider the poetic symbolism of his cemetery, which begins as a cultivated garden, to be progressively covered over with stone slabs, like those on the floor of an English church, until finally only the stone remains. The weakest point in Broadacre City is the design of the minimal house. Wright, who hates the very word "housing," has created a design for single-family houses for the lower-income groups which compares very unfavorably, I think, with the European and American "housing" he detests. He should have permitted himself to dream more generously. As soon as he reaches the level of the "two-car" house, he shows that he is still our most original architect, as capable of producing beauty in standardized units as in his favored materials that spring out of the earth. On the whole, Wright's philosophy of life and his mode of planning have never shown to better advantage.

T HERE is a nest of buildings in lower Manhattan that gives me more hope for architecture than I was ever able to derive from our late lamented skyscrapers. The central structure, in dignity and cost and elegance, is the new East River Savings Bank on Church Street, between Dey and Cortlandt Streets. Thanks to other examples by the same architects, Walker & Gillette, the general style of the building is by now pretty familiar: a monumental entrance, bayed inward, with an American eagle cut in stone over it, and monumental ornamented black-metal doors. The windows are great vertical panels. If the general effect is as pompous as a dozen columns, the means are not quite so stupid. The smart treatment of the setbacks of the upper floors, which one is scarcely conscious of from the street, could have been carried through the rest of the building with profit. Likewise the architects might have learned from Mies van der Rohe that they only diminish the charm and elegance of fine stone by dressing up the electroliers or going in for fancy metal grilles. The interior color scheme—black marble, red-brown marble, and a light buff travertine and granite—is good. Unfortunately, it dictated the color scheme of one of the dullest murals in New York. This mural is framed in five panels, each panel the size of the opposing window; it covers three thousand square feet of canvas, and it was based upon fourteen aërial shots of Manhattan Island. The serenity of the room, from its shallow barrel-vaulted ceiling to the details of its furnishing, is so satisfactory that one resents the stale and soporific features of the decoration almost as much as one resents its excessive monumentality. Perhaps someone will tell me, some day, why the operating part of the bank was placed opposite the windows, so that the work must be done under artificial light.

Even more significant than the East River Savings Bank are the two low shop buildings, one abutting on it, the other facing it. The structure on Church Street is of limestone, with an almost unbroken row of glass-fronted shops, topped by a second story defined by a row of sash windows, set close enough to give the effect of continuity. The Woolworth store, which forms an L within the building, punctuates the façade with its red horizontal signboard, which drops at the corner to the black glass bands of the other shops. The decorative effect is brisk and handsome. Where, as in the shop of I. Hess, the lettering is of metal, with good proportions and form, the result is fine. The largest slipup is the cornice over the door on Church Street. It should have been treated boldly as a louver, to define the entrance to the upper story.

As for the building next to the bank on the Dey Street side, its black-glass front sets off admirably the white limestone of the bank. There are two chief weaknesses: the dead white of the glass panel running above the shop windows, and the vertical aluminum fluting on each end. From the standpoint of developing a good contemporary vernacular, these two new shop buildings are very hopeful signs. It will be an even more hopeful sign when the presidents of banks really face the implications of making their august edifices look uncomfortably like swanky funeral parlors. The first bank done in a sound, unpretentious vernacular, built obviously for business rather than for public worship, will sweep the country as surely as the first motorcar manufactured to sell for two hundred dollars. One is probably as far away as the other.

1935~36

Public works continued to dominate "The Sky Line" in the fall of 1935. Mumford reviewed a zoo in Brooklyn's Prospect Park, Hudson River piers, and Fort Tryon Park in upper Manhattan. One of the chief legacies of La Guardia's first term was the creation of the New York City Housing Authority in 1934. Mumford reviewed several of the new public housing projects in December 1935, setting the stage for more intensive coverage of housing issues in coming seasons. Mumford's apprehension about the upcoming 1939 New York World's Fair is revealed in his June 1936 review of an exhibition at the Museum of Modern Art.

BROOKLYN has all the luck. After Olmsted had designed Central Park, he packed a dozen years' experience into his portfolio, crossed the East River, and designed Prospect Park, just to show how the job should really be done. Much the same thing has happened in our day. This time it's the Zoo. After a first stab at planning the Central Park menagerie, more to occupy the unemployed hastily than to exhibit animals, Mr. Aymar Embury II has gone to Brooklyn and has done one of the handsomest small zoos that the country can boast—the best, as far as the buildings go, that I have seen anywhere.

In both cases, Brooklyn deserved its luck because it offered better conditions to the planners. There was enough free space in Prospect Park, to begin with, to permit the choice of a finer site for the Zoo and to keep the animals in their old quarters till new ones were ready. The new Zoo is on the edge of Flatbush Avenue, just across from the Botanical Gardens; the Museum, the Gardens, the Zoo, and the Lefferts Mansion form an architecturally related group.

From the stairs that lead down to the Zoo, one can take in the plan at a glance. It is simple, logical, consistent, elegant—in a word, all the things that the plan of the Central Park Zoo, unfortunately, is not. The main group of buildings forms a low semicircle whose flat roofs are dominated by the ventilating stacks and dome of the elephant house on the axis that cuts through the entrance. The core of the semicircle is the seal pool, in the middle of a large plaza. Circulation through the buildings is on the inside arc of the semicircle, while the open-air cages, radiating from the buildings in long, narrow runs, serve the more rangy animals, like the deer and the elk, and provide a maximum space for observation and circulation in the open air. This is formal planning at its best, for the symmetry and regularity tell their story quickly and meet all the functional requirements.

Even the minor buildings are admirably placed and planned. Two large administration booths flank the stairs at the top. Going down, on the left there is a cafeteria building opening on a terrace set with tables; on the right, there is a public comfort station of the same general outlines, likewise provided with a terrace and benches. Equally admirable are the terrace and the benches.

In the treatment of his materials, Mr. Embury has surpassed what was indeed the strongest element in the Central Park design. He has used red brick throughout, with no limestone diapers or other patterns, and he has played the red off against the white rim of limestone, scarcely to be called a cornice, that cuts the building off at the top, and against the blue tiles which form a scalloped fret for the balustrade of the terraces and the clerestory of the houses. There are no indecisive gestures and small prettifications in the design. The mincing, conventional ventilator tops of the Central Park Zoo have given way to units with strong, clean, horizontal flanges; and this is only one instance of the general fact that Mr. Embury has left most of the whimsical tags of picture-book architecture behind him in these new buildings. As for sculpture, it is concentrated in a few great plaques of limestone, with representations of hunts, in low relief, over the entrances; the decoration not merely makes sense by itself but says, "Enter here!"

To look for flaws in a design so handsome is black ingratitude, for in all its important aspects the Zoo is a very distinguished success. Nevertheless it still seems to me that the use of arched windows above the open-air cages is a mistake. Here a horizontal bank would strengthen the positive note of the rest of the design and would permit more direct sunlight to enter the inside of the cages—important in the winter for the animals. And while most of the formal elements in the plan have the grace to be useful, I think Mr. Embury overplayed his hand in monumentalizing the central feature— the great stacks and the blue-tiled dome of the elephant house. Cut off the dome, reduce the size of the stacks, and the elephant house would still remain an imposing central mass, but the proportions between this house and the subordinate wings would be better, and all the buildings would sink—as they should sink—into this natural amphitheatre. These are more serious faults than the use of naturalistic rocks, in the fashion of the Buttes-Chaumont and the Hamburg zoo, for the bear dens. In such a formal composition the gneiss itself might have been handled a little more formally, I think. The bears would not have known the difference.

But let me end on a sweeter note, for there are no end of things to praise. Item: I like the moat of water at the bottom of the deer runs, the curve in the elephants' open-air cages, and the absence of bars wherever possible. Best of all, I like the fine French touch, probably unconscious, in the treatment of the ladies' restroom. From the outside, through a tall window, one may behold a dozen human females making up their faces. Somehow it reminds one of Théophile Gautier's suggestion that a pair of naked human animals should be installed at the Jardin des Plantes. At all events, that glass cage is in the best spirit of the Zoo, part of its animation, charm, frank animality. I trust my calling attention to it will not result in a pane of frosted glass.

To turn from the work of the Parks Department to the most recent structures put up by the Docks Department is to turn from a benefaction to a blight, and from a mood of civic pride to one of simmering rage. I am referring to the new pier for the Normandie at Forty-eighth Street and the North River, to say nothing of two other piers, prospectively as hideous, that are almost finished beside it. The east end of this monumental structure would give a stiff fight for first place in architectural ineptitude to anything that has been put up in our generation. It is not merely bad, but bad in the worst possible way, with a mediocre badness that lacks the vulgar energy and exultation that structures like the Chrysler Tower have.

The style of this fine municipal monument is Funeral Parlor Modernique. The dominating motif is a great upended casket of black tile over the motor entrance; the façade is of light-buff brick and limestone, worked into imbecile patterns, with minor mourning borders around the side entrances. All the mistakes that have been made in the decoration of third-rate loft buildings, cheap Broadway shops, and nondescript provincial department stores attempting metropolitan glitter have been concentrated in this façade. The lettering is in awful and exact harmony with the decoration; the words "City of New York Dep't [*sic*] of Docks" could not have been spaced worse if they had been put into the hands of the Gashouse Gang and thrown at the building. In short, the new dock is a howler; and there are two more howlers to come. Lack of time is no excuse for this disgrace; it took someone many valuable hours to achieve so many mistakes and to work up all the ludicrous details. If the Department of Docks could not lay its hands on the right architect for this job at short notice, it could at least have copied line by line the older piers. They are not the last word in architecture, but they are infinitely better than this bastard Modernique. If the city has a grain of self-respect left, it will tear down the present fronts and do the whole job over. That would be a genuine sign of a revival of art and civic spirit; and I should like to be there to handle the first crowbar and to pry off the lunchroom-tile picture of a steamship that alone proclaims the purpose of this structure.

A T last I have found something to admire in Rockefeller Center, and I hasten to express my feelings before any changes are made. This is the great entrance to the new unit on Fifth Avenue. When I first saw that high, narrow opening, with its austere columns, I wondered what plans might be afoot to mar its noble lines. (Did I not remember my original delight at beholding the great stone fountain in the Plaza, and did I not remember the sick feeling in the pit of the belly when the figure that symbolizes knee-action and floating power was hoisted into place?) Fortunately, the entrance is still unsmudged by ornament and decoration. And the interior is just as good, with its metal cascade of moving stairs, its great slabs of green polished marble, and its high, narrow marble-covered columns in oblong cross-section. One has only to see this luxurious but simple interior to know that it is the correct solution for a modern skyscraper—first used, I believe, in the white-marble halls of the Equitable Building. Whereas, all the stew about murals and sculptural decoration had no more point or sincerity than the hanging gardens; such things were not architectural features but newspaper features, the last ironic note in paper architecture.

THE SKY LINE
A PARK WITH A VIEW~M. LE CORBUSIER
INDIANS AND PLATTERS~NOVEMBER 9, 1935

THE best thing about Fort Tryon Park, which has just been opened, is the site. And to say this is not being unkind to the planners, the Olmsted Brothers, who have done, in the main, a pretty commendable job. But the point is that this site gives one of the most magnificent views in the world, with the Palisades on the opposite shore swerving northward to the bend facing Yonkers, and the George Washington Bridge curving against the sky to the south. I know no landscape near a big city that takes the breath away more completely. Edinburgh from Castle Hill or Arthur's Seat, the Havelsee from the heights above it in Berlin, and the Thames Valley from Richmond are fine; but this one view from Washington Heights freezes the heart, rips out the gizzard, and curdles the backbone—that is, if landscapes ever have that effect on you.

The first test of a landscape architect's competence is whether he has made the most of these sweeps and views; here Fort Tryon Park comes off well. There is a main entrance from Fort Washington Avenue, flanked by heavy butts of the native schist, and a broad promenade leads to the two terraces at the highest point, from the bigger of which one views the Hudson, from the smaller of which one looks eastward at the panic of bad building that has defaced the slopes and surrounding areas of Fort George. The benches along the promenade are above the level of the pedestrians, and the elms are planted only on the east side of the path, while the slope that falls toward the Hudson is treated as a naturalistic garden, covered with a profusion of low-lying plants. So you see the designers knew there was a view.

The observation terraces are surrounded by a low rampart of stone, and again the benches are elevated on successive levels to keep the view clear. Don't ask me why the designers used sand to cover the surface of this windy upland. That seems to me a major error, for the dust blows into the eyes and nullifies all the careful provisions for an unrestricted view. Cobblestones with grass growing between, such as those which now grace

Fifth Avenue along Central Park, would have been preferable. The architectural elements in this design are sincere but somewhat commonplace: if they do not spoil the view, they do not add to it. The refreshment house, with its high-gabled slate roof, seems to me definitely out of the picture; the old-fashioned masonry and the old-fashioned windows missed the opportunity for giving the people inside something to see. There is no poetry in the stone and no freshness in the architect's feeling for it. Had a man like Frank Lloyd Wright been given this great butte to play with, that would have been another story.

Still, the planting has been very pleasantly and intelligently handled, in a sort of orderly naturalism which did not hesitate to use the Japanese yew and the English ivy as well as the native fern—and, as I said, the view has been studiously respected. That is something; indeed, it is a great deal.

L E Corbusier's late exhibition at the Museum of Modern Art showed that his recent work is attempting more and more pathetically to escape the weaknesses of his early rationalism and mechanization. The latest building photographed, dated 1935, shows such curious stylistic atavisms as barrel-vaulted ceilings for a dwelling house and arched garden shelters that remind one oddly of the Maine carriage houses of the eighteen-forties. The fact is, as I pointed out long ago, that when an architect like Le Corbusier wishes to escape the rigorous restrictions of his formula, he is forced to become frivolous; the things which he excluded dogmatically from his original conception of the house as a "machine for habitation" now have to come back in the form of sheer caprice. He no longer tries to express everything in terms of cantilever construction and fabricated materials; but he uses curved lines and stone walls and natural materials in a way that a stage designer would use them. His influence as a polemic writer has been challenging and healthy, but in building I prefer his bleakest rationalism to his "poetry," even though the latter acknowledges belatedly the excellent principle that good building seeks not only efficiency but joy. That principle is not altogether new in a country that has had a Richardson, a Sullivan, a Gill, and a Frank Lloyd Wright.

Le Corbusier, I understand, has disclaimed being an architect for the future; he claims his place in the present. It would be well if the various houses for the future that are being shown about New York were equally modest. The one now on view in Rockefeller Center does not reach more than a step beyond current practice; hardly that. The good features of the latest example, based upon a prize design by Walker & Gillette, are that it is only one story high, and that the architects have not attempted to fake a lower cost by doing away with the cellar—that is, doing away with a family's eternal privilege of accumulating a certain amount of indispensable rubbish.

The square kitchen seems admirably planned—I speak as a cook—and I like the cork-tiled floors for looks as well as quiet. But there are a few weak features worth pondering before anyone imitates them. There is no vestibule, which means that the architects, in the interests of "economy," have forgotten about blasts of cold air, muddy shoes, wet overcoats, and dripping umbrellas. And the "modern" feature of a partial partition of glass tile to separate the dining-alcove from the living-room is worse than futile; it defeats the one real justification of this arrangement—the possibility of throwing the two rooms into one for dancing, or of blocking off one completely from the other for privacy, possibilities that require a removable partition, or, more simply, a double door. And while the furniture of the living-room is pretty handsome, I cannot say anything good for a dining-room table that doesn't fold up; that type no more fits the small house than does the separate, exclusive dining-room. Macy, incidentally, has been showing a fine new folding table, with drawers for silver in the central part, that would fill the bill exactly.

One more point. Nothing will ever convince me that a bathroom with a peephole instead of a full-sized window belongs to a modern house. The convention of the little bathroom window is one of the silliest tricks in the whole repertoire of American architectural practices. A bathroom ought to be a bright, cheerful place, with a horizontal window that begins at shoulder level and so avoids the need for curtains or frosted glass; it should have a pleasant view, preferably oriented southeast or east, and it should be wide enough to sun and ventilate the room quickly and completely. The efforts to treat a bathroom as a cross between a penitential cell and the Black Hole of Calcutta are more ridiculous than the stained-glass decorations of the eighties.

THE new Longchamps restaurant, where Reuben's used to be, on Madison Avenue finds me in a polite tussle with my colleague, Lipstick. We are probably both right, but that never makes it any easier. As far as I am concerned, the decoration is just a sizzling platter: the good architectural ingredients are spoiled for my squeamish taste by an excess of decorative parsley and the smell of scorching butter. (Now you know what I think about sizzling platters, too.) The elements of the new restaurant are fine: black and red and gold and yellow are a good combination for expressing smartness and style, all the more because vermilion walls are kind to girls' complexions. So, though the lighting is quiet, the gold and the mirrors and the red make a very vivacious ensemble. The long central bar with the double bank of tables on each side, at different levels, gives plenty of action to the picture, and I haven't a word against the curve that sets off the dining-room from the café proper; it is meant to be gay and capricious, and it is. But all the things that are done well are not a bit more exciting and effective for being overdone. The gold figures on the walls, the figures inset in the table tops, and the alternation of red and yellow in the chairbacks are excessive. As for the paintings of the Indians of North America in the back of the restaurant, all I can say is that if the Museum of Natural History is responsible for this innovation, it is pushing its policy of adult education a little too far. Fannie Brice and Joe Cook *as* American Indians might have been the making of the room; but surely Mr. Winold Reiss was mixing firewater and champagne when he put those specimen cases in this particular setting.

None of these excesses will keep the new Longchamps from being an extremely popular restaurant. Indeed, after a cursory glance at the really popular places about town, I've come to the conclusion that the two most important ingredients so far are architectural bad taste and the liberal use of the color red. Puritan though I am, I wish some born gambler would some day put all his money on the color red alone. It might be a winner.

THE SKY LINE
THE NEW HOUSING
DECEMBER 7, 1935

ALL the talk that has gone on during the last few years about "low-cost housing" and "low-rent housing" and "redeeming the blighted areas"—incidentally, they are three quite different matters—has probably left you with a headache. Those of us who have been doing the talking share your headache, too, for housing is in the same state as Mark Twain's weather: everybody complains about it, but nobody ever does anything.

Let us, before looking at a handful of examples of the new housing, get at least one fact clear. No dodge of architecture or mass production can solve the problem of providing decent quarters that rent for ten dollars a room per month for people whose wages only give them a claim to four dollars' worth. Most of the headaches are caused by bumping against that solid wall. The new housing doesn't solve that problem. What it does do is to give us a hint of what the city might look like if the economic groups that *can* afford to be housed decently were to refuse to go on living in the elegant pigsties, rabbit hutches, dungeons, and penal colonies that form our domestic environment from Henry Street to Park Avenue.

I shall begin with the best examples of the new publicly financed housing, and grade down to the worst. By far the most imposing and successful piece of domestic building is Hillside Homes in the Bronx, the great pile of red brick, capping a hill, that springs out of the low-lying land that faces you as you come down the Boston Post Road from New Rochelle. This is a seventeen-acre site; it has two and a half acres of playground. Most of the houses are four stories high, but at the topmost block they rise to six- and seven-story elevator apartments. There are 1,416 living units, or 4,948 rooms, built for about $1,000 a room.

Casually looking at the plans and the airplane photographs, I felt that the site was overcrowded, and I confess that my judgment was wrong. The existing street system, which unnecessarily cuts through the tract and wastes a lot of the taxpayers' money, was not changed till the houses were all built; for it takes endless political machinery to wipe out a street. So the architect, Mr. Clarence S. Stein, was forced to fit the buildings into the obsolete and obstructive street pattern. Otherwise all the old block and lot units and building lines have been broken down. In general, the apartment units form irregular double quadrangles, bound together by a building through which a wide passageway gives a vista toward the level just above.

Every element in the buildings has been sincerely handled, and the details, such as the circular handrailing at the doors, the finishing off of the stair and elevator towers on all four sides, and the type of steel-framed casement windows, are admirable. The brick used is the same orange-red brick from the kilns at Cornwall that was used in the Central Park Zoo. The vertical accents at the entrances are simple, well conceived, functional; from first to last, there is not a wasted touch, and the design of the connecting units, with their broad windows, has a very positive aesthetic quality. In the planning of the site, the difference of grade was utilized to permit the fuller occupation of the ground-floor level by apartments, giving them direct access to small private terraces, a feature which adds life and animation to the landscaping of the court.

In a few places, the architect seems to me to have missed an opportunity. One of them is the failure to use more positive colors for the doors, and perhaps even for the window frames; color could have been used to differentiate one block unit from another, with no loss of unity in the design. The other was in not taking advantage of the fine view over the surrounding country and over the interior gardens by using cantilevered windows at the corners. This has become a stale and laughable "modern" cliché of ordinary commercial apartment building, because the commercial builder does not bother to provide anything worth seeing from the windows. At Hillside, there is landscape, there is view, there is sunlight—and there are plenty of corner apartments. So what would ordinarily be a dull affectation of fashion would here have been a serviceable adaptation.

When Hillside was a-building, the children in the neighboring public school made a survey of the site in pictures and told about it in stories. One little girl wrote a prose poem about it, worthy to be put alongside Chekhov's "Cherry Orchard." Here it is: "This is the Hillside. We played in the grass. We sat on the rocks. We picked wild flowers. It is all gone." With the usual commercial development, this would have been a final epitaph; but in the present case she spoke too soon. The grass and the flowers are back; so is playing. There is an auditorium, a children's nursery, a whole series of wading pools, shops and studios.

The closest approach to Hillside is another PWA project, the Cord Meyer development at Boulevard Gardens, Woodside. The tract itself is a very large one, and the interior courts of the main unit are extremely generous. Unfortunately, after allowing too much space here, the planner found himself with a wedge of land to the east, facing railroad tracks and a dreary mixture of dumps and wretched houses; here he crowded the land with units whose long side faces the noise and the barren vista. Obviously, the apartments should have run parallel to the main avenue and at right angles to the railroad tracks. While the unit of building, a long unit with two short horizontal bars, seems economical, the architecture itself lacks positive conviction and gives no positive pleasure. Could the architect himself really have enjoyed the few half-hearted bastard Georgian touches, in the name of ornament, and the row of shutters—yes, shutters—at the fourth story, also presumably in the name of ornament?

Both these projects, in the use of open spaces and green, are miles ahead of the ordinary commercial development. The secret of their success is that the unit is not the single apartment house, but a whole group of houses combined in what the English call a housing estate. Hence the flexibility in site planning, limited only by the rigid street system; hence the open space. Hillside reaches a fairly high density: two hundred and fifty people per acre. This would be about the top limit for decent housing anywhere. Technically, neither development is overcrowded; but I am not convinced that on reasonably priced land saving in cost per unit justifies using six-story units instead of mainly three-story units. At three stories, both projects would have been in better scale, more livable, and human.

T HE last project is the so-called First Houses, built by the municipality as a project in slum clearance. The site is on Third Street between Avenue A and First Avenue, originally occupied by some old-law slums owned by Mr. Vincent Astor. Various innocent or deluded persons have during the last few years been advocating the salvaging of old-law tenements by removing one house in every two, thus leaving two exposed sides wherein windows could be punched. A very brilliant notion, apart from the fact that the wooden floors of these ancient structures, built in the seventies and eighties, are infested by rats, bedbugs, and roaches. Also, the cost of renovation is so great that one might as well tear down these lousy quarters and make a fresh start.

That is just what the New York City Housing Authority found it had to do: tear the buildings down. All that was utilized were a few foundations. Unfortunately, in making plans for the new houses, the architects kept to the limitations of the original scheme, and except for the three-story apartment group on Avenue A the result is downright terrible. Since this reconstruction consists only of an L-shaped tract occupying roughly half the block, the external environment remains exactly what it was before: bleak, filthy, ugly.

This is, in fact, an overwhelming demonstration of precisely how not to house the lower-paid workers, and, above all, how not to rebuild the blighted areas of New York. Unfortunately, it has been accompanied by the usual amount of bright, mendacious publicity. An account in the *Times* even said that "their sunny rooms will look out upon landscaped courts which will help to inspire in them [the tenants] a new outlook on life." If that happens, all one can say is that the tenants will have to be singularly susceptible to inspiration; and three-quarters of them will have to have X-ray eyes, too. By hook or crook, the Housing Authority has got down the rents on these apartments to $6.05 per room per month. That comes nearer to low-rent housing than anything the jerry-builder has been able to offer; hence it is bound to be touted as a "solution" of the housing problem. But from the standpoint of the standards of health, decency, and comfort accepted by every civilized country today, these new apartments bear the same relation to good housing that the dreadful model-tenement designs of 1879 did in their time. These new tenements would be expensive at half the price. This is "slum replacement" with a vengeance—it simply replaces an old slum with a new slum. Congratulations, Mr. Post!

THE ART GALLERIES
FIFTH AVENUE'S NEW MUSEUM
DECEMBER 28, 1935

T HANKS and rebellion contended for a place in my heart as I went through the newly opened Frick museum, and I am afraid that my baser feelings have won out. For the moment, I should like to look our new gift horse impolitely in the mouth, and not merely bite the hand that feeds us but take a nip or two at the ankles for good measure.

You must really visit the museum to see how effectually the directors have frustrated their obviously good intentions. Very wisely indeed, they decided to require applications for admission, in order to space attendance through the day. Since most American museums confuse education with mass attendance, this is a welcome departure, and I trust all small, over-visited museums will copy it. Unfortunately, this admirable provision was nullified by roping off the galleries in order to enforce one-way passage through the building. The result is to have all the evils of congestion without a colorable excuse for it; in action, the museum is an elegant counterpart of the Times Square subway station at six in the evening.

Crazy is the mildest word I can find to describe these regulations. They would be entirely appropriate if the sole object of the museum were to permit the maximum number of people to file respectfully past the mummy of the deceased steel manufacturer who gathered the collection together and once lived, in the fashion of his time, in this Renaissance palace. No doubt the barriers protect the carved chests, the Renaissance chairs, and the sculptural bric-a-brac from the prying hands of the curious, but unfortunately they completely sacrifice the paintings to these very minor works of art. The lover of paintings cannot see the bigger pictures without becoming walleyed, and the very essence of aesthetic communion—which involves the singling out of a picture, and its unembarrassed contemplation from various distances or angles—is lost. Indeed, one of the finest paintings in the whole collection, Giovanni Bellini's "St. Francis in Ecstasy," can be seen only from a forty-five-degree angle.

Precious little opportunity for enjoyment, or even effectual observation, lies in the present arrangement. And it is really too bad, for the Frick collection of paintings shows the influence of good, if conventional, judgment, and it boasts a generous handful of paintings of decidedly major magnitude. To my thinking, there is too much Romney and Gainsborough, and for the purpose of interior decoration Boucher and Fragonard were taken over wholesale. Above all, there is too much Whistler. (But "The Ocean" is surely one of his finest paintings; and if you have a liking for Proust, you'll be interested in his portrait of Comte Robert de Montesquiou, who was the original of the Baron de Charlus.) On the other hand, the Van Dyck portraits, particularly those of Frans and Margareta Snyders, are magnificent; the Veroneses are very good; Rembrandt's "The Polish Rider" is one of the best examples of his work in America; Goya's "The Forge" is top-notch, and the Limoges enamels are all that rumor ever said they were: a marvellous fusion of art and technical skill. So much for one's first hasty and badly handicapped impression.

Mischief like the misconceived administrative regulations can easily be repaired, even if this involves putting the bric-a-brac down in the cellar. But what shall one say of the general scheme of converting a private mansion into a public museum, and making the new galleries conform, in their general design and fulsome decorative background, to the rest of the house? The latter step, it seems to me, merely doubled the original error. A historical collection of paintings represents fifty different modes of life and physical settings; and the best background for the paintings and sculpture of the past is no background at all—the bare walls of a modern building, such as Barnard provided in the original Cloisters. While the scale of the Frick museum is fine, the decorative scheme—except in the Fragonard and Boucher rooms, where the rooms themselves are the frame—is a nuisance. The paintings are lost in the background. That may have satisfied the taste of Renaissance princes, or even that of American millionaires during the first part of the present century, but it no longer meets today's standard of presentation.

J ACQUES Lipchitz, whose sculpture has been given a handsome setting at
the Brummer Gallery, is one of the most original, if not most powerful,
influences of the last twenty-five years. On the surface, his work bears a
resemblance in motif and form to the paintings of Picasso's middle period;
there are the same Cubistic abstractions, the same utilization of musical
instruments as themes. But the musical element in Lipchitz's sculpture goes
deeper than the use of guitars as symbols, or even calling one of his finest
pieces "The Song of the Vowels." The transposition from the living form
to a plastic geometrical arrangement is as complete as the transformation
that takes place in music, but, as in music, the generating emotion itself is
not lost but intensified by its reduction to an abstract mathematical scale.
What disappears is the visible event; what emerges is a plastic equivalent,
sometimes in forms that have been made familiar by parallel explorations in
painting, sometimes in forms that remain curiously enigmatic—at first as
incomprehensible to the eye as Chinese music is to the Western ear. Still
other sculptures, however, show an interesting assimilation of tradition; the
complex rhythmic form of "The Song of the Vowels" possibly has its starting point in the Nike of Samothrace, and "Towards a New World" is a more
compact and muscular version of Rodin's dynamic figures and fluid surfaces. Lipchitz is a craftsman who works with equal ease in clay, in wrought
iron (note "She"), in stone, and in cast metal, but above all he is a man of
imagination, whose most abrupt departure from the outward forms of
things nevertheless has austere reason and workmanlike sobriety behind it.

N EW to these parts is the Walker Galleries' exhibition of the ceramic
sculpture of Russell Aitken, a young man who has been winning
prizes at the ceramics shows, and who is now rapidly catching up with the
pacemakers in this field, like Henry Varnum Poor and Carl Walters.
(Walters' pieces at the Downtown Gallery went so fast, incidentally, that I
didn't get around in time to see half of them.) Baked clay is an unpretentious medium: The fragility of the material and the devilish uncertainties
of the firing keep the potter from getting too pontifical about his forms.
Like Walters, Aitken is a plastic humorist, almost a cartoonist. His carica-
tures lean toward making pudgy people and animals, with eyes that bulge
like those of Japanese goldfish; his females run too easily, perhaps, toward

the Betty Boop model; and in his enamels on metal, where the plastic quality is lacking, these simplified cartoon outlines become trite. But "The Futility of a Well-Ordered Life," a legitimate satire on Surréalisme, is fine; "Godiva," a black wench on a zebra, is even better; and "Europa," on the back of a most lascivious old bull, is perhaps the best piece in the show. In short, Aitken's work is full of riotous vitality, and the color of his glazes is exceptionally juicy.

YEAR after year Peter Arno has been turning out the most brilliant comic drawing that has been done since the days of the oh-so-very-different Du Maurier. It is high time, *apropos* the show at the Marie Harriman Gallery, that someone stood up and said plainly how good it is in sheer technical command of its medium. There is nobody drawing in America that I can think of, except possibly Noguchi, who has shown anything like Arno's skill in sweeping a simple wash across a figure to create life and movement in the whole pattern after he has outlined its parts; and no one has dramatized so effectively the elementary battle of black and white, in a fashion that makes a face leap out of the picture like a jack-in-the-box, knocking one in the eye at the same time that the idea of the joke enters one's mind. Arno's freedom from set attitudes and his unlimited fertility in design come out plainly in a big exhibition like this. His invention is as unflagging as his wicked commentaries, though they both spring out of certain well-defined areas of metropolitan life, half-real, half-fantastic, altogether wild and unembarrassed and exuberant. The only fault I can find with him as an artist is this: a man with his perfectly savage gift of characterizing the human face—as deadly, in its way, as that of George Grosz—should not take refuge too often in lazy, pat forms like the white-whiskered major. Graphically these majors tend to leave a blur; but a face like that of the young lady sitting up tense in bed, beside her dormant, irresponsive male, damning the effect of the coffee that lets you sleep—a face like that one never forgets.

THE SKY LINE
OLD AND NEW
JANUARY 11, 1936

So much remodelling has been done around town during the last half-year that I can't pretend to have kept up with it. For the most part, however, the replacements have brightened the streets; the façades have been good, even if usually no profound improvement has been made in the structure itself. Some of the new building has gone even farther than this; the general layout has been improved, and the height has been again scaled to both the human form and the width of the streets. All this will probably come to an end presently, for if rumors from the draughting-rooms are right, we are in for another orgy of tall building. Before the big boys take to the air once more, let us examine a few samples of what the city might become if the boom were to be a gradual and modest and well-controlled one—which perhaps is pretty much like saying "if the tornado would only be tenderhearted."

For scale and arrangement, the best example of new building I know is the group of apartment houses between Fifteenth and Sixteenth Streets, just west of Fifth Avenue. Here the builders kept to an economical plan, based upon the original layout of the Manhattan block. The buildings for which our blocks were originally framed were three stories high and two rooms deep. This left plenty of open space behind the row, and when that open space is thrown into a single plot, it makes a very charming court and garden. By following this simple pattern, the architect was able to design small two- and three-room apartments, with excellent exposure, through ventilation, and a maximum of privacy, far more privacy than is possible in complicated plans whose projecting wings destroy the privacy of the adjacent sides. What is also important about this simple arrangement is that it provides a maximum insulation from noise, particularly on the interior court.

As far as layout and amenity go, here are quarters that are superior to most of those offered elsewhere within city limits at five times the rent. Except for people who have a taste for sky views, this kind of development answers every reasonable requirement for urban living; and a city built on this pattern would have all the tangible advantages of the suburb, in the matter of sunlight, fresh air, and gardens, with none of the inconveniences of being thirty miles away from one's best friend or one's favorite evening amusement. Real-estate brokers and banks who want some suggestions as to what is to be done to make over the slum properties of the East Side, with their high land values and their dwindling population, might consider the possibility of redeeming a whole neighborhood near the river, for middle-class occupancy, on precisely this general design. What Manhattan needs to overcome its present blight (caused mainly by an exodus to the outskirts and the suburbs) is a series of "internal suburbs."

It's something of a pity that the architecture in this particular development, though inoffensive, does not take full advantage of all its opportunities: the rough stucco smears on the outside walls will look pretty grimy in a few years, apart from the fact that they give one no pleasure now, and the southern exposures might have had even more generous windows than these. Nevertheless, both the owners and the architect deserve a special pat of encouragement for doing a very neat and workmanlike job; indeed, their farsightedness in planning these apartments for living, instead of greedily filling up each last square foot with allegedly rentable space, deserves public approbation.

NEARBY is another example of new building, not as good, but quite decent in another way. I mean the row of shops and apartments two stories high on Fourteenth Street, east of Fifth Avenue. This row consisted originally of vast, pretentious, dismal brownstones that were built around the sixties; thirty years ago they had become shops and offices for shabby business enterprises. Painters' studios, too; there were no conveniences, and in the winter the rooms were as cold as tombs, and many an artist's wife or sweetheart broke her heart and her back trying to make the high-ceiled rooms look clean. Now these gaunt horrors of antiquated gentility are gone, and the warm red brick and the low ceilings of the new buildings are a pleasant contrast for anyone who ever shivered in those old, makeshift apartments. One grants, of course, that the arched entrance in the middle is absurdly out of scale, and that the arch itself is out of place;

but for people who rather like to look out on noisy, vulgar, good-natured Fourteenth Street, the repetitive "U" plan of the buildings seems a good solution of the architectural problem.

AMONG the better remodelled façades I would put that of the apartment house at Fifty-seventh Street on the west side of Seventh Avenue. Here the architect, instead of lamely dodging the fact that the building had to have fire escapes, made them one of the principal components of the design; they are of bands of bright, rustless metal, which tie up decoratively with the horizontal emphasis of the new windows. The surface of the wall is a smooth, creamy stucco, and the bright-red sign of the five-and-ten-cent store below, instead of presenting itself as an intrusion, really fits into the design and completes the color scheme. (The old-fashioned way was to embellish a building with broken pediments or baroque urns, and then to affect horror, surprise, and indignation at finding that a five-and-ten-cent store was lodged below the architect's refined, decorative futilities.)

Just this positive note is what is lacking in the otherwise very acceptable low building at Fifty-fourth Street and the east side of Madison Avenue, partly occupied by the House of Morgan on the Fifty-fourth Street side. The sober limestone facing, an arched doorway in black glass, and the high shop fronts, with their black glass panels, are all good enough; but the effect is a little too heavy, and the panel of glass brick, by the entrance to the night club, is less amusing than it might have been, because the conventional treatment of the rest of the structure in no way prepares for it. Still, one must commend the uniform signs and lettering used for the various shops; this is a great improvement over the silly, competitive splurge that deprives our avenues of any collective dignity.

ON the other hand, look at the Hanscom Bake Shops that are now pretty much all over the city. They follow a general pattern of horizontal green enamelled sheets and neon lights and large windows and interiors finished in brown wood. In some ways they are admirable; the interior and the exterior of the shops are part of the same picture, and for small shops, whose entire inside can be seen from the street, this seems to me the correct treatment, both from the standpoint of the shopkeeper's own interest and that of the passerby. Where the site itself is helpful, as in the corner shop at Fifty-seventh Street and Second Avenue, for example, this type of design works out quite effectively. Its most serious defect is the oversized letters which outline the name in neon lights. There is simply no reason for making such a loud noise to identify a chain whose shops can, in fact—like the old-fashioned Childs restaurants—be easily identified even without the name. In many things, American architects should form the habit of scaling bigger and lighting more brightly; the numbers on house and apartment entrances are not nearly as prominent and legible as they should be. But this is a contrary example. If one Hanscom shop makes so many decibels of visual noise, what would a street of such shops sound like? Here is the weakness of competitive sign advertising; it really assumes that there will be no other competitors. As soon as there are, the shopkeepers might as well begin all over again, with a quiet, civilized, uniform design, like that of the Madison Avenue shops I have just mentioned.

B Y now almost everyone knows that Louis Sullivan is one of the three most important architects that America has produced—I am not counting that great Renaissance amateur, Thomas Jefferson. Up to now no complete account of Sullivan's works existed; the best essay on the work of Adler and Sullivan, that by Montgomery Schuyler, was published in 1895, before Sullivan had produced the Schlesinger & Mayer Building in Chicago. With great residuity, excellent technical insight, and good judgment, Professor Hugh Morrison of Dartmouth College has gathered together and analyzed Sullivan's lifework in a book called "Louis Sullivan: Prophet of Modern Architecture" ($4). Very properly, Morrison pays more attention to the buildings themselves than to the quirks and intricacies of Sullivan's own biography; and he has provided the reader for the first time with the material upon which any final judgment of Sullivan's work will have to be based. The book raises many interesting problems that I haven't space at the moment even to broach, but I can heartily recommend it. If you have been baffled by Sullivan's own "Autobiography of an Idea," here is an excellent place to take another try at the man.

DURING the last five years the Architectural League's exhibitions have been pretty melancholy affairs. In the midst of everything, the late Joseph Urban, with his characteristic generosity, put on one good show, but even Urban couldn't turn the funeral march of the building trades into a victory parade. Though plenty of new buildings have been planned or built during the last year, the present League show has the effect of a hangover. It is dull and confused, and demonstrates nothing whatever except that a lot of odd people got a lot of odd jobs.

The main reason the fiftieth-anniversary show fails is that no one apparently grasped the point of our development during the last ten years or saw how naturally it was bound up with the buried renaissance of the eighties. When the League was founded, the arts and crafts in America for the first time, thanks to Richardson, Hunt, and La Farge, were beginning to grow out of the ground from native seeds, instead of from sickly transplantations, preserved in boxes. Almost all that is significant in modern American architecture began in the eighties: the modern plan as evolved by Richardson and carried further by Sullivan and Wright; the modern elevation, springing out of the interior, altered in rhythm by the new modes of construction; the modern skyscraper, as conceived by Buffington, Jenney, and Sullivan; the modern auditorium, first evolved by Adler and Sullivan. To have given an alcove to an intelligent presentation of these beginnings would have been a modest but fitting way of celebrating the anniversary. Surely by now so much has been written about this development that even architects should be aware of it. During the last few months, Hitchcock's book on Richardson and Morrison's biography of Sullivan have driven home the point.

What the Architectural League has done is so silly it almost looks malicious. To depict the spirit of the eighties, it has exhumed an old-fashioned interior, a sort of Victorian Empire, with *chinoiseries* in bamboo, and has placed it opposite an allegedly modern room. Actually, the room of "1936"

is a characteristic example of the spiritless "good taste" that began to flourish around 1906, and ceased to be modern in any sense whatever after 1916.
In that touch one detects, perhaps, merely the influence of the American
Institute of Decorators; for these ladies and gentlemen, to judge by examples in the present show, will have to unlearn practically all their acquired
knowledge and taste before they will be of the least service to modern
architecture.

In order to underscore the failure to understand the eighties as the
seedbed of modern architecture, the designers have ransacked the magazines of 1886 for examples of the most awful monstrosities in domestic
buildings that they could find—and there were, of course, plenty. There is
no hint of the cottages of Richardson and Halsey Wood; not a breath of
Babb, Cook & Willard's De Vinne Building, one of the finest pieces of
industrial architecture this country has yet produced; no appreciation
whatever—except in a smudged photostat of the Tiffany Mansion—of the
superb brickwork that was introduced during this period, brickwork that
can still be found in neglected loft buildings around the Brooklyn Bridge.
No. What the League has done is to scatter over the walls a comic John
Held version of the eighteen-eighties. Was this to show what an advance
has been made since in taste or to hint slyly that the modern architecture of
today will one day seem as monstrous as the contorted cottages found
reproduced in color in the pages of the *Scientific American* for 1887?

Perhaps the main fact that emerges from this League show is that the
old guard is making one last, desperate stand. The finest example of traditional architecture here is the late Van Buren Magonigle's War Memorial in
Kansas City, none the worse because the silhouette reminds one of a gigantic chimney dominating a group of low factory buildings. Magonigle
demonstrated that one need not be afraid, aesthetically, of the more monumental aspects of industrialism. Perhaps the all-time low is struck in John
Russell Pope's National Archives Building in Washington, a building whose
complete irrelevance of design is accentuated by the howling lack of proportion between the facade and pediment and the great mass that rises in
the centre. Shades of Jefferson, Latrobe, and Mills! They could hardly have
anticipated the Supreme Court Building or the Archives, or they would
have torn up every classic steel engraving they possessed.

Between a liberal eclecticism and a mummified classicism stands the Newark station of the Pennsylvania Railroad, by McKim, Mead & White. This is in that style of deflowered classic, seen at its best in the Bronx County Building, in which some classic detail has been suppressed, and the rest has been turned into pastry cook's ornament—indeed, one can almost see the round molding about the entrances being pressed from the chef's tube. The result lacks the dignity of the ancient without achieving more than a faint, antiseptic aftertaste of a modern design. Meanwhile, in every architectural school and draughting-room in the country, young people are coming along who cannot even for the sake of a job pay lip service to the habit of botching every modern problem by attempting to couple it with some pious reference to the past. These young people will design modern buildings as inevitably as they will wear modern clothes. Many of them are represented in the current show; some, like Harold Sterner, by models, and some by photographs. One of them, Morris Sanders, even got a prize. But they do not belong with the rest of the company. They should either clean the barnacles off the ship or launch a new one.

THERE is only one part of the United States government that has caught even a glimmer of what modern design means. And that is the various departments in Washington that are concerned with housing. On a recent tour of inspection at the PWA and the Suburban Resettlement Division, I was surprised at the large number of sensible, straightforward designs, and at the generally high level of the work. (Incidentally, one of the best was by a Negro architect for one of the Negro housing projects in Washington.) And although the presentation of government-aided housing at the Architectural League show is a little pinched and confused, it forms one of the most interesting exhibits.

Apparently, the news about modern design has not yet got around to Mr. Farley's architectural aides—not by a long shot. If one had any delusions on this point, the new branch post office at 217 East Seventieth Street would cure one. This is a three-story building, done in what is called "modified Georgian;" that is, in the usual mishmash of red brick and limestone, with the usual traditional and now inconvenient windows. Architecturally, its nearest blood relative is the Georgian country house on Madison Avenue in which the Bank of the Manhattan Company successfully concealed its working quarters from the passerby a few years ago. You might mistake the new building for a Christian Science church or a D.A.R. clubhouse; by carefully watching the building for half an hour at a time, you can, however, accumulate evidence enough to favor the hypothesis that it's a post office. (There are more postmen than you usually find in a D.A.R. headquarters.)

What governed the choice of style in this building? Probably the notion that there is something peculiarly "American" about Georgian architecture. The very word "Georgian" should indicate what slight grounds there are for that belief, for this mode of building was the common upper-class idiom in the eighteenth century from Dublin to the Cape of Good Hope. The fact is that nothing distinctively American of any importance was contributed to architecture until Richardson began building his railroad stations in the eighties, a movement in thought and design that led directly into the vital but badly named "international style" of today. The trouble with our traditionalists is that they are at home with every part of the past except that which is still living; like undertakers, they have no concern with tradition until it is dead enough to be subject to their waxen ministrations and almost lifelike touches.

THE two modest architecture exhibitions of the Museum of Modern Art are easy to see and hard to digest. The show of Exposition Architecture, which the coming World's Fair in New York makes quite timely, is itself in the best spirit of modern fairs—an excellent job. That on Government Housing is below the standard of the Museum's usual presentation. I am sure that its experts on painting would never have permitted paintings as poor in quality as some of the plans that are shown to get into a show of moderns. And if the Museum was confining itself to mere façades—which might be excused, since that is what the public looks at—then the plans themselves are confusing, misleading, and sometimes altogether mischievous.

It is true that the Government Housing exhibition is in many ways better than one had reason to expect, even if one had memories that went back to the fine war housing done by the Shipping Board in 1918. At any moment up to 1930, such an exhibition might easily have been a chamber of horrors, full of grotesque embellishments, like those of a cheap suburb of the nineteen-twenties, or refined antiquities, like those of a more expensive suburb. To the credit of the government and its planners, the new housing is neither; it is merely a mountain of missed opportunities. Architects who had thirsted for years for the chance to break loose from random commercial requirements acted like a ballplayer who tries to bunt with the bases full; they played for safety at a moment that demanded a clean hit or an equally clean strike. If any real strides were to be made in housing, if new processes were to be introduced, if new house designs, new communal patterns, were to be developed, it was now or never. Today it looks as if it might be never—or not, at least, for another five or ten years.

What happened to the architects who worked on these projects? The stencils and red tape of bureaucracy partly account for the paralysis of their imaginations, no doubt; but what could have persuaded the able gentlemen who designed the Williamsburg project for New York to evolve in the interest of economy a complicated type of plan that wastes space and provides inadequate, half-lighted kitchens? What could have made Kastner and Stonorov create perhaps the cleanest architectural forms shown in the exhibition—needing only trees and gardens to enliven them—and then fail to provide the trees and gardens? What led a group of New York planners, headed by a man as eminent as Mr. Henry Wright, to create a plan for Greenbrook without a logical backbone, and with an old-fashioned English type of cul-de-sac layout that ignores orientation for sunlight—although Mr. Wright is himself an able student of orientation?

It is all very mysterious, this timidity, this failure to use knowledge, this lack of any positive expression as to what a new community might and could be. The plans of Kastner and Kahn for the Hightstown project in New Jersey show this paralysis of the imagination was not inevitable. Kastner, at least, saw that if land were abundant and cheap and communally owned—and those were the conditions—there was no reason the convenience of the flat and the bungalow should not be incorporated in one-story houses, spread along the ground—a design not very persuasive in its renderings, but perhaps the best on view, all things considered. If not the best, surely the most adventurous, the most stimulating.

What is the upshot of these experiments for architecture generally? Only two things seem to come out clearly, on the evidence of these models. One is the definite abandonment of the old-fashioned block, 200 by 600 feet or so, and the acceptance of the superblock, with a great reduction in paving costs and a considerable possibility of reduction in other utilities; likewise bigger and more usable open spaces. The other is the fact that it has at last dawned on American designers—witness particularly Churchill and Kastner—that the intense sunlight of our American climate demands a little shading for the eye; hence the return to the projecting roof used by Frank Lloyd Wright in his prairie architecture. I can cheerfully commend both innovations, but I wish there were more.

As for modern exhibition architecture, of which the stronger and more consistent examples are here shown, it has led me to ponder the whole theme of what fairs should be, in competition with the American Philosophical Society—the Fair directors being on *their* side; time and opportunity, and perhaps audacity, being upon mine. Expositions, as Mr. Henry-Russell Hitchcock points out, dramatize architecture to the general public. The first of the modern exhibitions was the great London Exhibition of 1851. This introduced the machine and the products of machine industry to the modern world, not alone in its exhibits, but in the glass-and-iron hothouse Paxton designed—now lying like a stranded dinosaur, sinking into the suburban marsh of Upper Norwood. (It was first reared in Hyde Park. So it illustrated the principle of take-down construction, too; and it was, in fact, the first definitive monument of modern architecture—as definitive, as challenging, as Le Corbusier's L'Esprit Nouveau building in the Paris Exposition of 1925.)

From that time on, each great industrial exhibition has acted like a stone in a pond, sometimes causing a ripple, sometimes a wave of architectural achievement in the style of the fair itself. The exhibition of 1889 in Paris, which gave the world the Eiffel Tower, dramatized the skyscraper skeleton and started the Art Nouveau movement; that of the White City of Chicago in 1893 resulted in laborious limestone counterfeits of civic grandeur in municipal centres from San Francisco to Springfield.

Perhaps I have said enough about the influence of fairs to indicate that the architects have a shocking amount of responsibility. And about the best suggestion I can put forward toward making an architectural success of the coming exposition is not to imitate Paris or Stockholm, but to eliminate architecture itself as far as possible from the picture. Up to now, every fair has suffered from the dullness of its promoters and the exhibitionism of its architects. The first lack any rational notion of a fair except the now completely tedious and unconvincing belief in the triumph of modern industry. The less said about *that* today, the better. The peace confidently promised in 1851 is now sour with war, and the plenty that industry seemed about to achieve now intermittently carries with it a threat of starvation.

Lacking any effective dramatization or rational purpose, most modern fairs are threatened at an early stage with bankruptcy. The symptom of this in America is a hasty transfer of attention from the agents of production to the organs of reproduction; a bevy of naked hussies remind the spectator that there are other wonders in Nature besides the harnessing of Niagara Falls, or the five-millionth Ford car. That is one way of dramatizing the facts of life, but it has the defect of being one-sided, and a good program for a modern fair would dramatize *all* the facts of modern life, our world of space and time, our science and our sport, our hygiene and our education and our psychology; all the things, which make us different from the people who built the Acropolis or Chartres, or even from those who wrote the Constitution.

In origin, a fair is a combination of a merchant's market, like a country fair today; a grand urban spectacle, like the return of a triumphant army; and a museum of curiosities and wonders. The architectural problem is to provide a setting that will make the fair pay, make the spectacle amusing, and make the museum interesting and profitable. Everybody who went to Chicago said that it was the visitors who really made the show interesting; there is a clue here. Everybody who went to the earlier Chicago fair carried back, besides sepulchral memories of Beauty, the image of Olmsted's beautiful water course in greenery; another hint there. In short, the fair, in every department, should speak the current American vernacular. Vernacular architecture today is based upon a popular acceptance of the machine; it demands the sort of technics and materials that the builder would use, as it were, without giving them a second thought.

This effortless, unemphatic style, as closely molded to life as the skin is molded to the flesh, is the precise antithesis to ancient theatricality and monumentality; that is, no doubt, the reason our monuments are for the most part grim failures, effortful but unheroic, while our subway stations, our lunch counters, and our kitchens are so unerringly good. When our architects try to be gay and fantastic, they are just silly; levity, fantasy, caprice, the qualities of the Dresden Baroque, say, are now at home only in motion pictures or musical comedies. Indeed, even our stage designers are usually best when they are most restricted, if not suppressed. But an architecture "molded to the flesh" can never be better than the idea and the program that have formed it. That's why the American Philosophical Society had better go into a quick huddle and give the Fair Committee an Idea. If they don't there won't be any exposition worth looking at or into in 1939.

1936~37

This was one of the quieter seasons, with Mumford chiefly writing omnibus pieces, including one about "taxpayers," small, commercial buildings that were beginning to rise again in the city's business districts. A major highlight of the spring of 1937 was his preview of the plans for the 1939 New York World's Fair. That summer, he examined several public works executed under Robert Moses' leadership, including the West Side Highway, the Triborough Bridge, and Jones Beach. The observations of Mumford, a pedestrian who did not drive a car, as he traversed the bridge by foot are especially poignant. This was also his last season as "The Art Galleries" columnist.

THE SKY LINE
MODERNITY AND COMMERCE
OCTOBER 3, 1936

THERE is an old line of sixteenth-century houses in Hamburg that is always photographed with the casement windows open. The houses look spacious and airy, despite their narrow fronts and high gables, because the windows cover the whole façade, and if you were a bird you'd want to fly in. That's the way you ought to feel, too, when you turn west on Fifth Avenue at Fifty-fourth or Fifty-fifth Street and see the parallel set of apartments designed by Harrison & Fouilhoux on those two streets. When the windows are open up and down the façade, the effect is like a sudden whirring of birds' wings out of a tree. And if anyone wants to know what is modern ornament, that's what it is—something built for use, which suddenly, when it hits you at the right angle, begins to sing like the four-and-twenty blackbirds.

A few fellow-archeologists may remember the time, about six years ago, when a distinguished critic of modern architecture, eager to have a local example to point to, picked out the Beaux-Arts Apartments on East Forty-fourth Street as the first capitulation to modern design in apartment houses. The chief proof of this was the fact that alternating bands of bricks accented the horizontal lines of the windows—one of the clichés of the "international style" that fortunately was done to an early death. What distinguishes these new apartment houses is that they are singularly free from this sort of superficial stylistic stereotype; even the four bulging bays can account for themselves as soon as one checks what they mean on the plan. The bays form dining alcoves at a corner of the living room next to the kitchen, and the banks of windows are thrust over to one side, instead of going completely around—a fine concession to privacy. I have singled out the bays because they are the most spectacular thing about the façade—and, as it happens, the most traditional. Houses on this pattern, with never a trace of exterior ornament, are spread all over Beacon Hill in Boston, and there are even a few on Sixteenth Street in Manhattan.

The materials out of which this elegant façade is composed are as simple and ingratiating as the manner of composition itself. The brick is a warm tan with a faint lilac tinge, which reminds one of some of the Dutch varieties; the wall is bonded without any attempt at accent or ornamental pattern, without any weak prettifying bands or spotty textures. This cleanness and vigor are altogether delightful. Furthermore, the simplicity of the main part of the façade deepens by contrast every little variation in the composition: the strong vertical of the chimney, the rondure of the wall of the penthouse and the curving glass band that keeps one from falling off the penthouse terrace. As for those glass copings, they are a tremendous and audacious piece of swank, and—saving someone's possible drunken lurch—they are, I think, pretty successful. A glass parapet should give a guest just the faint shiver of uneasiness that would accentuate the height of the topmost stories. That's a very fair way of restoring a primitive emotion to a world in which people arrive bored at the Newark airport and fly over a continent at ten thousand feet and waken bored next morning in Los Angeles.

But perhaps the most intelligent thing about the whole design is the quality and placement and general meaningfulness of the windows. For these new units are big enough to drown the interiors in light, and they seem actually capable of achieving ventilation. Four types of window are used in the design, but there is no attempt to make a fetish of either the horizontal or vertical arrangement; gone are the bands and spandrels and mullions that used to be used to give a sort of fake unity to the fenestration. The changing window pattern instead keeps the façade from becoming dull, without permitting the design to fall to pieces. There are no shadows or indentations in the wall, apart from the bays; and the setting of the windows flush with the outside wall creates a maximum amount of living space in the interior.

With respect to all those external choices that lay within the province of the architects, this building is surely the most brilliant and the most successful example of modern architecture in the city—at least in apartment houses. At one point, however, I think the architects have gone wrong; and their mistake is so typical it's time to say something about it. The kitchenettes have space and air on the scale one might expect in a small yacht. Speaking as a cook, I don't like this. If I were asked to cook a meal for more than four people in one of those kitchens, I'd try to jump out of the window—I wouldn't succeed because the window is too small, and I'd perish, instead, of asphyxiation. Are modern architects a race of sandwich-eaters and pill-swallowers that they treat with such contempt the august domains of the cook? Or do they think that an apartment designed for two people will never have more than two people in to dine? Planning like this can lead only to overdone food *en casserole* and warm salads and ratty, wilted-looking domestics.

On the other hand, a number of little things in planning and equipment have been carried through admirably in the rest of the works. The plain-surfaced door, once sacred only to hospitals, takes the place of the obsolete panelled door; there are sliding doors on the clothes closets, so that the entire closet is open and accessible; and in the bathroom, one gratefully notes, there has been a return to simple white fixtures. The last item shows that we have turned at least one corner, and need no longer worry about being threatened with art and gaiety and color at three o'clock in the morning whilst we are fumbling for an aspirin. Unless some interior decorator is permitted to go crazy in the lobby—which was unfinished when I looked at it—the total result will be very handsome indeed.

Two pieces of good architecture at once is a break indeed; and the second is even more startling than the first, because it is a bank building—the new Corn Exchange branch at 265 Broadway, done by Fellheimer & Wagner. The new deal in architecture has gradually been taking hold of the banks. One can trace the slow advance from the dead classic of the Greenwich Savings Bank to the ornate Romanesque of the Bowery Savings Bank, and from that to the still monumental style—theatric but vigorous—of the Walker & Gillette National City Banks, with its granite and its formalized eagle and its heavy block lettering. Now, thank heaven, the monumentality has been thrown to the winds; the American eagle has flown away, the last acanthus leaf has withered, and the result is a business building once more—no longer a cross between a funeral parlor and a monument erected by the Daughters of the American Revolution. (I hope that the financial gentlemen who passed favorably on that design for a Colonial mansion up on Madison Avenue are pretty well ashamed of themselves by now.)

The new building is distinguished by its absence of pretense. Two kinds of granite are used as sheathing for the façade—a light buff for the wall and a bluish gray for the spandrels; and two types of window are used—glass tiles for the first two floors and transparent glass for the rest. For decoration, there is the bank's name, in letters of gold, large and legible, with a single horizontal band of gold for emphasis over the second-story windows. The design is so chaste that every touch counts, and I am afraid that the rather clumsy-looking socket for the flagpole must stand as a fumble; it looks too heavy. By contrast, the interior is so pleasingly unemphatic that what one chiefly remembers about it is the time indicated by the clock and the conspicuous absence of august and authoritative-looking columns. That gave me a feeling of confidence that no amount of architectural plush and carving has ever been able to give. In short, this new building is not a Temple to Fortuna or one of Samuel Butler's musical banks; it looks like a place where one may conduct certain necessary business with a minimum of distraction. I have only one suggestion about decoration: I wish banks and telegraph offices and such places would repeat the current calendar date conspicuously on various wall surfaces. A calendar and a clock are a great comfort. But any bank that can bear to leave out a mural showing the purchase of Manhattan Island for twenty-four dollars obviously has a genius among its presiding officers.

PERHAPS you want to know what I think of the new Criterion Theatre block on Broadway between Forty-fourth and Forty-fifth Streets. What I'd like to know is what the architect himself thinks about it now. There are still a few uncovered patches of building on the sides which make one fancy he had a design originally, perhaps an honorable one. But what with the electric aquarium on top of the building, and the competitive barbaric yawps of Whelan and Woolworth, what is left is just so much pulp, and will never be anything else. At that, the upper windows at the Forty-fourth Street side are rather good, if just a shade too heavy. But that building was meant to be deflowered before it was conceived, and I am neither shocked nor daunted by its fate, even though it *may* be somebody's sister.

A s far as I am concerned, the tears that Mr. James J. Walker has been shedding over Little Old New York are wasted. However empty the heart, the eye is better treated now that it has been at any other time since New York ceased to be a homogeneous city. If you want a date for *that*, let's say since just before the Civil War, because it was then that the prevalent red brick began to be spotted with brownstone, and the two- and three-story buildings started their rise to five and seven stories and finally turned Al Smith into a flagpole-sitter on top of the highest skyscraper that never entertained a Zeppelin.

Most of the improvements of the last year or so have been rather minor, and yet they have turned out to be pretty important. Not so much a matter of individual buildings, but of trimming and tidying and renovating, most marked on those avenues where the car tracks have been dug up and the buses lunge and slither. Madison Avenue above the Sixties, for example, once was a sloppily dressed woman with her underskirt showing. Today it looks extremely suave and cosmopolitan, and I now realize that what used to make Fort Washington Avenue seem so elegantly "foreign" was the mere absence of trolley cars to break the surface of the asphalt and bulk into the picture.

Another plant that has burst into bloom is Central Park. Here the first prunings and plantings were done before Mr. Moses went into action, but one might as well admit that he has exchanged walking shoes for seven-league boots in the way of making improvements. Central Park began its career, curiously enough, in the midst of an earlier depression, and Olmsted, the first designer of the park, was helped and handicapped in the same way as Mr. Moses: he had to find work for a lot of unemployed. Unfortunately, Olmsted never saw his work finished. It began to decay on his hands, through knavery and corruption, before he had carried out the last details, and by 1920 it might have been used for a movie background of a shell-torn battle area. Olmsted's park will probably never entirely disappear, so long as no one gets a contract for blasting out the rocks and filling up the remaining lakes, but some mighty changes have nevertheless been taking place.

The original park was a romantic landscape. It was designed for gentle ladies who liked to take the air in their victorias and for well-behaved children whose morals were in the care of solicitous nursemaids—and vice versa—plus middle-class poets and mooners who could occasionally see a cardinal bird, a finch, or a thrush in the thickets. This old park was arranged primarily for the eye, and it was always at its best on weekdays, when there were not too many visitors, and when a few figures crossing the green in the distance or being whistled off by a policeman added a fleck of color to the scene. The new park (Mr. Moses' park) is what the Germans call a *Volkspark*. It is a place where crowds of people can meet and mingle; the landscape is just a fringe of verdure around the faces and bodies of the crowd.

What happened to Central Park is just the opposite of what happened to the Jardin du Luxembourg. The latter began as a stiff formal garden which, by the grace of the Parisian talent for play, has achieved the most friendly and informal kind of atmosphere; I know no other place where the enjoyment seems quite so dense on an afternoon in June. Central Park began with an informal and rambling kind of plan and has been tightened up into a concourse where thousands of people can meet to dance or sing or do most anything. It says something for Olmsted's original plan that it has been able to take on this new job, and it says something for Mr. Moses' reconstructions that he has introduced so many popular touches—including the neat little children's playgrounds that now skirt the park—without utterly destroying the original atmosphere.

So beneficent has been this new influence in our parks and playgrounds that I begin to hope that some fine morning the Commissioner will give an about-face order to the benches that are now lined up along Riverside Drive from the 160's upward. The view of the Hudson along this strip is among those exciting views one proudly shows to Japanese or Czechoslovakian architects after conducting them through the Medical Center. Presumably in order to reduce the strain on the heart, all the benches turn their backs to the view. Maybe that's the kind of people we are, people who like the smell of exhaust or the whizz of motorcars rather than great vistas of river and cliff and sky—true children of the Machine Age. But perhaps it's just that the minion who gave the order for placing those benches never saw this part of the Drive, or was born a fool.

Among the latest efforts of the Parks Department are the swimming pools and bathhouses for the neighborhood playgrounds, and if the Thomas Jefferson baths at 112th Street and First Avenue are a sample, the new work is very gracious indeed. The long brick buildings, with bands of windows that fill their bays, form an excellent frame for the pools. I don't like the weak festoons in brick or the overemphatic concrete bands or the baroque curves at the corners; and the windows, which are a bleak white to match the bands, might easily have been done in a positive color, with much more lively decorative effect than any of those other flourishes. But the entrance is effective, and the fine, clear lettering of all the signs and designations is a great help in every way. In short, this is so near to a sound vernacular modern architecture that one feels a little balked by the fact that the design has not been carried through to the last detail. With a little more positive conviction, or, if you will, with a little more doctrinaire narrowness, something completely consistent in detail as well as in the large would emerge.

LEAVING the parks and Mr. Moses' assistants out of account, the thing that continues to alter the looks of the city most rapidly is the multitude of two-story taxpayers that have steadily been replacing old buildings in the better-settled parts of town. Here chaos still prevails, but the fault is not entirely, or even mainly, that of the architects. What are the poor devils to do? A generation ago they could build in brick or terra cotta or stone or sheet iron. Today a half-dozen other materials compete for their patronage, with a much wider variation in texture and color than these older ones had. The problem of getting something consistent and decent established for as much as five blocks out of combinations of enamelled iron, opaque glass, tile, and glass bricks, in addition to all the old standbys, is insoluble. Art begins in limitations; today anyone who wants to achieve the effects of art in a street picture has to invent his own limitations and then prayerfully hope that he will have another chance nearby, or that the next man will adopt them too.

For this reason, I am inclined to give an extra pat on the back to the architect of the new two-story building at the northeast corner of Madison Avenue and Fifty-fifth Street, if only because he has kept to a limestone wall with gray metal frames and bands. There's a similar building on Madison Avenue and Fifty-fourth Street. Both buildings are in the tone of the neighborhood. Without being particularly distinguished, the new building shows plan and control over possibly offensive features: the height of the lettering and the amount of permissible advertisement have plainly been established. The result is a sightly building that will remain sightly. The variation in the window pattern in the second story, making the open windows narrow and short and the fixed middle window wider and taller, is perhaps a little effortful, since what is needed in such minor buildings is not distinction but reticence; still, until architects again have the opportunity to design blocks at a time, one must perhaps put up with these minor yearnings for individuality.

For contrast, consider the new Liggett building at Madison Avenue and Sixty-fifth Street. The most charitable thing one can say about this building is that it is misplaced. The architect apparently designed it under the impression that it was to compete for attention at Broadway and Forty-third Street, where the racket it makes would not so easily be heard. The framing of the windows was done to the tune of a bass drum; the black, gray, and orange yellow of the color scheme is a shriek of trombones and saxophones. As for the lettering, the "Liggett's" could probably be read with the naked eye at a distance of half a mile if the view were clear. In short, this building, architecturally speaking, is pretty much of a public nuisance, although the elements out of which it is composed are not in themselves objectionable.

Do not make the mistake of thinking that the architect's "modernism" is to blame. The same company has another two-story building, on Lexington Avenue at Seventy-ninth Street, which is quite decent. Its tan-enamelled front and its continuous second-story windows are as much in the contemporary mode as that of the black-and-yellow building, but the tan matches the brick wall behind it, and the lettering is restrained and decent, though it is legible at any reasonable distance.

The notion that modernism is fat and heavy and clumsy, the notion that a modern design must be dazzling and overemphatic and strident—all that really dates back to a few designers in the early nineteen-twenties, people like Erich Mendelsohn, in his Einstein Tower stage, who had been influenced by Expressionism. As a matter of fact, the best modern buildings I have seen—certain schools in Hamburg and Hilversum particularly—are extremely quiet and self-obliterating. They have a way of saying "*You* first" instead of interposing their masses and planes between the user of the building and the spectators. At the moment, the most recent and the best example of this tendency is the new front of the Essex House restaurant on Fifty-ninth Street, now that the artificial woodsiness of its summer decoration has been put away with the Christmas-tree ornaments. It is most charming by night: wide, unbroken fronts of glass window, set between lighted opaque glass columns, with the tables and the diners and the orchestra acting as the essentially decorative element. This is one of the best show windows in the city, and it has all the excitement, for those within, of open-air dining without the draughts and the dust and the tepid food. This is downright architectural nudism, but only the architectural dressmakers have any reason to complain if such nudism becomes fashionable.

I N his Utopian dialogue, "The Interpreters," A. E. pictured one of his characters, the young architect, designing all his separate buildings to fit in with an imaginary dream city he always kept in mind. The idea is not as romantic as it seems. Every vital period in architecture has had some collective pattern that guided the treatment of its individual buildings. Indeed, anyone can see now the hurtling skyscrapers of the twenties were not the product of sober financial calculation, still less of intelligent functional design; they were attempts to embody concretely an illusory Utopia of finance, whose shadowy outlines were to be seen in the charcoal sketches that Hugh Ferriss transmitted to paper.

Architecture today is in much the same position, relatively, that it was in the sixteenth century. It can no longer modify the order established in the past, because our new modes of life are not in keeping with that order. It must work toward an order that has still to be realized. In other words, it cannot rely upon old habits; it must formulate new desires. Architecture, to be effective, demands some common plan of living, and it needs this in small matters quite as much as in large ones. The dream city need not be a grandiose one; all one asks of it is that it should produce a certain consistency. The recent appearance of a new half-timbered business front on Madison Avenue (the timbers being done in metal, of course, to conform with the fire laws) should be resented because it is as willfully irrational as a surrealist painting; indeed, I looked a second time at the façade to be sure that a few jocose entrails were not hanging from a second-story window.

The chief question one should ask about a new building is not "Does it stand out?" but "Does it fit in?" Is it another ruffle on the surface of chaos, or is it something firm enough to be carried further, with appropriate modifications, in the next building? Every new structure, if it is really well designed, should be capable of becoming the nucleus of a whole city. I find myself asking such questions, too, about new materials—about the fashionable blue mirror glass, for example, that has been employed on so many shop fronts and restaurant fronts this last year. A city of brick or a city of limestone is fine, but how would one feel if so much as a single avenue were lined from end to end with blue mirrors? Doubtless there is little danger that this will happen. For one thing, this glass is apparently a tricky material to use: two of the panels in the new Foltis-Fischer restaurant on Fifty-seventh Street near Seventh Avenue are already cracked. Here, incidentally, is probably the best mirror-glass front that has so far been produced. The architect, Jack Aronowitz, has relied for his main decorative effect upon the use of yellow neon lights for the restaurant's name—the letters well designed and placed, with an upright instead of a horizontal light to indicate the hyphen and emphasize the entrance. The lettering is underscored by the shining ridged surface that forms the outside of the bank of lights above the windows. The curved blue glass that flanks the entrance is well conceived, too.

How good the Foltis-Fischer place is one may discover by taking a look at the new Stewart's on Sixth Avenue between Forty-fourth and Forty-fifth Streets, which is done on the same general pattern, and with the same general materials. But in the second lunchroom the red neon letters are overpowering, and the garish effect of the front is increased by carrying the blue-glass motif indoors in the fabric that covers the chairs; one feels as if one were sitting on Christmas-tree ornaments. The Foltis-Fischer chairs, on the other hand, are of an old-fashioned design that should have been modified for use in the new place. Blue is a hard color to use for architectural purposes, and blue mirrors are even harder. Except for dazzle in some place where only dazzle is required, I can't see the use of mirrors as outdoor decoration. But indoors, mirrors are far more serviceable than the kind of murals cafeterias affect. That large, crazy mirror pointed downward at the diners' heads in Lüchow's main dining room is one of the things that give the old place character.

Now that I've started again on lunchrooms, let me say a word about the new chain of restaurants that has been making its way about the city—the Little Whitehouse. Unlike the drab places of the late twenties, with their mahogany interiors, this chain has gone back to the original Childs tradition, with an emphasis upon a shiny whiteness, relieved by light apple-green surfaces. Unfortunately, the decorators are badly handicapped by the name of the restaurants. The proprietors or the architects are apparently entranced by the notion of attaching their trademark to the President's Mansion. So they have made a farce of the best restaurant they have so far done—that on Thirty-fourth Street, between Sixth and Seventh Avenues—by crowning the front with a two-story pediment in enamelled sheet iron with impressive columns of the same material. It reminds one of the White House as much as the Empire State Building reminds one of a log cabin.

At the street level, the exterior of this lunchroom is passable, but the effect of the whole façade is ridiculous. This is all the more irritating because the interior is very fine; the glary white surfaces have been abandoned in favor of a combination of terra cotta and green, with bright nickel fittings for the stools and counters. The clean, vigorous effect of the interior design is, however, smudged once again by a classical malapropism—the broken pediment over the wall mirrors. Still, to get anything like as pleasant an interior, one would have to go to the café-bar at Schrafft's on Fifty-seventh Street near Seventh Avenue, done in much the same colors, with more dark wood, less sparkle, and of course a totally different purpose and arrangement.

T HE best recent shop front has appeared on Fifth Avenue: the new Helena Rubinstein salon, between Fifty-fifth and Fifty-sixth Streets. The design is essentially a conventional one; the window opening is on the eye level, when it might have been carried high across the front, and the frame it forms for display is generous enough to serve a haberdasher's, whereas it might have been done on a miniature scale. Nevertheless, this is one of the cases in which the conventional thing, done rigorously, done cleanly, has a merit very similar to that of a design that makes a more conscious use of modern materials and constructional devices; in this it resembles the still-handsome Bonwit Teller Building. And since in the present example the shop's façade fits into the old-fashioned building above it without submitting to it, the design gets a good mark for tactful renovation, too. The architect is Harold Sterner.

The front of the Rubinstein salon is done in big limestone slabs. On each side of the squarish middle window is a rectangular entrance, one to the building, the other to the salon, both entrances being deeply recessed, but without a lintel or a louver above the opening. There is not a twitch or a tremor on the whole façade. Above the openings is an unbroken white surface, at the bottom of which, done in dark metal, are the widely spaced letters "helena rubinstein," all in lower case, small, well drawn, admirable. There is only one other mark on the front—the numerals 715 to the right of the building entrance. On the placing and the size of these numerals much depended, and I do not think that the result could have been improved, unless perhaps by the use of a "5" with a little more space between the horizontal stroke and the curve, so that it should not be mistaken for a "3." One point might have been revealed by the decorative treatment—the difference between the building's entrance and that of the salon's; perhaps the shop's glass door might have been framed in painted wood, carrying out into the street the bold blue of the floor of the interior.

Maybe I am singularly taken with this façade because it embodies two points which must be generally accepted if our shopping streets are to become endurable to the eye. One of them is that the name of a place need not be paraded in letters thirty inches high with a special orchestral accompaniment of lights in order to attract attention to itself. Observe here how the architect has used the blank space above the lettering to achieve an even greater emphasis than he would have had had he emblazoned the name over the entire space. The other happy touch is that the avenue number should be bold and easily singled out; the number of a building should not be a dark secret known only to the postman and the doorman. Such a simple exterior as this, of course, puts a great burden on the window decorator; it is one of the few places on the Avenue that might effectively use a nude figure sculpture or a well-composed abstraction of cosmetic bottles to suggest in austere fashion the holy Corinthian rites that are practiced within. Actually, the first window made one think of Dennison's Christmas wrappings, and the second one contrived, with the aid of a triptych and a fat, greasy candle and some fake frosting, to look like an insurance-calendar lithograph. Once the window decoration catches up with the façade, it will be very fine.

Harlem Houses
"The sculpture is 'functional' in a practical as well as an aesthetic sense, since the cast stone which composes it will be improved in finish by being handled and climbed over by children."
—from "The New Order," February 26, 1938

Red Hook Houses, Brooklyn
"Some people have criticized the façades of the individual Red Hook apartment houses because they are devoid of ornament. One might as well criticize the eighteenth-century façades of Bloomsbury for the same reason." —from "Versailles for the Millions," February 17, 1940

Fort Tryon Park and Cloisters Museum
"At a distance the Cloisters looks not like the excellent museum that it is but like a transplanted building, picked up by the jinn and whisked through the sky—not so much an honest relic as a wish." —from "Pax in Urbe," May 21, 1938

Cuxa Cloister at the Cloisters Museum
"A little of that ancient peace still broods over this museum; you can walk around one of these quiet gardens and even discover whether or not you have a soul."—from "Pax in Urbe," May 21, 1938

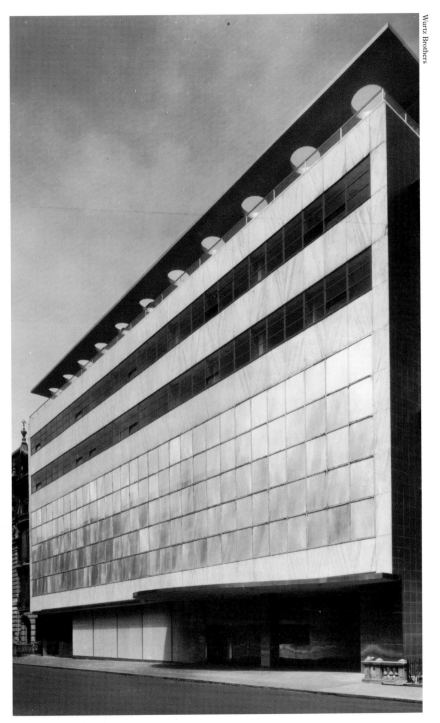

Wurtz Brothers

Museum of Modern Art
"For those who have been brought up on the American tradition there is nothing to identify the new Museum of Modern Art as a museum. There are no classic columns or cornices; the place does not look like a temple or a palace." —from "The New Museum," June 3, 1939

P. L. Sperr

General View of the 1939 World's Fair
"The World of Tomorrow, so far from exhibiting false forms, has a sort of veracious formlessness.
The architects in charge of the project plainly despaired of imposing any kind of order upon either
the plans or the elevations or the competing industrialists." —from "West Is East," June 17, 1939

P. L. Sperr

General Motors Futurama
"What the Futurama really demonstrates is that by 1960 all jaunts of more than fifty miles will be
as deadly as they now are in parts of New Jersey and in the Farther West." —from "Genuine
Bootleg," July 29, 1939

Castle Village
"Aesthetically, this X plan is more successful in single units than it is in repetition. One building, properly supported with minor masses, might have a superb place in the landscape; five such are just a barricade." —from "Modern Housing, from A to X," October 28, 1939

La Guardia Field Administration Building
"It is a series of bungles, missed opportunities, and hideous misapplications of ornament.... If you don't like the Administration Building's architecture any better than I do, you can at least fly away from it." —from "Millions for Mausoleums," December 30, 1939

WPA Photograph, Federal Writers Project

Rockefeller Center
"In spite of all [its] handicaps, Rockefeller Center has turned into an impressive collection of structures; they form a composition in which unity and coherence have to a considerable degree diminished the fault of overemphasis." —from "Rockefeller Center Revisted," May 4, 1940

Radio City Music Hall
"The Rockefeller Center signs are, I regret to say, failures. They attempt monumentality and merely look elephantine." —from "Rockefeller Center Revisited," May 4, 1940

RCA Building

"Many of the camera views of the buildings are striking, but then a camera doesn't mind being tilted at a forty-five-degree angle for as much as five minutes, while the human neck does object."
—from "Rockefeller Center Revisited," May 4, 1940

I T is hardly possible to walk three blocks in any direction this spring without stumbling across a model of a building for the 1939 World's Fair. I hope to have something to say about these models and plans when the grand fashion parade opens at the Architectural League Exhibition on April 21st. But recently a group of sculptors and painters and architects put on a special exhibit at the Architectural League's rooms, and the flock of them that collaborated on the Community Centre unit threw out one or two bright hints that are worth mulling over.

The unit consisted of three cleanly designed low buildings, one an auditorium, one a museum, library, and laboratory, and the other an athletics building. They were grouped around a circular swimming pool. I have doubts as to whether all these buildings should have been united on the same site—certainly I should want my library half a mile from the nearest tennis court or swimming pool—but at this moment the aesthetic conception is more important than the sociological one, and the formal relationship, with the buildings spreading outward instead of forming a walled court, was admirable. (The architect was Oscar Stonorov.) Most of the murals were spread over the walls surrounding the glass-covered peristyle which formed the margin of the swimming pool. This would give them outdoor light, a maximum amount of attention, and protection against the weather; even Duco is the better for a little protection. In other words, the murals were treated in somewhat the same fashion as the billboards on Broadway, or the shop windows on Fifth Avenue—as a background for the promenade.

The most important innovation in wall decoration, however, was the design for a colored sign by Louis Ferstadt for the whole outside wall of a building. This is the first time, so far as I know, that a serious artist has attempted a wall decoration in electric lights, and though Ferstadt's design was in the nature of a comic strip, I think this sort of thing need not be passed off with a Wrigley laugh. Is there any reason glass or pre-cast concrete tile should not be equipped with sockets so that entirely new effects could be worked out in colored lights, using smaller bulbs, placed more closely together?

The other really stunning innovation was José Rivera's models for abstract sculpture in the form of three islands for the swimming pool. These boldly modelled forms showed that there is still a place for the monumental sculptor when he makes new opportunities for himself, instead of lazily designing heroic forms for nonexistent tombs and impossible arches of triumph. It would be fun to bask on the abstract flanks and bosoms of Rivera's beautiful forms, and the bathers themselves would compose into far more interesting patterns on the uneven platforms and elevations than they would rolling on the flat surface of a float. Noguchi pointed the way last year with his model for an abstractly designed play mound for children, and there have been lesser attempts at such modelling, as in the seals' diving platform at the Central Park Zoo, but Rivera's statues drive home the idea in a ten-strike.

THIS season is unusually prolific in good books about modern architecture and its related fields. The most important is Dr. Walter Curt Behrendt's handsomely designed and illustrated volume on "Modern Building: Its Nature, Problems, and Forms." Dr. Behrendt was the first editor of *Die Form*, that once-brilliant organ of the *Deutscher Werkbund*, and he is one of that group of talented men, loyal to the best elements in the German tradition, who are now planting the seeds of Germany's post-war renascence in countries that can make more grateful use of the new culture than the *Dritte Reich*. He is now lecturer on housing and city planning in the Art Department of Dartmouth College.

Dr. Behrendt's approach to modern form and structure is a fundamental one. His first chapter opens up the general problem of order and develops the idea of two types of expression inherent in the creative spirit itself. One kind is formal, geometrical, externally imposed, the product of reason in the Platonic sense. The other is more inward, more intuitional, more vital, more responsive to time, place, function, change, and the human demands that grow out of the complicated processes of life itself. The first sort of order is typified in the legend about Procrustes: it lops off a limb in order to fit its preconceived bed. The second kind of order makes the bed fit the sleeper even if it is forced to "spoil" the bed's appearance by breaking out a panel. One is architecture; the other is building. And while the creative instinct embraces both, it is building that is inevitably uppermost today.

No other book on modern architecture that I know says so much in so small a compass, and spreads so far in every relevant direction. In contrast to formalistic critics like Geoffrey Scott, Dr. Behrendt knows that organic design today cannot derive from a purely visual theory of architectural form; it is tied up with economic and moral and practical matters that inevitably condition that architect's success, even as they modify his forms in the process of creation. Dr. Behrendt himself is a unique combination of the architect, the engineer, the administrator, and the scholar, and his treatment of the development of modern form is far more evenhanded and delicately weighted than most contemporary treatises. If you wish to find out how modern building came into existence and what it means in terms of form and life, "Modern Building" is your book.

Professor Hudnut, the new dean of the School of Architecture at Harvard, appropriately introduces the American edition of Walter Gropius's little essay on "The New Architecture and the Bauhaus." Gropius's succinct account of his own development in relation to the development of the modern architectural movement in pre-Nazi Germany is most stimulating. Though his mind seems to work by nature from principles of abstract order down into reality, he is a man sensitively harmonized with the realities of modern life, and the kind of teaching he developed at the Bauhaus tended to develop from the abstract-formal into the organic-actual—if I may permit myself a few Germanisms you will not find in Gropius's essay. To find an architect and a thinker of Gropius's calibre welcome in what was once a very old-fashioned architectural school is an exceedingly cheering sign— even though one Gropius does not make a school.

Japanese architecture has been praised by people as diverse as Ralph Adams Cram and Frank Lloyd Wright. No architecture has been more completely standardized in essential design than the traditional Japanese dwelling house; no architecture, not even that of the New England farmhouse, is more free from extraneous ornament; and yet none is so close to nature and so refined in its formal aesthetic effects. Fortunately, an admirable book on the Japanese dwelling house has at last appeared, in German: "Das Japanische Wohnhaus," by Tetsuro Yoshida. It is so full of illustrations and plans that I can recommend it even to those who have to spell out the legends under the pictures with the aid of a dictionary. Here is that combination of the organic and the formal, the vital and the mechanical, that the best modern work in the Western world also aspires toward.

"Adventures in Light and Color," by Charles J. Connick, is the work of the modern master in traditional glass decoration in America—a man whose stained-glass windows have brought into dozens of contemporary churches some of the ecstatic brilliance of the early medieval windows. The present volume, sumptuously illustrated, with many colored plates, is a friendly, discursive introduction to the subject, the sort of observation, technical, historic, autobiographic, that one could get otherwise only through close association in the workshop. So far, the interest in stained glass has been persistently ecclesiastical—if one excepts that brief spell in the eighties when no bathroom was complete without its colored-glass window. Modern architects, even when under no financial restrictions, have not explored the possibilities of using glass of different colors and textures for other purposes than that of religious symbolism. But I have a notion that a time will come when master craftsmen like Mr. Connick and modern architects who wish to add to their decorative resources in the structure itself will have something to say to each other.

THE SKY LINE
THE WORLD'S FAIR
MAY 8, 1937

THE Architectural League show this year is dominated by the plans and models of the New York World's Fair of 1939. That is pretty fortunate for everyone concerned, particularly for the Architectural League and me. For I can omit, without dutiful misgivings, any further comment on the Georgian post offices designed to make us believe that nothing has happened to the world since the Constitution was signed, and I need not say how ghastly most of the handicraft is, or how vapid the larger mural paintings seem. Here and there a good modern design slipped into the exhibition—a modest meteorite from another world. To ask for more than this would be to demand that the League should become an American version of the *Deutscher Werkbund*, which is exactly what I would demand if I thought anyone were listening to me.

The World's Fair, unfortunately, is now in that embryonic shape which makes criticism impossible. Being an embryo, it can no longer be affected by any suggestions one might make about choosing a new set of parents; at the same time, its various organs may now show defects that will disappear before it is born. Nevertheless, the heart and the beginnings of the bony structure are visible, and at the risk of saying things about the aesthetic organization of the Fair that will look silly later on, I will plunge in, having held myself in a state of benign innocence for more than a year.

THE key to the Fair is its plan. In essence, a World's Fair is a miniature city, a very special kind of city, more in the nature of a Washington than a Pittsburgh, but still a city. If one is going to portray the possibilities of communal life in the remaining decades of the twentieth century—and that seems to be the general idea—it is with the primary visualization of the structure of the modern city, *any* modern city, that the designers might well have begun. From this standpoint, the skeleton plan is incredibly old-fashioned. The outline of the site is roughly in the form of a horseshoe. At the base is a wide avenue that leads to the amusement section, set on a lake outside the curve of the horseshoe, and at right angles to this is the main axis that connects the Theme Building with the government buildings ranged around the upper part of the curve. From the Theme Building centre two other avenues radiate, cutting the Fair into rough, wedge-shaped areas. These areas are devoted to communication, clothing, cosmetics, to production and food, and also, in the northeast corner, to what is called the Community Centre, on the extreme edge of which is a housing project.

So far there have been two logical schemes for a World's Fair. One was the Paris scheme of 1867, which had the exhibits ranged in concentric structures, so that the visitor could either follow the arc of the perimeter or cut through to the centre. The other type was that of Chicago, 1893, which had the buildings grouped in a formal pattern around the main watercourse, in something of the fashion in which public buildings were later grouped on either side of the Mall in Washington. Both these modes of planning were on well-tried Renaissance lines, and they had the great advantage of such abstract planning—complete and immediate legibility. The designers of the present plan clung to these ancient precedents, but having committed themselves to a stale plan of organization, they did not, unfortunately, cling hard enough. For what they did in elaborating this bare skeleton was to superimpose upon the abstract Renaissance formalism the informal, disconnected rambling plan (with irregular spottings of buildings) that was popular in suburban developments a generation ago. The result is a plan so weak in conception that it is valueless as a precedent, and if I am not mistaken, it will not even work effectively as a traffic plan in facilitating the passage of visitors through the grounds.

This is the first visible muff, and I think it is a serious one, for it shows that the architects on the Board of Design have not successfully thought out for themselves the implications of modern building, either as it affects plan or as it affects design. They know no alternative to the half-baked order of a Renaissance plan—no alternative except disorder or planned caprice. Working in the big metropolis, where the sense of the whole has all but disappeared, these architects have been trained by their environment to accept, and indeed to overvalue, the irregular street picture produced by unplanned building. When they find a uniform façade for as much as a couple of hundred feet, their impulse (to use their favorite expression) is to break it up. On the surface plan of the Fair the designers have accordingly produced the maximum amount of "breakage" with the minimum amount of clarity and coherence. What the plan sadly lacks is a fresh organic sense of order.

Now, it happens that one of the great achievements in modern community planning has been the introduction of the notion of orientation as a guiding line for design. Primarily buildings are oriented to take advantage of sunlight, breezes, and views, but in a Fair the principle might legitimately be introduced for still another purpose—the purpose of keeping the visitor clear as to his general movement, and to make it possible for him to explore the Fair thoroughly and to reach a desired destination with a minimum of strain and confusion. The point is doubly important because many of the projected buildings are, perhaps for functional reasons, designed in irregular shapes, with exits at points which may be relatively close to the place of entry. The plan, instead of giving the visitor a clue to his position, simply aggravates his difficulty, so that, even after a short tour, he may find himself helplessly at the place where he started, wondering why he is not at least half a mile away. The architects have apparently decided to ease the visitor's embarrassment by providing pools of quiet, with trees, fountains, refreshments, at suitable intervals, but they might have made these rest spots even more available on a more systematic and intelligible plan.

THE plan, in short, is an opportunity missed. It is one of those feeble composite designs that reveal an absence of creative leadership, or, what is perhaps as serious, the absence of strong convictions and an underlying consensus among the designers whose resources were pooled. What, then, shall one say of the buildings? To the extent that modern buildings need to be grouped together on a modern plan in order to function effectively, the layout seriously hampers good design. Nevertheless, there are good points. The main type of exhibition building is relatively low, rather than high and monumental, and as far as the treatment of the structures goes, a negative victory has been won by getting away from the classic or neo-Georgian designs which were first suggested as being especially appropriate for the Fair. But such a victory is meaningless unless it signifies that

a new order is being worked out. As yet, there are no signs of such a positive advance. Sculpture and paintings will probably be used in concentrated masses about the entrances of the buildings, and the buildings themselves will be frankly bold and showy, instead of being content to be a harmonious but inconspicuous background for the human pageant itself.
Scalloped walls, fluted pilasters, and old-fashioned columns will probably
not be altogether taboo, unless the designers suffer a change of heart. In
short, the "modernism" will be of the school of Paul Cret and Ralph
Walker rather than the school of Frank Lloyd Wright.

All this indicates, I think, a certain fuzziness, a certain lack of clear
intellectual discipline and positive leadership in the Board of Design and
among the associated architects. They have not been working on fundamental principles, but on hunches, hopes, compromises, affabilities; they
lack the cold, hard vigor of youth. It is not a matter of birthdays but of
spirit. The future is not yet in these men, and in designing a Fair to exhibit life as it may be, they have fallen back upon the easy cushion of what was.
They will not make the swaggering blunders of the Chicago Fair. What
they do will be in decent scale, it will be graced and mollified by generous
landscape gardening; but their architectural virtues will not be those
springing out of a robust faith. They will be emblems of discretion.
Architecturally, the two most promising symbols of the Fair are at the formal entrance: two great, stark elements, male and female, a high obelisk and
a hollow globe, within which the visitor will be introduced to the theme of
the Fair. But the strength of those symbols will, I am afraid, be lost in triv-
ial fantasy.

As the Fair now stands, the one place where a fresh architectural beginning may perhaps still be made is in the Community section. A few million
dollars well spent in this department will send thousands of Americans
back to their Main Streets and their Middletowns with a clear, decisive
vision of what life in rural and urban communities might be. There is nothing in the Architectural League exhibits to show, in any detail, what has
been done here or what is contemplated, but the opportunity is a challenging one, and it will determine, once and for all, if the directors and designers are capable of rising above the embarrassing limitations they carry over
from their several pasts.

THE SKY LINE
BRIDGES AND BEACHES
JULY 17, 1937

T HE public architecture of the city of New York reached an all-
time low in the North River steamship piers that were finished a
couple of years ago. Since then it has been on the upgrade, and
this is partly because so much of the new work has been done under the
astute and energetic Commissioner of Parks. There was a time when I had
hoped to give a report on Mr. Moses' varied improvements taken as a
whole, but who can keep pace with the sweep of his projects? Before I could
polish off the Triborough Bridge he was making fresh improvements in the
islands it sweeps over; and now he has finished the Jacob Riis Park at
Neponsit, where I haven't yet had time to follow him.

East Side, West Side, all around the town, Mr. Moses' improvements
are creating the framework of a new city; he will even probably get credit
for the East River Drive, though the initiative for that belongs to the
Borough President of Manhattan. From the standpoint of town planning,
the best single improvement is probably the lower stretch of the Riverside
improvement, covering the old railroad tracks, by-passing the city's streets
in an express highway with widely separated points of entrance, and spot-
ting the lately claimed area with playgrounds given to the more active varieties of sport. This new, swift outlet to the north was so necessary that one
can easily imagine Mr. Moses' defences, if he thought they were needed,
for the invasion of Inwood Hill Park. Anyone who has had to go through
land-condemnation and street-closing proceedings, even vicariously, can
understand why the highway engineers kept to the direct outside route.
The steel arched bridge over the Spuyten Duyvil looks light and graceful,
and the type of wooden lamp standard employed on the highway, while
almost the same as the simple form used on the original Bronx River
Parkway, is an improvement; the tree trunk has been squared, instead of
being left in the raw.

The new Mary Harriman Rumsey Playground in Central Park, which
takes the place of the ramshackle mess that was the Casino, is a happy

replacement. Not merely was the old structure an eyesore, but it obscured, even from its own windows, one of the unexpectedly fine views of the Park, which has now been opened up. A short flight of steps, broken by a circle, leads from the east to the open area; the axis runs through the dome of the orchestra platform that faces the Mall. The whole playground is very gracefully done, from the little sculptured figures on the entrance posts to the sober, grayish-pink brick that is used for the resthouse. The brickwork in the wall is a little finicking, as so often happens in the present activities of the Parks Department—indeed, I wish that someone would send the architects on a trip to Holland and England just to learn a lesson or two in freshness and simplicity—but the only sizable blunder is the emphasis of the gabled roof of the resthouse. Here every aesthetic consideration demanded a flat roof.

The same interesting grayish brick, which has not to my knowledge been used to any extent in New York before, was employed in the new buildings that have just been put up near the Stadium on Randall's Island. And that brings me to the Triborough Bridge itself, about whose features I have been slowly making up my mind. My final verdict is that it is an essentially honest but not highly inspired job. The piers of the suspension span are probably what one should expect of a well-braced design in steel, but quite apart from size and scale, they lack the exciting quality of the George Washington Bridge. Furthermore, the engineers made a great mistake by putting skyscraper lanterns on the crest of the cables, thus breaking the beautiful nonchalant curve of the suspension. Granting that these lights are necessary, another form should have been found for them, more in the rhythm of the bridge, less in the fashion of that departed day when even bookcases were built to imitate skyscrapers. On the other hand, the toll booths and accessory structures are clean mechanical designs; and as an inveterate pedestrian, I also thank the engineers for putting the pedestrians' walk high above the motor traffic.

The way to see the bridge itself and to get a view of New York is to hoof it back from the Astoria end. Here is one of the few places, outside Governors Island, where one can see New York across a foreground of verdure and water, and it must be counted one of the most dazzling urban views in the world. I shall, however, confess that the last mile, as one approaches Manhattan, is extremely tedious; I also regret that there is no point—even at the most natural place, the toll station—where a tired pedestrian may catch a bus. Worst of all, the designers so despised the whole notion of walking that they have not even had the grace or the good manners to provide benches, where one might rest and take in the view. To create one of the greatest of metropolitan promenades and then not stock it with benches seems to me almost feeble-minded—not least because over Ward's Island one can look down from the bridge on a sight exceptionally rare in New York: a well-ordered formal garden. I am happy to say that these ideas are shared by an aged Italian woman (a Mrs. Bernardino Tutti) whom I encountered halfway over, one hot afternoon in June. It seemed to both of us that we had been wandering around with Mr. Moses for forty years.

B UT so far Mr. Moses' greatest achievements are his marine parks, and the great landscaped highways that parallel and connect with the barrier beaches of Long Island. Since I hope he will go on building these to the end of his days, and mostly in the same fashion that he is doing now, I want to say a few belated but critical words about the most magnificent of these achievements: Jones Beach. It is all the more important to appraise this place intelligently because the good parts are so superb that they will tend to carry the bad parts along with them, as no less essential to the design, especially when other people begin to imitate them.

The landscaping of the highway and the beach leaves me in a state of ecstatic admiration. The landscape architects have used for the most part the native heath vegetation of the coast, and they have made the most of even the salt marshes, either by leaving them undisturbed or by planting a grass that I have not been conscious of hitherto in America—a superb grass with a long, pointed blade, like bamboo, with a fluffy efflorescence, a variety I recognize as being similar to the species that grows so handsomely around the inland lakes of Holland. As one approaches the bathhouses and pavilions, the low shrubbery forms borders and background masses that are as lush as they are varied in their quality of green and their contrasting textures. The effect mainly depends upon the use of bayberry, untrimmed privet, and dwarf pine. They fit the scene and flourish in the salt air.

Such intelligent planting has its reward in requiring a minimum of care once it is well started; this makes it possible to expend a little extra time and attention upon such fine superfluities as green lawns that meet, in an abrupt line, the dazzling white sand—a sweet gift to the eyes when the sunlight is too intense. As for the floral borders, they show the same high order of aesthetic imagination. At one place, in June, there was a rich, unexpected contrast of white and yellow violas, and at other points a colorful mixture of petunias and ageratum. Nowhere was there a touch too much; nowhere was there a note out of key. The word "heavenly" should be reserved for such complete achievements.

The general planning of the grounds and buildings, the clean separation of the parking spaces from the recreation areas, the ordering of terraces for eating and lounging, the low, curving boardwalk, the disposition and variety of the play spaces are all no less admirable than the landscaping. But the architecture, to speak frankly, is terrible, and if it spoils no one's pleasure, that is simply because the perfection of everything else keeps one in a pleasant, uncritical coma. Now, it happens that in the architecture of seaside places, there is in America a long, honorable tradition, which reaches its peak, probably, in the buildings and color combinations that are used on Cape Cod and in nearby coastal territory. Our lighthouses in particular have an appropriateness to the locale that should set the standard for every other kind of seashore building, and it was only natural that the designers of Jones Beach should want some such tall structure to dominate the scene. Unfortunately, they sought to improve upon tradition, and in doing so they showed no better taste than the suburban builder who rusticates brick cottages with heavy, warty field stones. Instead of the tapering cylinder of the lighthouse, the architects designed an obelisk, and instead of sticking to the traditional colors of white and gray, which could be achieved in concrete or in white brick, they used an orangey field stone at the base and carried the rest of the structure up in a dark-red brick, an atrocious combination that would be bad enough a thousand miles away from the white sand and the green waters of the Atlantic.

That sort of thing happened in all the other buildings, with variations, and when one examines the results carefully, one could weep. I am no blind worshipper of concrete, but here, by the sea, was above all the place to use it; here, if anywhere, concrete might be called a native material, all the more because it enables the architect to achieve in a modern, permanent material the color combinations that our earlier coastal architecture achieved in gray shingles and white trim. Compare any of these pavilions with Mendelsohn & Chermayeff's design for the building at Bexhill-on-Sea in England—the English work is clean, bright, and gay, while the Jones Beach designs are tedious and mediocre. The tradition that the latter represent is that of the suburban builder in Jamaica and Canarsie. Indeed, the only things that can be called positive architecture on Jones Beach, harmonious with the landscape and with the spirit of the place, are the white lifeguard stands and the rows of wire baskets for wastepaper. Both these utilities are crisp and shipshape, as the buildings themselves should be; and, incidentally, they give scale to the foreshore. If the buildings had been done in the same key, Jones Beach would have been a spectacle the modern world has been waiting long to see: a complete and harmonized whole, as fine in every part as it actually is when one turns one's back to the clumsy, arty buildings.

1937~38

Mayor La Guardia was handily reelected in the fall of 1937. With the charter reforms he had initiated earlier, which included the establishment of a city council, his position was strengthened considerably during his second term. Moreover, the city's finances had finally stabilized. A combination of public and private works—including shops along Fifth Avenue, two public health centers, and housing projects in Harlem and the Williamsburg section of Brooklyn—merited Mumford's coverage that season. His review of the Cloisters Museum in Fort Tryon Park is a masterly reflection on the role of modern architecture in an increasingly disordered world.

T HE most gratifying piece of architecture at the moment is the new formal gardens in Central Park at 106th Street, where the old hothouses used to be. I say "architecture" advisedly, not simply because the gardens are formally designed, but because perhaps the most significant thing that has happened in New York during the last few years is the increase in the quantity of open spaces and the improvement in their quality. These new gardens do not, of course, add to the amount of public green in the city, but they suggest what might be done, on a modest scale, if ever the city gets poor enough to afford to raze a block of tenements every ten blocks and set aside such an area. Another shattering economic crisis, with tenement properties falling into the city's hands for non-payment of taxes, and plenty of WPA workers to effect their demolition, might turn the trick. Manhattan would be more fit to live in, even if one still needed Flents to get to sleep.

The site of the new gardens is admirable, for the plot itself is sunk below the level of Fifth Avenue, and its western end is backed abruptly by a hill. The central element in the new design is a wide, velvety greensward, edged with low Japanese yews; on each side is a broad path closely lined with short trees in a double row which forms a parallel alley, and against the semi-circular brick parapet and retaining wall are clipped evergreens in three rows, closely planted one above the other. The top of this amphitheatre is a wide terrace, lined with benches, which give a marvellous sweep over the gardens; at each end the construction embraces a public comfort station in red brick, with octagonal windows. At present the one weak note in this composition is the high iron lattice, fancy but unentertaining, which bounds the terrace, but fortunately this will be obliterated, in the fullness of time, by the huge wistarias that have already been planted at the base. Between the greensward and this terrace is a basin curved in the Renaissance fashion.

The main mass, whose visual axis runs east and west, is separated, by the tree-lined alleys of approach, from the two other gardens, one on each side, gardens whose more intimate scale gives the right relationship for the close-at-hand enjoyment of flowers. On the north side, emphasizing again the approach from above, so effective in a geometrical arrangement of beds, there is a fine circular planting in the middle; at about the time these comments come out, it should be radiant with chrysanthemums. On the south side there is a different kind of planting, whose central point is a pool, with sculpture, enclosed by a firm, dark-green boxwood hedge. Splendid purple asters, of the variety that's closest to the wild sort, make this spot, in the twilight of an October evening, the very embodiment of autumn's sensuous melancholy. It is a place for lovers to moon in; and speaking on behalf of those who know the difficulties of expressing love on a Fifth Avenue bus or in a traffic-blocked taxicab, I would say that the city has need for a great many other such enchanting places. They would do more toward promoting sweetness and light than another express highway.

Even in the waning season these gardens are aesthetically alive, for the landscape gardener knows how to handle his greens, and make the most of both his borders and his masses, with a span of variations which ranges from the gray greens of the catnip family through the bright-emerald grass to the crisp, blackish definitions of the evergreens. The whole design has been carried through scrupulously, even in details like the green-and-lavender mixture of flagstones on the terrace, and it is so successful that one wishes a trace or two of a non-contemporary order of thinking had been sloughed off. There was no reason to hamper such a spacious design with piddling Renaissance touches—the iron lattice, the scroll formed by the border of yew, the shape of the basin beneath the terrace—for who can really take pleasure in the involved geometry of the seventeenth century? Moreover, such tags traduce the essential breadth and simplicity of the architect's design. For what is fine in these new gardens is the sense of peace and order and completeness; every superfluous touch, from another century, from another culture, detracts from the integrity of one's impression. Fortunately, there are few such touches.

PERHAPS it is not altogether accidental that one's very minor criticism of these gardens should coincide pretty closely with one's feeling about the new Corning Building at Fifty-sixth Street and Fifth Avenue. The general elements in this structure are simple and excellent. In a frame of broad Indiana limestone slabs, two great vitreous masses are placed: a single, long, rectangular bay in the narrow façade on Fifth Avenue, and a broad, horizontally placed rectangle, of five bays, on the street side. These glass walls—they are no longer openings—are composed of translucent, square blocks, thirty-eight hundred of them; they were put in place by bricklayers, and they are sealed with fibrous glass insulation to the handsome nickel-silver framework, a yellowish metal that is just the right binding link between the glass and the stone. Blocks with a fine interior fluting, which give a different effect of texture, are used to conceal the floor members and the columns; this is emphasized in the crisscross of the metal frame. Beneath the glass wall on Fifth Avenue is a high show window—the only clear glass used in the building. A narrow black granite band protectively edges the base from scuffling feet. The architects are William and Geoffrey Platt.

The general conception of such a building, apart from the use of glass walls and complete insulation against direct sunlight and clear vision and open air, was first achieved in factory buildings, and its rationale was systematically worked out for museum buildings by Mr. Clarence S. Stein. The great advantage of the glass wall is that it makes for the maximum amount of flexibility in the arrangement of the interior space. Such a design does not essentially depend upon the use of glass tiles, and it does not depend, either, upon that great new American toy, air-conditioning—a toy which, in its present form, will probably go the way of Tom Thumb golf and crossword puzzles. What the glass tile has done, by reason of its insulating qualities, is to permit the architect to use great light openings without bankrupting his client through the increased cost of heating. The main elements in such a design would remain valid even if transparent glass and openable windows were used.

In the main, the architects did their job well. They visibly dramatized the use of glass; they even employed it for acoustic tiles in the ceilings. But the spirit in which the building was conceived is frustrated by the decoration the architects superimposed upon their otherwise handsome main façade: the floating figure at the top, the old-fashioned lettering of "Steuben Glass" over the show window, the carving at the upper corners of the façade. Such ornamental fly buzzing distracts one's attention; it is evidence of a failure to feel the building as an aesthetic whole. Someday, perhaps, there will be space enough around our buildings to permit the use of detached sculpture as a counter-accent to the planes of the structure itself; but the day when sculpture will thus become part of a new architectural whole is not hastened by piously attaching lumps of sculpture to a building in which they can have no integral part. Attached sculpture, like fixed mural painting, belongs to a departed order of design. The sooner the architect and the sculptor discover that fact, the quicker they will make use of—or demand—more vital opportunities.

O N the same scale as the five-story Corning Building are a number of other structures that have been rising in the upper Forties and the Fifties; and what is more, these buildings are being carried through in the same general materials, with the result that this section is beginning to have a new architectural identity—the first sign of coherence since the old brownstone rows were broken up. The latest example is a "taxpayer," still in process of building, at the northeast corner of Madison Avenue and Forty-eighth Street. The architects are Cross & Cross. Like its predecessors, it shows the same triad of short-long-short windows on the second story, as if afraid to meet contemporary design full-face; but the shiny, chrome-finished metal frame of the central shop windows is handled with a somewhat greater boldness than the earlier designs. Aesthetically halfway between this new set of shops and the Helena Rubinstein shop around the corner is a little building (Chez Rosette) at 10 East Fifty-sixth Street. Though it is not without a certain modest excellence, its chief defect is that there is no common bond between the horizontal windows of the upper floor and the display window below. Probably it would have been better to alter the proportions of the show window, and even to divide its plate glass into a number of horizontal lights. In addition, all the windows should have been flush with the walls, instead of being set back for a shallow reveal. The architects are Scachetti & Siegel.

What is important about these buildings, however, is that they show a sense of the neighborhood. They manifest concretely what New York is most in need of—a belief in the possibility of order. It may be that Radio City, despite its many extravagant mistakes, has contributed to this sense, and has even set the pattern in its specific use of limestone slabs and glass. Small buildings, indeed, can utilize its good qualities without imitating its pattern of congestion. In Stockholm, I believe, there are block committees that are devoted to keeping up the general character and manners of street and neighborhood; every new building must have their approval before being built. There are dangers in this sort of supervision, for these committees tend to lay too heavy a stress on mere conformity, and they might oppose, even more effectually than current building regulations, experimental departures like the Corning Building. It would be better if each architect and owner acquired for himself a notion of his aesthetic responsibilities, a belief in orderly and urbane building. Such order is the very foundation of individuality in neighborhoods.

Q UIETLY—and the word "quietly" has happy implications— Fifth Avenue has been having its face altered during the last six months. It is at the eye level or thereabouts that most of the changes have taken place—not new buildings so much as new show windows and shop fronts. This is mainly the work of the department stores, the specialty shops, and those particular friends of a rather blatant form of modernism, the shoe shops.

The quietest of all these alterations is that just finished by Best & Co.; the architect is Harold Butterfield. This is perhaps the best piece of refurbishing that has been done lately, and it is also one of the most exasperating, just because the architect has made the wrong choices in those final details where a false motion spoils a good effect almost as completely as a streak of lipstick carried too far out of the general curve of the mouth can spoil a woman's makeup. The Best building is one of those structures which one may pass a hundred times without really noticing if they are good or bad. It happens, when one finally looks at it, to be a good example of an unobtrusive modern vernacular—except for the moth-eaten lintels and moldings, it is a clean design.

As the result of the alterations, the façade of the main floor has been opened up and further simplified; the windows are now framed delicately in a metallic green, and the Roman lettering above the entrance is brilliantly simple and effective. What happened to the architect's imagination when he reached the door frames, I can't fathom. Maybe the use of a verdantique finish suggested worse things. At all events, the horizontal line above the door is spoiled by some tedious spiky ornament, and the stone between the bays of the windows is cut into that characteristic form of the pseudo-modern, a fat bundle of fasces (or what resembles fasces), without the lictor's axe. I would favor adding the axe, if only to demolish the fasces. Note that there is only a hairsbreadth difference between the design as actually carried out and a straightforward architectural statement without benefit of these time-worn quotations from Caesar. Aesthetically, what has been added by way of ornament has about the same high emotional value as *Gallia est omnis divisa in partes tres.*

The shoe shops are in a class by themselves. They suggest what happens to modern architecture when its slogans and catchwords, instead of going to the head, descend to the feet. More perhaps than any other type of store, they are designed, like a cunning flower that traps insects, to lure the pedestrian off the Avenue and draw him, by persuasive curves, into the dark corolla of the shop itself. This accounts for the billowing window bays and the sinuous streamers on the pavement that point inward. Psychological— you follow your feet. The Stetson Shoe Shop, at Thirty-sixth Street, shows its wares under a lush, pink-grained marble band that turns the corner in a bland curve; the upright at the corner of the window is a greenish-black block of marble, also curved. I could swallow the strawberry-sundae effect of the marble, but I draw the line at the point where the architect went out of the room and gave the office boy a chance to play with the draughtsman's compass and draw circles, or portholes, all over the design. I don't know yet if it was the portholes or the strawberry-sundae frame that made me feel a little unsteady on my feet.

My vote goes to the new Cammeyer shop, at 448 Fifth Avenue, done in essentially the same order of design—shoe-shop modernism—and with almost the same general materials. Here the great, smooth plaque above the window consists of white marble, cut in squares, and the name Cammeyer is spelled in heavy, green script letters, raised and gilded at the edges. The legend is overbold—letters half this size would have been equally effective and much more handsome in the street picture—but I must say a special word of praise for the architects (the firm is Telchin & Gina) who are intelligent enough to repeat the name of the store and to display the avenue number in readable letters and numerals above the door.

There are a number of things about the new Betty Wales shop, at 394 Fifth Avenue, that I like; mainly, perhaps, the fact that the architects have not suddenly been persuaded by the air-conditioning people to design the premises with poky, windowless interiors, to give an effect as much as possible like that of E Deck on an ocean liner. There are two continuous banks of windows at the front, with continuous horizontal spandrels of stone above and below, and the display windows, instead of being big and over-powering, are more intimate in scale—an excellent notion. The material used is a slaty blue stone, and the whole design, though not brilliant, is direct and unforced, which is perhaps even more important for the health of modern building. The name of the shop appears twice on the front and once at the corner at eye level—a model of effective reticence, even though in general I must deplore the use of script for such purposes. The big windows on the side street are worth more than a glance, for here the architects, Bell & Goodman, used slats of opaque glass at either side of the Venetian blinds, thus recognizing that control of light and air, rather than their wholesale acceptance or rejection, is what constitutes the modern solution of the problem of fenestration.

Compared with the Betty Wales Shop, A. Sulka & Co.'s new premises at 661 Fifth Avenue are a more ingratiating design. The choice of a polished stone, which is an olive yellow-gray in color, is admirable, and the fine brass trimmings, like the bars that define the lights of the upper windows, are admirable, too; while the change in the window composition, from the divided space of the upper part to the unbroken plate-glass fronts of the show windows is the work of an architect (Alfred Freeman) who plainly knows how to vary his pace and not let a formula run away with him. Unfortunately, at the most critical place—the two entrances—the design slips from modern into neo-romantic rococo; the formidable frames of the two entrances are done in a shape usually reserved for goldfish pools in Renaissance gardens. The fact that these two frames jut out is not necessarily a defect, even though every other part of the composition is essentially two-dimensional; but the absence of differentiation between the frames of the building entrance and of the shop shows that a purely formal concept of design interfered with a useful functional expression. And the shape is wrong because it contradicts the order that exists in the rest of the design. Otherwise it's a handsome façade, and I would commend the scale of the lettering to most shoe-shop designers.

UNLIKE Samuel Butler, who always wiped the knives before the forks, I have kept the best building to almost the end. This is the handsome little structure that W. H. Hall, Inc. (furs), has erected on West

Fortieth Street, just off Fifth Avenue. The architects are Starrett & Van
Vleck. Perhaps the thing that makes me feel especially warm about this
building is the architects' combination of white limestone with a few
sharply incised gold lines between the upper floors, for one night when I
was young I dreamed of a miraculous white city with brilliant red roofs,
touched with gold spires and pinnacles, and though I have seen the
Goldenes Dachl at Innsbruck and have beheld the Sacré-Coeur on
Montmartre with the sun slanting against a backdrop of dark clouds, I
have not yet had my fill of golden magnificence. (I almost forgive the new
courthouse on Foley Square its stitling classic colonnades, now that the
tower is pyramided with gold.)

The unit of design in the Hall building is the upright rectangle. This
contradicts all the superficial dogmas about horizontality and modernism,
but in such a small structure, this choice was perhaps a wise one. It creates
a spacious frame for what otherwise might have seemed a cramped façade.
Beside the low entrance, capped by a small carved and colored coat of arms
(squirrels rampant), there is a huge two-story window divided into nine big
lights, held together by flat metal bands. Above this there is a generous
swath of stone before a row of windows is reached, and within that space
the name of the shop conspicuously but decently calls attention to itself.
Then there come two floors, with four small rectangular windows on each
floor. These windows are of that useful type with horizontal divisions top
and bottom and two vertical casements. In fact, they are a distinct improvement on the type, since all the elements—not just the casements—may be
opened. This greatly increases the usefulness of this sort of fenestration
from the standpoint of effective ventilation in winter.

Above the top windows there is a quite unnecessary touch of delicate
scalloped carving—like the irregular weathering marks that shade a stone
surface where an awning has been used—and the top course terminates in
a slight, round flare. The front has an excellent balance, owing to its good
proportions, and it has the quiet, self-respecting character that wine merchants sometimes recommend in a good wine of undistinguished vintage.
The label tells you nothing about the bottle; you must taste the wine. This
is a quite traditional building, but its feeling is fresh—far more "modern,"
and far more sound, than the teasing antics of the shoe-shop family.

IN comparison with this structure, the new National City Bank building, which has been tucked away back of Rockefeller Center on Fifty-first Street, off Fifth Avenue, is something of a disappointment. The architect's problem was a difficult one. The narrow plot makes the building seem high, even though it is only three stories. But unfortunately the use of a single rectangular opening in the façade above the entrance increases the sense of leanness, and this is further accentuated by the vertical stone projection on the left, by the deep inset of the windows, and by the curious vertical brass fin that divides up the great fenestral bay. The interior is very ingenious; there are three sets of levels for the various departments of the bank, and the fittings are well conceived and well carried out. But the circular murals of clouds do not solve the problem of relieving the formidable wall and keeping it from pressing too near; a mirror on one wall might have helped. Still, the general treatment, by Walker & Gillette, is straightforward and sensible enough to symbolize, perhaps, the end of funeral-parlor pomp and mausoleum security in the design of banks.

THE SKY LINE
FOR THE COMMON GOOD
JANUARY 8, 1938

THE battle of the styles, as I have undoubtedly remarked before, has been over a long time. The fancy-dress architects are still hanging on, but the sort of costume-room eclecticism for which they stand will probably have its last great opportunity at the World's Fair of 1939, where it will be zealously publicized as "modern." But another battle of a more important kind is still being fought: that between the monument and the building, between the showplace that doesn't work and the workplace that refuses to sacrifice a single need to the traditional requirements of show. Perhaps the worst obstruction to modern architecture in the United States is the notion that public buildings must be of a monumental order: solid, grandiose, imposing, futile. This tradition has even governed the design of some very exciting buildings that the municipality of New York has been strewing over its boroughs during the past year: the new health centres. Someone should put an end to this quickly before it spoils any more new public buildings.

If you have never been poor and ill there is no reason you should be even dimly conscious of the existence of municipal health centres in New York. They have usually been in battered, broken-down buildings, with a dusty area outside and a dingy sign, as of some abandoned undertaker's shop, indicating the purpose of the structure, or have been in empty grocery stores that could be rented cheaply. All that is being changed. In the midst of a drab neighborhood like East 115th Street, one of the most congested areas in the city, the new East Harlem Health Centre stands out smartly, breaking into the dark squalor of the streets with the promise of another kind of city, another way of living—no longer makeshift services in makeshift quarters.

I have gone carefully over two of these buildings, once in the company of a nurse, once with a doctor, and the scope and reach of the work done within these centres so excites my admiration, to say nothing of my native pride, that I could be easily tempted to pass over the shortcomings of the structures themselves. Here is preventive medicine on a grand scale, with a new efficiency, a new politeness, even a new tone of voice that must strike anyone who knows what clinics for the poor were in the good old days, when a self-respecting patient would die of humiliation, if not of his original disease. The doctors and nurses are, I gather, very proud of these structures, which give them a sense of making a new start. Not merely are the various dispersed clinics (for tuberculosis, for sexual diseases, for maternity) brought together in a single building but all the voluntary and official agents for helping the sick have their headquarters there too.

This whole effort is so important that one would be doing it a serious injustice to accept the buildings that have so far been designed as adequate to their purpose. Aesthetically they are scarcely halfway to being attractive; functionally they are inadequate to present needs and will be even more inadequate to meet future ones; hygienically the design is nothing short of a disgrace.

Take the one I have just mentioned, that at 160 East 115th Street. Like the Chelsea Centre, it was built on the site of a new public playground, and in order to put up the building it was necessary to wipe out a badly needed breathing space. Even though Mr. Moses made a bargain with the Health Department providing that another playground would be constructed on the roof of the structure, no one can pretend that it's the full equivalent. The amount of land is entirely inadequate: the site is crowded and only the front and rear façades have even the beginnings of adequate ventilation. The plan resembles that of the old dumbbell tenement, the all-time low in New York housing. Though the Chelsea Centre has a much more favorable site and is open on four sides, the interior plan is no less defective than that of the East Harlem Centre. The rooms in both buildings are grouped around a square central corridor. There is no through ventilation; there are many interior rooms and cubicles without any light or ventilation at all. If these are health centres, the architects were the last people to demonstrate it. These buildings, in fact, embody the very hygienic evils against which the doctors and nurses must fight.

Here is a pretty tough paradox. All the equipment in these buildings is the very latest: the dentists' chairs are as fine as you will find on Fifty-ninth Street, the radiograph service is what you would have in the best Saranac

Lake sanatorium. But the quarters provided for the physicians and their instruments and their patients do not measure up to these standards of efficiency. The waiting rooms are too small, and in the Chelsea clinic the waiting room for tubercular patients is worse than inadequate. The lack of air and ventilation, considering the number of benches provided for the waiting patients, is below a reasonable factory standard. The dressing cubicles will be either stuffy or drafty in winter, and little Black Holes of Calcutta in the summer. The windows in the examination offices in the tuberculosis clinic at the Chelsea Centre reach down to the level of the examination table, which is beside them. Don't tell me that Park Avenue specialists are often as careless of the comfort and safety of their patients. I know they are. That is no excuse.

The defects in these sites and building plans are probably partly due to the haste to get hold of WPA appropriations, which might be withdrawn, and partly to the fact that either the architects or the administrators lacked rational standards of design—standards expressed in terms of light, sun, air, comfort, and efficiency. A good plan would have called for shallow buildings. There would have been no dark, deep, unventilated spaces; and even the dressing cubicles would have had light and air and heat. Instead of a monumental front, the continuous ribbon window would have been used, so that the interior space could be flexibly partitioned and new arrangements easily made when conditions altered. Finally, a health centre should have spacious waiting rooms with a cubic air content equal to that of a public-school classroom; it should have individual, well-spaced seats, not benches where people may be so crowded that they exchange ailments in their discomfort. The building itself, in short, should dramatize the facts of modern sanitation, hygiene, and health, and not be a reminder of how difficult these things are to achieve in a congested city. Despite the WPA easel pictures on the walls of the East Harlem Health Centre, the result of the architecture is dull and depressing. Compared to the old slum quarters, the new health centre is a palace, but compared to adequately designed modern buildings, these structures have too much the quality of being slums.

T HE same betrayal of the living function by the sacrifice to mass and monumentality is observable in the new Post Office and Federal Office Building on Church Street. Again the interior functions of the building are exciting: window after window, eighty-one of them, for the expediting of public business, twelve hundred lock boxes, a whole floor dedicated to the assortment of mail, two miles of observation galleries where postal inspectors on patrol keep the entire works under surveillance, to say nothing of a floor from which run twenty-seven miles of pneumatic tubes that serve to connect this building with Brooklyn and other Manhattan stations. Here is the system and order and rationalization of modern life at its efficient best; it needs only to be translated into modern terms. And what have the architects—Cross & Cross, and Pennington, Lewis & Mills—done to dramatize these activities? Nothing at all. They have succumbed to the corpselike classicism of Washington.

All these activities are masked behind a monument designed as if it were to face the Lincoln Memorial at the other end of the water course in the national capital. Given the architects' premises, one might describe the post-office section even without seeing it—the square, ill-lighted structure, the vertical bays, the six square columns on Church Street, the deep reveals, the shield-and-darts molding, and of course the hatchet-faced eagles at the corners; the interior of gray marble and silvered metal, with all the little details chastely classicized. Did I say chastely? I forgot the electroliers, which have been tediously converted into an elaborately classic design, with a fasces—axe and all—as an upright, with eagles fluttering around the bowl and swirly metal supports underneath.

When one remembers the positive sense of exhilaration one got on going into one of the new German post offices built before 1933, one realizes that the blame for the present tedious and expensive affectations cannot be placed at the door of mere bureaucracy. What is at fault here is just a common failure of the American imagination—a failure to realize that a mode of building that was in international vogue in 1789 is neither appropriately international nor properly expressive of our much broader and richer national tradition in 1937. The present combination of ponderousness and marmoreal sublimity should appeal to the imagination of a New Jersey burial-vault proprietor. It is a mighty expensive substitute for living architecture.

I T should be a great blow to a New Yorker's pride to realize that none of the important things that have happened in modern architecture have taken place here. Don't mention the skyscrapers or the Radio City Music Hall. All the decisive improvements in the design of skyscrapers were made in Chicago before 1900. When, the other day, I sat for the first time in Adler & Sullivan's Auditorium Theatre, listening under perfect acoustic conditions to the worst opera in the world, I realized that any theatre design that followed this stunning building might perhaps claim to be as good, but could not in essentials be better, for these architects were both masters of technique and poets of space.

All these humble reflections were started by looking at the photographs of a new house by Frank Lloyd Wright, built for Mr. and Mrs. Edgar Kaufmann at Bear Run, Pennsylvania. The exhibition of these pictures will be on at the Museum of Modern Art till March 1st.

Whether it was Wright or his client who thought of building a house over a waterfall I do not know, but Wright's imagination played with the opportunity as freely as Michelangelo's played with the decoration of the Sistine Chapel. The perpetual youngness and freshness of his mind were never better shown than in his treatment of this extraordinary problem. The site would have frightened any conventional architect out of his wits. Wright uses the opportunity to demonstrate that when the need arises he can swing a cantilever across space, using the method of construction not as a cliché of modernism but as a rational engineering solution of a real problem.

The house is anchored against the side of a hill and juts out in a series of concrete terraces that hang over the waterfall, commanding the view along the stream, achieving the fullest intimacy from within, with the wooded banks and the running water swishing over the rocks. The main horizontal elements are great reinforced-concrete monolithic slabs, with finely rounded edges. Wright handles these masses as cleanly as if he were building a dam for a hydroelectric works. They are set into the vertical elements—the hillside itself and the great stone columns and walls.

The masonry construction, especially in the side views along the hill, is no less exciting than the engineering. As for the stone itself, laid in irregular horizontal blocks, thick and thin, it is rugged and strong in its own right, but does not attempt to counterfeit the irregular forms of nature. The stones represent, as it were, the earth theme; the concrete slabs are the water theme. From the bottom of the falls one sees the bold, smooth slabs, and not the least beautiful of the photographic views is that which shows the flaring concrete piers under the living-room balcony. Between the jutting slabs are the living spaces of the house. Steel casement windows, emphatically horizontal, give an almost unbroken outlook, though the light that comes into the rooms is softened by the wide overhangs; the rocks, the trees, the big rhododendron bushes, the swirling water form the main decoration.

The structural elements are strong and handsome, but Wright's genius shows itself no less conspicuously in the little touches. One of the best of these is the rectangular pool of quiet water above the river level, proof that Wright never thinks of architectural design except in relation to the third dimension, plus movement through space. Hence the perpetual breathless sense of surprise one receives in becoming acquainted with Wright's work. One looks at two-dimensional compositions and exhausts them in a view or two, but one must go through Wright's work, finding new compositions, new revelations, new relationships at every step. Even abstractly considered, the planes and the profiles in Fallingwater (as the place is called) are in a state of continuous animation.

I HAVE not seen this house on the spot, but I did spend a few hours in Wright's new Willey house in Minneapolis: a modest one-story structure on a bluff overlooking the Mississippi at the outskirts of the city, where Minneapolis becomes St. Paul without anyone but the taxpayer being the wiser. The opportunities for such a house were much less striking, but Wright's imagination displays here the same creativeness, the same human warmth, the same poetic sublimation of materials. The Willey house is done in a reddish brick laid in bands of contrasting textures— brick outside and brick within, brick walls, brick floors. The living room is

wide and high; through its great sweep of windows it absorbs the outside
world without being overpowered by it, for a great bank of plants, growing
lushly indoors, removes any touch of winter bleakness.

In the Willey house, too, the little touches emphasize Wright's general
mastery. One of them is the corner window in the main bedroom, which,
when opened, presents unobstructed space without even a thin post for
support; another is the lantern that Wright forms out of a simple pattern of
bricks by the fireplace. The workmen were mystified by the plans for this
house, and the masons predicted that the chimney would not work, because
the top of the fireplace was twice the usual height above the floor. But the
chimney was working well on a mean, windy day when I was there. The
touch I liked best—I speak as a cook—is the wide glass window that sepa-
rates the kitchen from the living room; to see the pots and pans hanging in
serial pattern at the far end of the kitchen, and the head and shoulders of
the pretty Swedish cook, was to have a grateful sense of intimacy with one
of the most important parts of a house; it was like being in a farmhouse
kitchen. It took a man of Wright's sensibilities to give Cinderella a glass
window instead of the usual glass slippers.

These two houses show Frank Lloyd Wright at the top of his powers,
undoubtedly the world's greatest living architect, a man who can dance circles around any of his contemporaries. In a city that boasts its leadership
over the rest of the country, particularly in aesthetic matters, you would
naturally expect to come upon at least a few good samples of Wright's work.
The fact is that while we do have one of Sullivan's loft buildings, there is
not, I believe, a single structure by Wright this side of Buffalo. And when
a friend of mine suggested to the eminent architects who are designing the
World's Fair that a World's Fair without Wright, especially after the architectural fiasco of Chicago, would look foolish, he was greeted with gentle-
manly jeers. I grant that the suggestion was certainly ill-advised. One does
not improve a rhinestone necklace by setting a real diamond in it.
Architecturally, however, the chief claim of the World's Fair on the attention of posterity will be the preposterous fact that Wright was not called in
to design it.

THE two big PWA housing projects that have recently opened are worth going out of your way to see. Until the present administration in Washington began building these demonstrations, it was necessary to go to London, Amsterdam, or Paris to discover the outlines of the new order of building. Now the example is at our own doorway. If the standards in these new quarters do not ultimately affect the methods of even commercial builders within the city it will be because we are a race of Caspar Milquetoasts.

The words "model housing" have a bad flavor and the sooner we drop them the better. Model housing began in New York in 1854, when a group of philanthropic gentlemen built a model tenement for the poor which had so many unventilated and unlighted interior rooms that the place became almost overnight a natural harborage for thieves and thugs. So model housing got off to a bad start, and some of the worst misdemeanors in building, like the old dumbbell flats (designed *as* dumbbells *by* dumbbells) were committed in its name. It was impossible to solve the problem on a lot twenty by one hundred feet, and both the builder and the architect found it hard to overcome the handicap of those artificial boundaries.

What was required in order to improve the layout and outlook of the single apartment unit was a large tract of cheap land, not a few overpriced building lots. In the Harlem River Houses and the Williamsburg Houses in Williamsburg, space is what the architects were given; it is the secret of their success. Superficially the Williamsburg project shows the greater number of innovations. The area was a slum site of twenty-five acres. Like all the rest of the city, it had been laid out in rectangular blocks in order to permit the maximum amount of traffic to stream through. The district was a backwater and there wasn't much traffic, but the streets were there, numerous, dusty, expensive—waiting for the increase in traffic and land values that never came.

Now, the first principle of modern neighborhood planning is to reduce the number of streets, convert more open space into gardens and play-grounds, and route traffic around, not through, the neighborhood. Unfor-tunately it takes endless patience and a great deal of legal procedure to close up a street that has once been legally opened, and you have to fight the fire department, too, which thinks no house is really safe unless a fire truck can dash up to its door. But the results justify the effort. In Williamsburg nine acres of useful land were added by closing up two streets; money that would have been wasted on maintaining paving could go into gardens.

One thing seems a bit queer to the eye in this development: the apart-ments are not parallel to the street; instead, row after row slants across the area. Two new principles are involved in this. One is the separation, as far as possible, of traffic from residences; the streetless house and the house-less street are what the planners are after. The other principle is the orien-tation of the rows to achieve a maximum amount of sunlight in winter and a minimum amount in summer. The second principle seems simple, but it is somewhat difficult to carry out, and has been the subject of a lot of shal-low dogmatism. Orientation for sunlight works best when you have dwellings in plain rows; it looks a little silly in the Williamsburg project, where the architects have used not a straight row but a T-unit, in which, if the main axis is correct, all the buildings at right angles to it are incorrect-ly oriented. Still, the architects were *thinking* about sunlight; they had learned their ABC's. Besides, the distinction between front and rear approach disappears; there is not one kind of architecture for the street façade and another for the back yards. Every side of the building must be finished. (The architects, incidentally, were a group of ten headed by Mr. R. H. Shreve.)

The dwellings in Williamsburg are four-story walk-up apartments. They are done in a yellowish brick, with the horizontal ribs of the structure forming continuous bands of concrete. The cantilevered corner window, with a clear view on two sides, has been used in numerous corner units. There is no variation in the height or the placement of the units; the same formula has been kept throughout. The only variation, indeed, is in the angular placement of shops, which run parallel to the avenues and thereby form wedges in relation to the building to which they are attached. When the trees have had time to grow, the effect will be pleasanter. But I feel that a site of this size should have had a greater variety of units in it. The one building that might have saved the day was the new public school, in the middle of the site, but that structure, for which these architects were not responsible, descends to a staleness and mediocrity and inept planning which have become habitual in New York public schools.

T HE Harlem Houses project doesn't illustrate all the new principles, but both the site and the architectural treatment make it a much more exhilarating design. It occupies a plot of nine acres, previously vacant, bounded by 151st and 153rd Streets between Macombs Dam Road and the Harlem River, with Seventh Avenue running in between. There is a triangular area on the east side of the plot, and a triangular park, recently donated to the city by Mr. Rockefeller, gives a handsome approach from the north. It was a magnificent site on which to build and the architects made the most of their opportunities; everything that touches architectural choice was straightforwardly and imaginatively done. Mr. Archibald Manning Brown and his six associates, the architects, deserve a medal.

The theme is red brick and broad steel-framed windows with horizontal lights. The variations are the corner stairs, with a ribbon wall of glass, and touches of strong blue in the doorways, with flat-roofed porticoes that actually shelter the person who stands under them; the house numbers, plainly enough marked to win the approval of F.P.A.; the trees set about the ample open spaces in the fashion of the Luxembourg Gardens; and the handsome sculpture by Heinz Warneke, the penguins round about the central wading pool and the wrestling bears on the east side of Seventh Avenue. The gracious austerity of the architecture magnifies the importance of each variation, and the sculpture is "functional" in a practical as well as an aesthetic sense, since the cast stone which composes it will be improved in finish by being handled and climbed over by children.

The planning of the site is equally good. There are two main levels; the higher is west of Seventh Avenue and the lower on the side next the river. Seventh Avenue itself drops considerably as it goes southward; this leaves a wedge between the street level and the terrace on which the apartments are set, and the architects have cleverly used this space by inserting a short row of shops. As for the part of the project that faces the Harlem River, with a natural amphitheatre for concerts in one corner and a park and a playground below, it is about the best setting any dwellings have in the city, and should make Sutton Place bilious with envy.

Two blocks away from Harlem Houses are the Dunbar Apartments, built by Mr. Rockefeller a few years ago as a model limited-dividend housing project for Negroes. Already the standards of light and open space in the Dunbar Apartments belong to the past. The cramped, U-shaped apartment units are, from the standpoint of good housing design, deplorable. While they represent only a loosening of the old congested pattern, Harlem Houses represent a vigorously different method of neighborhood organization, building, and design.

So much for what is plainly visible from the outside. What are less visible in the Harlem Houses, but no less important for decent family living, are four social units for adults, four rooms for occupational use and children's inside play, a nursery school that can accommodate sixty children, and a health clinic. Here, in short, is the equipment for decent living that every modern neighborhood needs: sunlight, air, safety, play space, meeting space, and living space. The families in the Williamsburg or Harlem Houses have higher standards of housing, measured in tangible benefit, than most of those on Park Avenue. By contrast every other section of the city is a makeshift, congested, disorderly, dismally inadequate.

There was a time when the Sunday magazine sections were full of windy plans for the City of the Future. A lot of these projected a city hundreds of stories high, with the proletariat living in artificial light and air beneath the multiple avenues and terraces that served the needs of those who were literally the upper classes. Many such crazy dreams disappeared with the depression—although I hear rumors that they are to be exhumed for the World's Fair—and their disappearance left a blank spot in the imagination. Here is something to fill it up with, samples of what New York might be if we wanted to make it rival the richer suburbs as a place to live and bring up children. I have only one further suggestion: the PWA projects in future should be three stories high, as in Chicago, not four. Most of the city is obsolete now by even minimum standards of health and beauty. Why not cart it away and begin all over?

I CONFESS to an original dislike for the new Cloisters as a figure in the landscape. This south European building, with its tawny, tiled roof, caps the northerly one of the twin hills in Fort Tryon Park and confronts the George Washington Bridge as the Virgin of Chartres, in Henry Adams' parable, might have confronted the Dynamo. But in this case the Virgin loses out. At a distance the Cloisters looks not like the excellent museum that it is but like a transplanted building, picked up by the jinn and whisked through the sky—not so much an honest relic as a wish.

Indeed, the very virtue of this structure, its fidelity to history, only accentuates one's feeling of being bewitched. For whereas fake Gothic like that of the Riverside Church is plainly a fake at any distance, cast in one piece, built all at the same time, this new building is full of authentic disharmonies. The designers have not only skillfully incorporated the window openings of various periods, they have even added a Gothic chapel which looks as uncomfortably new in relation to the rest as such an addition might well have looked in the thirteenth century. The building is much closer to being a real monument altered to suit the needs of succeeding generations than anything else we have in America today. If people drew the proper moral from this, it might be a healthy influence. They would learn that there are no periods to respect in history—only men, who must live in their own way, in accord with their own needs.

I have not lost my fondness for the architectural rightness of the original Cloisters contrived by Barnard. But the execution of the new job seems to me magnificent. The designers might well, though, have avoided the studious Mediterranean accent of the round-tiled roofs; above all, they might have done away with the tower, which is an archeological reminiscence rather than a natural evolution of the museum as museum. This would have reduced the bulk of the building in the landscape. It is conspicuous enough in its lordly isolation without any vertical features; the tower brings the building too close to the important vista from the esplanade of the park.

But here my objections come abruptly to an end. For, granting its purpose, the museum seems to me one of the most thoughtfully studied and ably executed monuments we have seen in a long time.

Primarily, the central elements in this museum's collection are not individual works of art, pieces of statuary, screens, fountains, sarcophagi, although one room is exclusively and wisely devoted to splendid unicorn tapestries, among the finest now in existence. If such scattered individual objects had been the key to the collection one might well quarrel with the housing of them in anything but a modern building, arranged principally for light, for circulation, for storage, and for quiet study and enjoyment. But the important thing about the Cloisters is the cloisters themselves. There are five of them, with a chapter house for good measure. In this collection of cloisters, some dismembered by revolutionary uprisings, from the Huguenots' to the Jacobins', and now pieced together and reconstructed with loving care, is the main theme. The building itself is essentially a setting for the cloisters.

T HE curving driveway that brings the buses and motorcars to the north entrance gives an admirable approach, and that, by foot is even better. Above the dark Manhattan schists of the base the lavender-gray New London granite, mingled with more rosy blocks, looks very much alive, more pleasing close at hand than from a distance that reveals the motley russets of the tiles. The time-battered Gothic windows at the east side are frankly set in the masonry wall without any attempt to make the whole unnaturally homogeneous. This candor is repeated within. The handrail of the stairs is simple and severe; the side lights and the overhead lights are honest and modern, harmonious with the objects on view because they make no effort to bridge the gap between the flickering candle and the implacably steady electric light. There are no useless baseboards; the oak beams of the ceiling are neither painted nor carved; the functional elements of the design are either authentic or unobtrusive. The refusal to build up fake medieval pedestals for the statuary, or fake canopies for sculpture that originally rested under canopies, in the unhappy fashion of London's Albert Memorial, shows good judgment. The fragments of medieval art are plainly indicated on charts in each room: sometimes the piece is rounded out, as in the Romanesque chapel, sometimes it is left fragmentary.

The centre of the plan itself is the Cuxa cloister—a great square, with a fountain basin in the middle, open to the sky. The halls and chapels of the main floor are grouped around this cloister. The rooms are of varying size, and by the use of a series of models—thanks to the indispensable aid of a corps of WPA craftsmen—the axial vistas, the openings, and the lighting were thoroughly studied in advance; hence the great difference between the first plans and the much sturdier three-dimensional design that was finally worked out, with due regard to the eye's need for an occasional glimpse of a garden, a sunlit space, or a patch of sky. Further legitimate variations are achieved, through changes of form in the ceilings, now barrel vaulting, now beams; differences in the texture and color of the floors, now stone, now tile, now wood.

The studied absence of the superfluous characterizes both the setting and the display; it is this that emphasizes the underlying kinship between modern and Romanesque art, a feeling quite different from the confident complexities of high Gothic or the boisterous motley of the waning Middle Ages. Each object is shown at full value, because it is not surrounded, for dubious educational purposes, by a dozen other objects. This rigor of selection is responsible for the clean, spacious sense that the building has even on a day of crowds. It is the least cluttered of museums.

T HE designers of the Cloisters, fortunately, have not forgotten that the setting of the building is as much a refreshment for the spirit as are its finest memorials from the past. Mr. Rockefeller, with great imagination and generosity, acquired the top sweep of the Palisades opposite, to ensure that this stunning view would never be marred by hideous architectural encroachments. The setting of the Bonnefont and the Trie cloisters, looking south toward the lush hillside of the park and west to the river, is worth a periodic pilgrimage, if only that one may realize what nature and the art of man can do when they work harmoniously. The handsome touch of the contemporary world, in the curving driveways, the steel cables, the swooping yellow-and-green buses, provides the necessary counterpoint as well as a space scale and a time scale for the cloisters themselves. As for the medieval checkerboard garden in the Bonnefont cloister, it is a particular delight. The plants arrayed here are those Giotto or St. Francis might have looked on.

Except for the excessive emphasis of tower and roof, I give this building a pretty high rating, not as a model for other American museums—heaven forbid!—but as the highly special solution of the almost unique problem offered by the materials that were to be preserved and reëmbodied and by the site. One doesn't have to be an adept in medieval symbolism to see in the Cloisters the extreme opposite, in position, in sense of life, in feeling, of all that exists architecturally in the insolent towers at the other end of the island. The difference between faith and credit finance, between holy dying and profane living, is written there; likewise the difference between pious monks celebrating the glory of God and the faithful female secretary increasing, like Joseph in Thomas Mann's story, the uneasy self-esteem of the Big Boss.

A cloister was originally a covered walk around a rectangular space, open to the air and forming a garden, protected and sheltered by the walls of the abbey church, the chapter house, the refectory, and the other working parts of the monastery. There the monks copied manuscripts, sometimes conversed, often meditated in this quiet pool of life within the monastery, whose walls and whose regulations kept the brutalities of life at bay. A little of that ancient peace still broods over this museum; you can walk around one of these quiet gardens and even discover whether or not you have a soul. I am reminded of a remark overheard on my first visit to this new building. "People might not have to go to sanitariums and hospitals for medical care," a thoughtful voice behind me said, "if they could get a little time to themselves in a place like these cloisters." One remembers how people went in for the collective security of these retreats when the power of Rome was dwindling and the proud stones of Rome had become a mockery, and one doesn't have to read Stephen Benét's creepy verses about the barren women or the steel-eating termites to realize how close the barbarian has already crept up on us today. Maybe Mr. Rockefeller hasn't given us just a museum. Maybe this is an experimental model to help us face more cheerfully the Dark Ages. If the crowds on the opening day are any indication, most of the sons and daughters of the machine age are willing to give the new prescription a try. Or was it just the publicity?

1938~39

The construction of the World's Fair dominated the architectural scene this season, but Mumford waited until the fairgrounds had opened before unleashing two caustic reviews. Otherwise, "The Sky Line" covered an eclectic array of subjects, ranging from improvements to Riverside Park to the new building of the Museum of Modern Art.

THE most exciting thing on the horizon at the moment is the Bauhaus show at the Museum of Modern Art. This school, which took shape under Dr. Walter Gropius and existed between 1919 and 1933, first at Weimar, then at Dessau, was a historic experiment. We all have a lot still to learn from it; indeed, it will probably take our schools of architecture another half-generation to catch up with it fully.

The Bauhaus arose during a period of collapse and disintegration far more devastating than anything the world has known since. It was part of that grand revival of the German spirit, in which both the intellectuals and the workers in Germany participated, which by 1930 had placed Germany back again in the forefront of civilization. All the old molds were broken. Gropius himself, whose work in the Cologne Exposition in 1914 was so serene, so mature, so far ahead of that of most of his European contemporaries, relapsed briefly into expressionism before he got back on a more constructive path. But his instincts were sound; he realized it was necessary to rebuild both architect and architecture from the ground up. The courses in the Bauhaus began not with buildings but with the materials and processes and personalities and ideas out of which buildings are formed. The Bauhaus demonstrated the unity of the arts and crafts and mechanical processes of manufacture; above all, it showed that good machine designs can be achieved only by people who can use their eyes, their hands, their fingertips, their muscles.

Thanks to the fundamental retraining that Gropius and his colleagues gave, they unleashed the imagination of the students; their experimental work was resourceful, impudent, sometimes a little mad. But instead of leading toward surrealist disintegration, the discipline of the Bauhaus school led in just the other direction—to the conquest of the machine. Gropius's apartment houses, Breuer's chairs, Marianne Brandt's lighting fixtures set new standards for machine design. At the present Bauhaus exhibition one is impressed not merely by the quality of the final achievement but by the gusto and high spirits that accompanied it. If Gropius, Moholy-Nagy, and Breuer, who are now teaching in America, can reëstablish the spirit of the Bauhaus here, they will be doing a good job. For this combination of imagination and logic is what our architects mainly lack; they tend to substitute memory for the first and precedent for the second.

C ONSIDERING the number of restaurants that have been built in New York, one would think that by now either the managers or the architects would have discovered how to design them. Chain establishments, forever opening up new places and revising past efforts, should long ago have reached perfection, but neither the new Automat on Fifty-seventh Street near Sixth Avenue nor the new Schrafft's at Thirteenth Street and Fifth Avenue indicates that the architecture has yet caught up with the food.

These new restaurants have two qualities in common: they both have curved fronts and their exteriors are both pretty bad. I suspect that we owe the curved front to the coming World's Fair; at any rate, it is the new cliché and it will soon belong in the done-to-death department. Sometimes it is called modern, sometimes it is called Regency, sometimes it is called just plain bull. With the price of land what it is on Manhattan Island, one may predict that the space-wasting business of rounding off the corners—that, in essence, is what the curve really is—won't be carried very far; indeed, the one on the Schrafft's building is just an abrupt arc, which merely gives the front a screwy appearance.

In general, this Schrafft building is a pretty sorry mishmash. The ill-assorted windows look as if they had been picked out of a catalogue and fitted on the façade at random; they reach a pitch of futility in the window at the Fifth Avenue curve, with a pediment on top of a crazy little "balcony" in front. The interior is much better, mainly because of the decent design of the leather-covered chairs and the tables. But who, one wonders, was responsible for the creation of a "period" building?

I have heard the new Automat ostracized because it offers the inmates more privacy in dining than the monkeys' cage at the Zoo. But, from an observer's point of view, the trouble is not so much that the diners are visible, as that in material, in form, and in incidental decorative detail the façade is just a very dull job, more in keeping with 125th Street than with

Fifty-seventh Street. If a huge window such as the new Automat presents is worth having at all, it certainly shouldn't be wasted in a one-story structure; to be fully justified, there should be two floors and double the number of window seats. In its present stage, the Automat represents the emptily monumental; it glares and glowers at the passer-by without making an aesthetic gesture that satisfies the eye. Yet with any delicacy of line, with any sense of the value of materials, this mediocre building might have been turned into an extremely gracious one.

If my criticism of these buildings seems stern, it is only because there are so many good small examples of clean design about now; one does not have to point to some tiny and obscure building in Amsterdam or Vienna to show how the job should be done. Take the new little shop of Mosse's, at 659 Fifth Avenue, done by Paul Frankl and Morris Ketchum. The design is so simply put together that it can scarcely be described, and each part has been so well chosen, so delicately poised in the ensemble, that one cannot suggest an improvement. The legend above, "Mosse, Linen," is not composed of particularly beautiful elements, but because of their size, their balance, their method of combination, the result is excellent. There, Mr. Shattuck, Mr. Horn, Mr. Hardart, there is what is missing in the buildings you so frequently put up. This straightforwardness, this elegant simplicity, do not require expensive materials.

THE exterior design of the new Normandie Theatre, on Fifty-third Street west of Park Avenue, has just a little of the preciousness one once associated with the drawings of Robert Mallet-Stevens. The great panel of glass bricks gives the impression that a grander building has been unevenly scaled down, and that some of the parts have been left bigger than they should be. The vertical fin that the designers, Rosario Candela and Ben Schlanger, have used instead of a detached sign to indicate the theatre's whereabouts is in the tradition of some of the new London Underground stations, and is bound to be copied pretty often in similar structures.

One enters a circular foyer glowing with rose-colored furniture, comfortable, spacious, and from there one either moves downstairs to the lavatories and telephones or, to the right, into the theatre itself. Though the auditorium is rather wide for so small a theatre, the distortion on the screen is negligible from a side seat, and the arrangement of the proscenium arch, which curves into the auditorium and permits the use of indirect lights at several levels, is admirable. The golden yellow of the walls and ceiling, deftly patterned and textured, is very pleasant in effect—and very economical. The seats are extraordinarily spacious and comfortable. The neutral carpet of the floor mediates between the rose of the chair coverings and the gold of the surrounding hall. Altogether, this is perhaps the best-looking small movie house in New York. The effect is elegant, feminine—Park Avenue at its best.

THE post office on Twenty-third Street between Lexington Avenue and Third is so much better than the run-of-the-mill ones that I hesitate to mention the one or two points which are not up to the standard set by the rest of the building. Very definitely, I like the treatment of the overhead lights; I like the character of the service windows and their plainly lettered grilles; I like the indicative arrows that really tell people where to go; and I like the spacious and orderly interior. The Twenty-third Street façade is not, thank heaven, either Georgian or Federal in design; it is only faintly reminiscent of the classical, and I could wish that the architect, Lorimer Rich, having gone so far, had made it as direct an expression of the interior as the red-brick rear on Twenty-fourth Street is. The material on the front is a polished brown granite; this brown, carried into the interior of the post office, makes it a trifle sombre. Probably the intent was to blend the structure with the dingy buildings that surround it, but the result is not altogether happy. If the front were as businesslike, as demonumentalized as the rear, the design would have set a valuable precedent for all future post-office buildings. As it is, it goes halfway. Considering past efforts, that's a lot.

THE SKY LINE
WESTWARD HO!
FEBRUARY 25, 1939

I F you look at an old map of Manhattan Island, you'll find that its out-line was once as full of spines and prickly edges as a sea horse. That was the time when Water Street was really on the water and when Front Street was actually in front. Strip by strip, these indentations are being filled up. The latest and most important job in rounding out the island is the West Side Improvement; it is also the finest single piece of large-scale planning the city can point to since the original development of Central Park.

To understand the extent of this improvement one ought to go back to the time before Riverside Park had even been thought of. The City Plan Commission of 1811, which chopped New York into a gridiron of uniform blocks and streets, had prepared a map of the island. Having carefully mapped the depressions, the high places, the swamps, the approaches from the water, and the scraggly foreshore, they promptly forgot them and pre-pared a plan for the city that ignored their existence.

Fortunately for this rocky island, it refused to fit into the rectangular strait-jacket. From Seventy-second Street northward a steep slope rises above the Hudson; paralleling it, but facing east, there is another slope, from Morningside Park north. Olmsted, one of the designers of Central Park, saw that these slopes were just so much lost real estate; no one could build on them, and he planned to turn them into a series of narrow parks. Riverside Park is the lowest member of the chain; Inwood Hill Park is now the highest.

The original Riverside Park has almost disappeared from memory. A lit-tle while ago, when I said something about the bicycle path that, in my boy-hood, used to hum with wheels, a few people thought that the wheels were in my head. I began gently to wonder myself when I discovered that the Parks Department had no record of such a path. Happily, the city's brochure on the West Side Improvement shows a photograph of the bicy-cle path in use. This path was paralleled by a bridle path and a driveway. On the river side, the land fell away, and the park was informally landscaped in naturalistic fashion.

As early as 1891, a proposal was made by a Board of Advisory Commissioners to reclaim land under water between Seventy-second and Ninety-sixth Street, to build a commercial-transit avenue on it, and to place on a terrain thirty feet above, a road for fast drivers and an equestrian promenade, a Riverside Rotten Row. The railroad trains were to run through a cut and be shut off by a high wall, trees, and shrubbery. Nobody then bothered particularly about playgrounds for the Eastern cities, any more than anyone bothered about automobiles, though both had been invented. But in those early suggestions lay the germs of the present plan. In its final form as carried through by Mr. Moses, the West Side Improvement does all that the original proposers conceived and a good deal more. At a cost of $24,000,000 the railroad tracks have been put under cover, with space to spare for another two tracks; two railway grade crossings have been eliminated; a series of playgrounds has been created for a neglected part of the city and a great traffic parkway has been built. This eases the load on the avenue and makes the open country really accessible.

One's first broad impression of the new work is that the original park has been wiped off the map. Visually that is true. For the green area, no longer descending abruptly to the river, now widens into lawns and playgrounds; instead of being a hillside park, Riverside is really a wide, open pleasance. Actually 132 acres have been added to the park by railroad-covering and filling operations; the assessed value of this new land is about equal to the amount expended on the improvement. Unlike what often happens when an avenue is widened within a built-up area of the city—take Park Avenue—the gain in traffic speed has not been accomplished through wiping out open space used for other equally important purposes.

Following the new pattern set in Central Park, a group of playgrounds has been spread along the park. Some of these are for small children; some are for older football and baseball players; there will be a stadium for track sports; there are special esplanades for roller skaters, and even a path for bicyclists between 100th and 116th Streets. At Seventy-ninth Street there is not only a boat basin for pleasure craft—there is to be a grand one at Spuyten Duyvil eventually, too—but also a garage, located in the basement

of the traffic circle, is provided for the cars of boaters. All these improvements mean a vast multiplication of opportunities for use and enjoyment.
But the old-fashioned pedestrian, out for a saunter with a dog or a baby carriage, is not forgotten. At intervals solid lines of benches, with an unobstructed view of the river, sweep along the footpaths.

S o much for the origins and purposes of this improvement. What about
its architectural form? (Clinton F. Loyd was chief of architectural
design and Gilmore D. Clarke consulting landscape architect.) In all its
larger essentials this is thoroughly modern planning. The visual key to the
design is the great traffic intersections, with their clover-leaf form, their
changes of level, their vigorous curves postulated by the necessity for swift,
uninterrupted motion. If there is no place here for studied irregularities,
there is no place, either, for the purely formal figures used in Renaissance
park-planning. Nevertheless, in a spirit of harmony, the designers have not
been averse to using curved outlines for their playgrounds; they even used
round arches in the many opportunities for bold masonry bridges and
ramps that the roadway improvement provides. The masonry walls, in
brown and gray granite with grayish copings, are clean and vigorous; they
have a quality of aesthetic permanence that bare concrete, even at its very
best, cannot promise. The use of similar materials and similar forms in the
smaller park structures, like the rest houses, powerfully contributes to the
impression of unity.

Compared with the architecture of Mr. Moses' earliest masterpiece,
Jones Beach, the West Side Improvement shows a decisive advance. At last
the cheap eclectic ornament has disappeared, likewise most of the straining
after incongruous traditional forms. Here and there, however, a little of the
old spirit remains. What is perhaps the most striking piece of masonry of
all seems to me the most dubious. This is the circular cloisters and fountain
that now stand where a grade crossing was eliminated at the traffic intersection at Seventy-ninth Street. I am not as keen about this as Mr. Moses'
architects undoubtedly were. There seems to be something blankly contra-
dictory about a cloister formed out of a traffic circle; it is as arbitrary as a
business building made to look like a cathedral because it happens to be tall.
It serves a purpose in the scheme, but a lot of money was spent to achieve

this archaic effect, and I am not sure that it was worth achieving or that something better could not have been done by more modern means.

While I haven't the space to point out all the felicities of detail, there are a few that must be mentioned. One is the low iron fence, with curved uprights, at, for instance, the Seventy-ninth Street entrance; another is the nonchalant ship's railing, with a wooden top, along the waterfront. I like the broad black walks of crushed stone set in a tarry composition; the dull bronze green of the rails and ventilator openings; the rich texture and color of the granite. I like the complete separation of pedestrian and motor traffic within the park. The small lamp standards, on the other hand, are disgraceful; and the architects, in designing the broad steps that sweep down to the Drive, forgot to provide for baby carriages.

But the whole design is bold and forceful; the architects have not been afraid of long straight lines, decisive curves, paths and esplanades meant obviously to lure and to hold thousands of people at a time; they haven't niggled and overrefined their effects; they haven't pretended to create a refuge for the solitary lover of nature. This is a grand collective design. It will be at its best when ten thousand people are there to share it with you, but it is not without a windy grandeur when you take it, by early morning, alone.

Incidentally, there is one visual prospect no visitor to the park should miss. It is best achieved toward twilight as one approaches the lower end of the Drive, where the automobiles mount from the parkway to the street level and one can peer below into the vast railway tunnel. The scale of the place, with its huge arches and the air of brooding darkness, makes one think of Piranesi immediately; concentrated here, one feels, are the cyclopean dimensions of the whole project. And the imposing effect is entirely legitimate, an accidental paralleling of old forms rather than an imitation.

In a few years, when the planting has had time to assert itself, one will, I think, be gratefully conscious of two things: the noble scale of the main lines of the park, and the more intimate quality of the smaller playgrounds. The designers have given to the walker along the riverfront some of that clean exaltation one could achieve before only by a walk westward over the Brooklyn Bridge. This is not the kind of romanticism one finds in Olmsted's coyly naturalistic parks, but Paul Bunyan would have liked the sheer dramatic swagger of it—and there is a lot of Paul Bunyan left in all of us.

THE Fifth Avenue Association distributed a number of prizes for architecture recently. Some of them were obvious, some were not so obvious, and at least one of them could be justified only if, by some mistake, the committee imagined it was voting for the worst new building in the district.

The obvious award was, of course, that to Rockefeller Center. Purely as a visual contribution to the midtown section, this group of buildings has turned out so well that one can afford to forget about all the little stunts that have accompanied its exploitation, from the roof gardens to the rejected Rivera murals. I am speaking, though, just of the outside. The gloomy magnificence of the interior of the R.C.A. Building still strikes me as unnecessarily sombre, and there are a lot of features in the general plan and layout that reveal how ill-prepared New York architects were, at the end of the twenties, to take over such a comprehensive scheme. But none of these things shows from the outside, and externally the Center is a serene eyeful.

In the not-so-obvious class was the Lilly Daché building, on Fifty-sixth Street west of Park, done by Shreve, Lamb & Harmon. This is a narrow façade with a deep, oblong panel of glass tiles running down the front. There are small, square windows at each side, and at the bottom are two portholes, circular for no particular reason. The entrance is the most decent part of the job, but even here the window box above, with a few melancholy little cedars to serve as excuse for its existence through the winter, is on the finicking side. No one has yet solved the problem of making a presentable transparent window to set in a wall of square glass tiles, and I predict that this particular problem will remain pretty hopeless until the glass manufacturers get out a rectangular tile. The only trouble about this building is that it is carefully dressed up to look like something besides a simple box, and the dressing wasn't worth the trouble. You cannot make a three-dimensional building out of a two-dimensional façade. What is more, no one should try.

A T the moment there are two architectural exhibitions at the Museum of Modern Art. One shows the awards in a competition to design a theatre and exhibition hall for William and Mary College at Williamsburg. It was won by three young men who had been under Mr. Eliel Saarinen's able wing: Eero Saarinen, Ralph Rapson, and Frederick James. The fact that the winning design was "modern" and that all the rest were equally without reference to the tastes and trimmings of another age is not exactly news. By now the only people who think there is any other way to design a building are the old-timers who haven't died off yet and the suburban real-estate speculators who have never sold a modern building for the good reason that they have never built one and don't believe it can be done. The real news is that competitions are now being held in which the judges refuse to be bamboozled by elegant renderings in color, whose greatest architectural achievement is the sky. Instead, the critics attempt to arrive at their decision on the basis of plan and a small-scale elevation. This makes the show a little dry for the spectator, who must examine the designs critically if he is to form an opinion of them, but it should be very helpful to architecture.

The fact that no one was tempted to fit the new building into seventeenth-century Williamsburg by even adding as much as a wooden pineapple to the forthright façades is, naturally, all to the good. Williamsburg, after the Rockefeller restoration, is a large-scale outdoor museum. William and Mary, on the other hand, is a living institution; to house its new activities in Wren buildings would be just as false to the spirit of the restoration as it would be to the activities themselves. The greatest mistakes committed in the Rockefeller restoration were the creation of an inn in the Regency fashion and the building of a marketing centre in which Ye Olde A. & P. does business behind a Georgian front. That was faking, not restoration. If once this lesson was really learned, the future of American architecture would be safe—at least from the perversities and misconceptions of building committees.

A s for the other exhibition, the pictorial history of American architecture put together for last year's Jeu de Paume in Paris, it is a very able and gratifying presentation of a subject that no one—I said no one—has yet fully encompassed in print. What is unique about this show is that it gives due place to the various regional traditions in our architecture, including the belatedly recognized Early Spanish, and that it is particularly good in dealing with those vernacular buildings whose importance architectural historians, despite the influence of William Morris, have never fully accepted. Here the handsome barns of Lancaster County, Pennsylvania, to say nothing of the virile medieval beginnings in Topsfield and Salem, show how foolish it has been to think of the American tradition as being solely the mincing Georgian one.

There are still certain phases of American architecture that are unrepresented here, as they are unrepresented even in the WPA guidebooks. No one has yet done justice to the miraculously fine brickwork that went into the loft buildings and warehouses put up in New York and Baltimore, in Chicago and Minneapolis, during the eighties. Likewise, no one has yet appraised the important contribution made by the late Leroy Buffington, the man who, at least on paper, "invented" the modern skyscraper, if anyone can be called the inventor. Buffington's work in Minneapolis, particularly one of the buildings he did on the University of Minnesota's campus, has been curiously neglected. Then, too, there is a strong tradition in urban domestic architecture, seen at its best in houses built in Washington in the late eighties and early nineties. So far as I know, these buildings have never been illustrated or even referred to in print. In short, architecturally speaking, we don't known our country yet.

One of the things for which I am especially grateful to the Museum's architectural curator is the show's clear demonstration of the continuity between H. H. Richardson and Louis Sullivan. The late Werner Heggemann went out of his way in his posthumous books on American city planning and architecture to discredit Richardson and to cast all manner of doubt on his contribution. But although Heggemann was no doubt an earnest scholar, he had apparently never read Sullivan's "Kindergarten Chats," in which Sullivan magnificently acknowledged the debt of all the Chicago architects to the man who built the Marshall Field Building and the Glessner house. The relationship is plain enough here, and like our vernacular tradition, it gives depth and continuity to all that the modern architects are attempting. Some of the best of the new work shown, by the way, is in wood, inventively used in novel structural forms, as in Wright's little house and Lescaze's dining hall and the Forest Products laboratory.

A T the International Building in Rockefeller Center one can see the work done by Antonin Raymond, chiefly in Japan, to which he went in 1911 as an assistant to Frank Lloyd Wright. It consists of photographs, floor plans, renderings, and a model of his sliding sash, which should help solve the problem of adjusting window openings and interior space to the varied demands of living. Some of the buildings are rigorously mechanical; some are close to ancient Japanese forms. This show dramatizes a fact of which we will be increasingly conscious, I have no doubt, during the next generation: that the United States faces the Orient as well as Europe and that a rapid give-and-take is going on between the cultures that line the Pacific. How far the Orient touched Mr. Wright's imagination before he went to Tokio it is hard to determine, but there is no doubt at all that the austere, delicate forms of the traditional Japanese house, with its highly rationalized scheme of design based upon the width of its floor mattings, found a quick echo in the best Western minds.

Some of the finest modern work I have seen—in domestic design, at all events—is what has been done during the last five years in Hawaii and in the Pacific Northwest; it is based not on any copying of traditional Oriental forms but upon an understanding of the principles behind them. I have never liked to hear the epithet "International Style" applied to modern form, since it seemed to imply a uniformity, an externality, that were without regional color or variation, but the sources of good modern form are indeed international. And the fact is that the wider the sources we draw on the more likely we are to find just those combinations that are exquisitely fitted to local conditions. The last way to achieve a good regional style is by practicing cultural isolation.

THE SKY LINE
GROWING PAINS~THE NEW MUSEUM
JUNE 3, 1939

ARCHITECTURALLY, New York is in a grand turmoil. The city has been refurbished lately in such a number of spots that one can hardly keep pace with the changes. Much of the improvement has been due to the waterfront developments pushed forward by Mr. Moses. But it takes more than such leadership to reach the promised land—one also needs a little land. And actually Mr. Moses has had nothing whatever to do with the main source of our architectural renovation, which has happened because during the last fifteen years a few hundred thousand Manhattanites have permanently left the island. As a result, the rest of us have a little *Lebensraum.*

But among these brighter possibilities, Mr. Moses' bridge across the Bay certainly cannot be counted. The army engineers did us a good turn when they sent Mr. Moses' original plans back to him. The fact is that, architecturally, the bridge in any form would be a howler. At one sweep Mr. Moses would ruthlessly demolish the beauty and splendor—above all, the imposing scale—of New York's chief architectural asset: the sky line that greets the traveller as his ship noses up the Bay.

Admittedly the sky line of Manhattan is a stupendous accident of nature, like the Grand Canyon. No collective intelligence presided over its development; it is the result of competition, cross-purposes, and economic chicane. Indeed, it has no rational justification for existence, except that it is, from the purely pictorial standpoint, probably the finest urban silhouette on a great scale one can behold anywhere in the world.

All this is so commonplace that Mr. Moses and his colleagues, including Mayor La Guardia, have apparently forgotten it. For the sake of the few million dollars extra that a tunnel would demand, the planners of the new bridge propose to disfigure the approach to Manhattan's greatest monument—its collective shell as seen from the upper Bay. If Mr. Moses had a scheme for tearing down all skyscrapers south of Canal Street, in order to supplant them with more rational structures, I would be with him. But what he proposes is mere aesthetic demolition, and no amount of alteration in the design of the bridge will keep it from being simply out of place. In short, this is one of those plans that should be firmly discarded and never mentioned in anyone's presence again.

T HE area that is now crying for a little prompt intelligent planning is Sixth Avenue. The tearing down of the "L" has given the City Planning Commission an opportunity it might well have prayed for. The dreary mess of buildings that loitered beside the old "L"—much of it dating back to the seventies—has long been ready for demolition. Doubtless plans are afoot to build high apartment houses or business buildings above Forty-second Street, if anyone thinks they can be rented. And this is precisely what should not be built. If the midtown area is not to be strangled to death by traffic congestion, the load of buildings in this area must be kept light, and a type of development radically different from that on any other avenue should be instituted.

What is needed first of all is a zoning ordinance to keep the new buildings along Sixth Avenue below four stories in height. In addition to this, the City Planning Commission should select an experimental block or two and get an intelligent architect to design a new type of building which would utilize the major part of the ground area at street level for parking. A new plan for this area means a new kind of structure. One might have shallow shops on the avenue front, with parking space in the rear; another might utilize the entire plot for parking, with restaurants and offices on the upper two floors. The main feature in all these possible forms would be the fact that they provide parking space; and if this were done consistently on both sides of the avenue, an enormous parking area might be added at precisely the point where it can be used to best advantage.

Curiously enough, the precedent for modestly doing over Sixth Avenue is already being set in the East Fifties by a quite spontaneous development. Most of the new buildings around Madison Avenue are two-story structures. These—the new fish restaurant, Colbert's, on Forty-ninth Street, is the latest of them—are taking the place of the old-fashioned brownstones. Such two-story buildings fill a real need: they make it possible, since they cover more than one building lot, to plan a restaurant interior or a showroom on a scale hitherto feasible only in hotels and department stores. Unfortunately, there has been very little freshness or inventiveness in the design of these structures.

F OR those who have been brought up on the American tradition there is nothing to identify the new Museum of Modern Art as a museum. There are no classic columns or cornices; the place does not look like a temple or a palace. The building belongs as visibly to our day as do the Rockefeller Apartments, which face its rear, or garden, side.

Nor does the Museum remind one of any other structure in New York, if only for one reason: it possesses, to a degree not dreamed of even by the designers of Rockefeller Center, the luxury of space. There is nothing cramped about either the ground plan or the setting. On the contrary, though the building itself is modest in dimensions, the eye has an opportunity to roam.

Now, it happens that the unity of interior and exterior is one of the defining principles of modern architecture; at all events, it is the key to its design. Where the architect has no control over the site as a whole and no opportunity to utilize the exterior setting, he can create only a fake modern building, with none of the sense of spatial freedom that a good modern design gives. In the Museum, thanks mainly to the Rockefellers' munifence, there was space in plentiful measure. And the first happy thing to note about this six-story building is that the architects, Messrs. Philip L. Goodwin and Edward D. Stone, have taken full advantage of it.

Approaching the building along Fifty-third Street, one is aware of the blue tile of the side wall, a color that is carried into the topmost story. The front façade consists mainly of an enormous window, of opaque spun glass, which gives light to every part of the second- and third-gallery floors. Above this, in continuous strips, are the windows of the administration floors. The topmost story, which is set back, consists of a terrace, with eleven round skylights in the roof where it overhangs the third floor; this gives the façade an accent of shadow that terminates it as decisively as a cornice. Both in the garden and on the top floor, the architects' plan shows recognition of the fact that New Yorkers may spend the better part of six months comfortably out of doors, if they have a mind to. On the top floor, dedicated to members of the Museum, they have made the most of the opportunity. For all the talk about using roofs, this is one of the few places in the city in which a roof has been successfully employed.

One enters the building under a curved marquee from the side; the entrance itself is bowed inward and forms an outside lobby for slowly circulating crowds. This is a very happy introduction to the building, and it calls attention to another fact—the generally intelligent and gracious use of curved forms throughout the building. In the development of modern architecture in Europe after 1915, the influence of Cubism in painting undoubtedly had an effect on formal design. But one result of this was an overinsistence upon straight lines, even where they were not needed or where they actually defeated the functional purposes of the building.

Partly because of Oud's happy instinct for curved forms (the Dutch long before him had the knack of it in building their windmills), partly because of the influence of abstract painters like Arp and the later Picasso, curves have come back in modern forms. Their effect is to restore that sense of freedom and of the unexpected which purely rational design sometimes too austerely avoids. In the Modern Museum the curves are sometimes used functionally, as in the entrance and in the catalogue counter. In the latter, the inflaring curve gives more space for circulation on the cloakroom side, by the doors, where it is needed. Sometimes curves are used for purely decorative reasons, as in the tubular lights on the ceilings by the elevators. Sometimes curves are used for both purposes, as in the flowing patterns of the garden, where the blue and ochre pebbles form an independent ground design, very handsome when seen from above, and the curves of the garden plots are further used in the creation of a wooden background and shelters for the sculpture displayed there.

Dramatically, there are two specially rewarding spots in the building. One is on the ground floor, where, as one turns a corner to go into the exhibition halls, one immediately beholds a wide expanse of garden. Here the sense of air, space, and light is in absolute contrast to the marmoreal bleakness affected by most museums—not least because the marble wall on the left is a brilliant red. The other spot that gives one sharp pleasure is the main stairs as they mount upward past a stunning frieze of statuesque green plants, which stand out against the filtered light of the great window.

The combination of appropriate materials, light, color, and living forms here demonstrates the rich decorative resources of modern architecture.

Functionally, there are two instances in which the design of this structure especially justifies itself. The use of overhead daylight for the display of sculpture has been made feasible in the exhibition gallery on the third floor because the setback of the fourth floor permits the insertion of skylights. Overhead lighting for sculpture has also, naturally, been achieved in the garden. The other instance is the entirely flexible arrangement of the exposition space, made possible by the absence of permanent partitions and by the presence of unbroken glass windows.

This permits the reshuffling of the space without regard for the façade. Accordingly, the picture galleries are actually designed to fit the pictures; they consist of a series of irregularly shaped rooms, small but with plenty of space for the spectator to get his distance. These galleries are arranged in such a fashion that, at whatever angle one turns, one is always facing a picture and never being hastily drawn toward an exit. The result is the display of a maximum number of paintings with a minimum of crowding. So far as I know, this is the one instance in which the principle of flexible interior space, first worked out for museums by Mr. Clarence S. Stein, the architect, has been utilized in thoroughgoing fashion. This innovation is bound to affect every future program for museum building.

As an exhibition museum, the present building seems to me a pretty complete success. Visually, my chief criticism would centre on the architects' choice of white marble as the main exterior sheathing, along with chrome metal and blue tile. The two dominant notes in the immediate neighborhood are the limestone of Rockefeller Center and the handsome lavender-tan bricks of the Rockefeller Apartments across the way. With a little keener sense of the need for civic order, the architects would, I think, have chosen one or the other of these materials. As it is, the building has a needlessly Italianate air, which makes it seem less fresh and native than it actually is. But that is a minor flaw in what constitutes, as a whole, a real triumph.

THE SKY LINE IN FLUSHING
WEST IS EAST
JUNE 17, 1939

C ALIFORNIA, always prolific, gave birth to two fairs this year. San Francisco's fair, monumental and aristocratic, kept quietly to its anchorage in the middle of its bay. Los Angeles, however, contrived a surprise setting by placing its fair in one of the remoter portions of the country—in the middle of a swampy No Man's Land once claimed by New York: Flushing Meadows. The contrast between the styles of the two cities is, as usual, terrific, but as I haven't actually seen the San Francisco fair, I won't go into that.

Architecturally, the World of Tomorrow has a simple pedigree. It is by Coney Island out of Los Angeles. This accounts for the fact that it has buildings as good as the drive-in markets of Los Angeles, and that it has monuments to salesmanship vying with the incredible milk bottles and ice-cream freezers that line the great highways of movieland. It accounts for the fact that provision for the circulation of traffic at the World's Fair is as ample as that along Wilshire Boulevard, and that everyone must spend the greater part of his day circulating over needless distances. It accounts for the bright feeling that almost anything might happen at the next turn of the road; it also accounts for the fact that almost everything does happen. The ultimate California touch is the oil derrick busily chugging in the midst of nowhere. It's just the thing to make a resident of Hollywood feel at home.

A S for the Fair as a whole, it has no architectural character whatever. It is just a cozy sector of chaos. The vices and virtues of New York 1939 are indeed the precise opposite of the most imposing fair produced in America before this, that in Chicago in 1893. That earlier fair suffered from a false sense of order which stifled the creative impulse of the individual architects. While it put on an effective front, there was no connection between the outward form of the building and the marvels which were displayed inside. The shell was that of ancient Rome, the exhibits were those of modern industrialism. The unity of those white buildings, in their formal, orderly grouping, pleased the eye, but the architecture did not embody forms that could be carried out successfully in new buildings.

The World of Tomorrow, so far from exhibiting false forms, has a sort of veracious formlessness. The architects in charge of the project plainly despaired of imposing any kind of order upon either the plans or the elevations or the competing industrialists. The buildings sprawl, billow, leap, perambulate, following no order except the sweet will of the exhibitor and his architect. Though the Fair spreads to gigantic distances, just like the modern metropolis itself, it has the air of being cluttered, even congested. Here, too, there is a contradiction between the formlessness of the architecture and the mechanical equipment and the devices of large-scale organization shown by the exhibits, with their sober, ingenious demonstrations of the way tires are fabricated, motorcars built, cows milked, or statistics tabulated. From the standpoint of modern form, this veracious formlessness is just as dead as the faked forms of the Fair of 1893.

Where the Fair succeeds architecturally is not in interpreting the World of Tomorrow but in desperately running away from it: the best moments are those of carnival, gay, irresponsible, exotic, full of color. By day the buildings are a little seedy, for strong sunlight is unkind to most temporary materials, but at night it is entirely a different matter. As darkness falls, a dream world becomes reality. Then the buildings one by one awake with color and light; then the Perisphere is a blue moon hovering over the water; then the tower of the Glass Center shines crisply and the blue flanges of the Petroleum Building spread outward like an inverted pagoda; then, in the distance, the brass plaques of the Polish Tower gleam against the haze. The effect becomes just what a carnival should be—a splendid riot. Whatever architectural sense the Fair has in the large, it achieves at night.

For the nocturnal Fair I have copious admiration. Here is the architecture of light, projected in a way that makes Broadway seem pallid and feeble, because at the Fair the buildings themselves are as colorful as the pylons that decorate them, and the play of light through glass towers, through sprays of falling water, and through neon tubes, and the heightening of color on flat surfaces achieve a richness and a radiance that no ordinary architecture can boast. Undoubtedly, a good part of this success with light belongs not to the architects but to the engineer, Mr. Bassett Jones, who laid down the law on this point.

Mr. Jones is one of the few masters of lighting—Mr. Claude Bragdon, the American architect and stage designer, is another—who realized that the sheer intensity of illumination has no bearing directly upon its success. Mr. Jones did not make the mistake of floodlighting the buildings and trees in such a fashion as to turn night into day; he may have realized that this would merely unfold all the weaknesses of the design. Instead, he used light to accentuate the character of night itself. So there is light, but no irritating overhead glare; on the contrary, one walks about in a mellow twilight that intensifies every line and surface of illuminated color. Set off by indirect lighting shooting up out of the ground, the foliage of the trees takes on exciting depths of green one never sees in daylight. While most systems of illumination tend to wipe out color, Mr. Jones has used lighting for just the opposite effect—to make color more vivid.

At night, then, the Fair is designed to fit every possible mood, from bibulous public hilarity to the twilight tenderness of two lovers who want to be conscious only of each other. That is an achievement, an achievement of first magnitude. If this scheme of illumination from below does not revolutionize the lighting of parks and public buildings, that will merely be a proof that the manufacturers of lamp standards have a stranglehold upon us, or that we just lack taste. All this skill in using light comes to a climax in the special illumination of the fountains. And that, somehow, is right, too, for here two of the oldest pleasures for the sophisticated eye—fountains and fireworks—unite in a mighty spectacle.

UNFORTUNATELY, there is nothing like the same reason for congratulation and delight when one considers the daylight Fair. For the general ground plan of the Fair I am still unable to say a good word: it works out in practice quite as badly as it originally promised. Its sole good feature is that the avenues are scaled on such generous lines that even the largest crowd will never be seriously jammed. The weakness of the layout was accentuated by the fact that the planners gave only the most perfunctory consideration to the principle of zoning. As a result, the Academy of

Sports backs up against the Heinz (57 Varieties) dome, while the visitor is led by the nearby Borden plant toward Turkey and thence, via Sweden, to Standard Brands.

With no disrespect to Mr. Whalen's professional interests, one must point out that though this may be a canny principle for organizing a department store, it is a terrible way to put together a fair. It is impossible, without a map, a special sense of direction, and the benign guidance of providence, to know where one is or where one is going; at the end of a day one feels like a frustrated rat in a psychologist's maze. Worst of all, the buildings are scrambled together in such a fashion that it is impossible to make short cuts. It's no wonder that all the trains out to the Fair are filled with advertisements of remedies for sore and aching feet.

Since the Fair contains practically everything, it even contains a good specimen of what an intelligent plan and a coherent style of architecture might have worked out into. This is in the buildings devoted to the separate national exhibits, grouped around the Court of Peace and centring in the Federal Government Building, which holds the end of the main axis of the Fair opposite to the Perisphere. Certainly, the architecture here is not inspired, but it is at least very decent and it shows how well order and intelligence and an urbane sense of the whole can perform by themselves, even when they are not backed by originality. In a really modern plan, these buildings would have been at right angles to the Court instead of facing it, and the Court itself would perhaps have been narrower, to shorten the walking distances. But even as it is, this group shows that chaos was not inevitable. The fact is that beauty was sacrificed to competitive advertisement. That is why even the best visual effects, such as that around the Lagoon of Nations, are spoiled by the assertive name plate of some nationally advertised brand.

If the designers of the Fair had kept a sure hold on the simple principles of modern city planning, they might have saved the visitors a lot of grief without taking a single man-hour of attention away from the commercial exhibitors. For some of the industrial exhibits are the best things the Fair can show, and to imagine that these displays had to be sandwiched among other spectacles, as one puts the perfume counter and the neckties all jumbled in with underwear and stationery in the design of a department store, was sheer folly. This sort of overemphasis on the business motive fails to appreciate either the ingenuity of American industry or the natural curiosity of the machine-minded American. And the proof of this is that General Motors and Ford, which are in effect zoned off by themselves in a far corner of the grounds, attract visitors the way honey attracts wasps.

THE buildings of the Fair are mainly of two kinds, those with and those without windows; and there is still another division, between those in permanent materials, like the Russian and Belgian Buildings, and those in more transitory materials, sometimes stucco, sometimes sheet metal, sometimes fabricated plates of one stuff or another. On the matter of windows, I am for the structures with natural lighting, exposed to the sea breezes. I predict that by the middle of the summer everyone else will be of the same opinion, when the difference between breezes and fans, between the natural heat of the sun and the same heat plus the heat of electric-light bulbs, will make the difference between comfort and irritation. Too few of the architects used the principle of the glass-walled show window to attract the visitor and draw him inside; where this was done, even at the entrance, as in the Borden and the Contemporary Arts Buildings, the result in every way seems much happier than in buildings in which only a mural or a piece of sculpture indicates what goes on within the dark interior. But there are instances in which, because of the special nature of the exhibits, the windowless building works well, so one can hardly lay down any rule about it.

As for the painting and sculpture outside the buildings, the Fair is for me an altogether convincing demonstration of the fact that modern architecture has nothing to hope from these accessories. The mural that is frankly designed as an elementary public signboard, modest in aesthetic pretensions but easy to read—like Miss Hildreth Meiere's mural on the Public Health Building—comes off much better than more esoteric compositions. For poster art, for signboard art, there is still a place in modern architecture, though I don't recollect any portion of the Fair where these were authoritatively used; but painting and sculpture are no longer part of the essential fabric of modern architecture, and the sooner that fact is realized, the less frustration there will be among painters and sculptors.

P ROBABLY the most talked about building in the Fair is that put up by the
U.S.S.R. If there were a theme song for this building, it would have to
be "I dreamt that I dwelt in marble halls." For the Soviets have outdone
themselves in their use of fine materials. This building is conceived in the
same fashion as their subway stations in Moscow, one of which is here
reproduced in section; and these in turn were conceived in the fashion of
an ancient palace. For those who love classic monumental effects, this
building turns on the works: the horseshoe curve, the imposing steps to the
first-floor level, the full-red porphyry pylon on which the imposing metal
statue of a Soviet worker stands, to say nothing of the juicy marble plating.
All this spells richness and grandeur of a very orthodox kind.

Now, the exhibits and movies inside the building are fascinating, and
some of the contrast models—Russia before and after the Soviet regime
took over—are extremely good. But I cannot speak as enthusiastically about
the architecture, for the form of this building is stale and the language that
it speaks carries as little of the overtones of a new world as the Lincoln
Memorial. This building belongs to the imperial past. If you want a
glimpse of the World of Tomorrow, you will have to look at it through the
more modest but far more eloquent eyes of the Swedes, the Belgians, the
Czecho-Slovaks, or even the English.

The Belgian Building, with its dark slate tower and its unglazed, slightly rough-textured red tiles, is one of the handsomest pieces of real architecture at the Fair. The great bay of windows that faces the water display,
reflecting it at night as in a mirror, is a dramatic point of emphasis that vies
with its own open-terraced restaurant on the Lagoon. Belgium produced
some of the best of the early modern architectural leaders, particularly Van
de Velde and Horta, and it has no reason, on this showing, to be ashamed
of its present generation. In fact, the Belgian Building puts the fussily
respectable Netherlands Pavilion hopelessly in the ruck. One wonders,
indeed, who or what was responsible for either the Netherlands Building
itself or the quite inadequate picture of the nation's modern architectural
development in the exhibits.

The Swedish Building is a miracle of elegant simplicity. It is built around
an open court and utilizes that fact in the manner of conceiving and compos-
ing its exhibits, which are all meant for daylight display and easy, quick read-

ing. The only unsatisfactory touch in this fine structure is that the garden in the centre looks as if it were bargain day at a Long Island nursery. With a little solid-green turf and Hudson bluestone in the centre, this building would take first prize for a maximum result with a minimum expenditure of effort.

The interior of the British Building also deserves very honorable mention; it is good enough to live down the inane female colossus (gilded) who towers over the staircase. (The statue is a libel on British womanhood, but perhaps no true Englishman would ever stare long enough at a girl to realize it.) With its color and its imposing composition of space, to say nothing of the beautiful corrugated ceiling, the building sets a lively pace.

The honors for comic ineptitude are divided fairly equally between the cramped group of buildings representing states of the American Union and the Italian Building. The first is a monument to the disheartening effects of competitive individualism; even the worst building in the lot, repeated sixteen times, would have been better than the present ill-assorted show. The Italian Building is funny almost to the point of pathos. The dominant motif is the figure of Roma, perched on top of a thin sheet of falling water. This lady will remind a younger generation of Lady Peel imitating a tired charwoman; to old New Yorkers it will bring back recollections of the golden goddess affected by Siegel-Cooper's department store—"Meet Me at the Fountain." Coming from a country whose architects recently designed the Naples post office and the Florence railroad station, this building is bad enough to make one suspect purposeful sabotage.

A RE you exhausted? I am, too, but there must be dozens of other buildings equally worth comment. I speak after only two days of exploration. Among the architectural odds and ends no one should miss, however, are these: the stunning blue windows in the Temple of Religion; the entrance of the Contemporary Arts Building, which, were it not for the highly superfluous metallic decorations, would be one of the most successful American buildings in the Fair; the topless brass tower of the Polish Building, particularly at night, when looking up at the sky from within. This one, by the way, is good enough to serve as a permanent memorial tower in the park, once the Fair is gone. Technically and aesthetically, it is the nearest thing to a purely architectural modern monument I have seen anywhere.

THE SKY LINE IN FLUSHING
GENUINE BOOTLEG
JULY 29, 1939

NYONE who is interested in the City of Tomorrow might as well take off his shoes and rest his feet before he goes to the World's Fair. He will have to do a lot of waiting and shuffling in order to get a glimpse of what Mr. Henry Dreyfuss and Mr. Norman Bel Geddes think the city of tomorrow will be like. And he had better provide himself with some rose-colored, one-way Polaroid glasses, so that he will really be convinced he has something to look forward to if he lives another generation. For, like so many other features of the Fair, the City of Tomorrow is a melancholy might-have-been.

While the idea of the Fair was still unformed, a group of young architects, backed by some sympathetic older men—the late Henry Wright was one of them—had the excellent notion of designing a whole community along modern lines. The Museum of Modern Art started to play along with them; it prepared to foster a competition for new community designs. The aim was to make as decisive an innovation in city building as Le Corbusier made in his individual "machine for habitation" at the Decorative Arts Exposition in Paris in 1925. In the original sketches for the Fair, a considerable tract was set aside for just such a development. For a few sanguine moments those who had never met the prima donnas and sentimentalists who run many of our great business enterprises were convinced that a bold, large scheme might be carried out by their cooperative efforts.

As the months went by, these hopes and proposals for a major contribution to urban design were progressively defeated. Today their wreckage is strewed about the Fair, so thoroughly smashed and disfigured that their own fathers could scarcely identify the corpses. Democracity, in the Perisphere, is one of these wrecks; the Town of Tomorrow is another. As for the film "The City," which is now being shown at the Science and Education Building, it is a belated attempt at salvage. But although the city shown there is more human and more up-to-date and more close to actuality than the others, it necessarily leaves off, in the real town of Greenbelt,

Maryland, at the point where a new demonstration should properly begin.

But the young architects who thought the exhibition of modern urban units would be a huge attraction were right. For in attendance, the Futurama, which is an essay in modern urban and regional design, beats every other show. As presented in the Fair, Democracity, the Futurama, and the Town of Tomorrow have absolutely no relation to each other; they are scattered across the great spaces, quite innocent of each other's existence. If they were assembled, they would tell, oddly enough, a continuous story. That story would not be very new or very exciting or very promising, but it would at least have a beginning, a middle, and an end.

To be logical, one should begin with the Perisphere—that great egg out of which the new civilization is to be born. Dawn breaks over this slick new world; one sees in the centre of the hall, somewhat below its equator, a great metropolis, separated by wedges of countryside from the satellite towns and villages that stretch into the distance. Here, masquerading as the future, is the stale conception of the capital city developed by the centralized despotisms of Europe from the sixteenth century on—a pretty moth-eaten conception. It belongs to the universe of Newton, in which the planets swing around the sun; it has nothing to do with the universe of Einstein and Alexander Graham Bell and De Forest, in which each person or each place may become at any moment the centre from which everything else is reckoned, or observed, or broadcast.

Mr. Kaltenborn's voice says all the right things about this city—how it is full of sunlight and open spaces and beauty—but somehow the city doesn't more than half say the same things that the voice is uttering. One keeps on wanting to draw closer to this remote urban spectacle in order to examine its workings in detail—and just as one's expectation is fully whetted, one finds oneself shoved out into the open, to perform one's remaining duty to the future by heliclining slowly toward earth. Less than half a mile away, provided you find the right crossing, Mr. Geddes continues the story in the General Motors display.

One enters the Futurama—I am careful not to say how soon—by way of a great hall. Again one is on a spiral ramp—"Helicline" to Mr.

Whalen—and this time the void is filled with a voice and a lighted map of the United States showing how completely the world of tomorrow will depend on transcontinental transportation. Mr. Geddes is a great showman, and the solemn, thoughtful introduction, in the coolness and darkness of a great hall, almost wipes out the tedious minutes, or hours of waiting; it gets one ready for the great journey into the future. Everyone knows about the admirable mechanics of that journey: the smooth jaunting car, the persuasive voice at one's elbow, the final moment when one staggers away from the model street intersection to its full-scale replica. Mr. Geddes is a great magician, and he makes the carrot in the goldfish bowl look like a real goldfish. One has to rub one's eyes before one remembers that the future, as presented here, is old enough to be somebody's grandfather. In fact, this future is so much like the past that people have not yet given up trying to raise flowers on the roofs of office buildings, just like Mr. Rockefeller.

If you combined Mr. Dreyfuss' clouds, which are fine, and Mr. Geddes' landscape, which is marvellously good, you would have a pretty faithful model of the real world. In the Futurama one gets the nearer view of things one misses in the Perisphere: here are farms, houses, roads, cities, near enough to make one feel that the airplane had better go up another couple of thousand feet, just to be safe. At first the main emphasis is upon a rural world rather than an urban one: General Motors demonstrates how the new main-line motor roads will link the farmer with the consumer.

But the great new theme of the Futurama is the importance and character of the many-laned, transcontinental express highways of 1960. Each one-way lane permits travel at one speed, somewhere between fifty and a hundred miles an hour. Circulation is controlled by car-dispatchers in signal towers communicating by radio with the cars and directing them. Long, curving ramps make it possible to enter and leave the highways at high speeds. I am not sure how Mr. Geddes would get rid of the snow if a blizzard struck one of these highways or how he could keep the lighting system from being paralyzed then, but he has done a lot of research on the problem, according to report, so probably he knows.

Sitting in the cozy *cabinet à deux*, watching the future unroll, one can enjoy Mr. Geddes' countryside. But he has designed a traffic artery that will effectually prevent a motorist from enjoying anything except the speed of his journey and the prospect of getting to his destination soon. If the railways had wanted to convince people that sensible travellers would always go long distances by rail, they would have subsidized the Futurama before General Motors got the chance. For what the Futurama really demonstrates is that by 1960 all jaunts of more than fifty miles will be as deadly as they now are in parts of New Jersey and in the Farther West.

Mind you, Mr. Geddes is on the right track, but the joke on General Motors is that it is a railroad with lighted barriers to keep the motor trains on the track. It was back in 1927 or thereabouts that Mr. Benton MacKaye first called attention to the fact that the motorcar is just a private locomotive and that our main highroads must therefore be designed with the same safety features and traffic devices as a railroad. He even made the further provision, which U. S. highway engineers still resolutely try to ignore, that these new motor roads must not repeat the railroad's costly mistake of attempting to go into the middle of a town. A good highway plan should hit the main arteries of a town at a tangent, distributing its traffic into feeder streets and avenues, as, by a great piece of good luck, the new express highways do in New York.

Now, Mr. Geddes has caught the first point about modern highways clearly enough: the major roads are correctly designed for heavy traffic— although I somehow missed the toll stations which would be necessary for paying the interest on these extremely costly public works. But Mr. Geddes still dreams of continuing, on such a scheme, our present system of individually driven locomotives. The truth is that these express highways will by their very nature create a new type of motor transportation— *trains* of motorcars, beside which our present feeble attempts at trailers will look piffling.

Once you cancel out the motorist's freedom of speed and movement, his sense of power at the wheel, and his opportunity to enjoy, if only faintly, the scenery, you have reduced motoring to a chore. The main problem on long journeys will be what it already is on many Western roads today through lonely desert country: how to keep awake. In short, efficiency and safety and speed, if pushed as far as Mr. Geddes proposes, will abolish the individual motorist again. The task of driving will go back to men professionally inured to keeping awake, to minding the signals, to facing sudden emergencies. Just as we have at last got around to the point of building great scenic highways, like the new Eastern State Parkway in New York, which sweep and climb with all the freedom the motorcar gives, the people who put speed above pleasure are proposing just the opposite ideal. If the Futurama program wins out, it should do more to undermine the individual use of the motorcar than the most drastic reductions in railroad fares. If I were a General Motors executive, I'd want to look these facts in the eye and begin thinking pretty fast.

So much for the effect of speed in the world of tomorrow. As soon as the Futurama approaches the city, however, one gets a different kind of letdown. The closer Mr. Geddes gets to the city, the more old-fashioned his imagination becomes. By the time one reaches his remodelled towns, one enters the tinny world of a Jules Verne romance, or one of those brittle nightmares Mr. Wells used to picture in the early nineteen-hundreds. And when one finally debouches on the upper level of a double-decked street, surrounded by an apartment house, a department store, an auditorium, and an automobile salesroom, one is back in the jumbled world of yesterday— yesterday's reality and yesterday's dream.

In the face of a population that is approaching stability. Mr. Geddes still imagines that the city of 1960 will be bigger than that of 1940. And despite all that town planners have been demonstrating during the past twenty years, he still cannot pull himself away from the old-fashioned Renaissance city plan, in which traffic is combined with business and residence. The saddest joke of all, however, is that the Futurama fails to demonstrate some of the most obvious uses of motor transportation. Take the industrial town of the future, with its steelworks brightly dominating the sky and some realistic smoke issuing from the chimneys. Here is a town that brazenly repeats the bad planning of Gary, Indiana, or Lackawanna, Pennsylvania, by placing the workers right under the dirt and fumes of the steel plant, within *walking* distance. Already there is plenty of actual precedent for putting such hygienic nuisances as steelworks or cement-making plants two or three miles away from the domestic quarters of even the unskilled workers. What is a motorcar for if not for that very purpose? I say nothing of Mr. Geddes' 1,500-foot skyscrapers, except to note that by 1960 they will all have to be thrown down as public nuisances—obstructions to aviation.

B Y the time one reaches the Town of Tomorrow, which is where one is supposed to have landed when one leaves the Futurama, one is prepared for the worst. Between Mr. Geddes' worst and the nondescript real-estate development labelled the Town of Tomorrow by the great industrial organizations which collectively show their products in it, there is hardly much choice. One is brittle; the other is mushy. No one apparently told the designers of the Town of Tomorrow that there is such a thing as a new kind of neighborhood plan, still less that in modern architecture the common plan and the individual house must be developed together. The result of this innocence, or negligence, is just the usual suburban wilderness, what is called in the seed catalogues the wildflower package. You may get a forget-me-not beside a castor-oil plant. That is called the charm of the unexpected.

The best house in the lot is probably the plywood house, designed by Mr. A. Lawrence Kocher. The runners-up are the Pittsburgh House of Glass and the more urban type called the House of Vistas, which might easily be adapted to a row unit. The plywood house has been done with a little of the real inventiveness that has been conspicuously lacking in house design, even among the advocates of prefabrication. Its narrow ventilating windows at the top of the living room are a useful innovation; they probably would have been even more so with a slanting roof, like the one Harrison and Fouilhoux used in their admirable farmhouse in the nearby Electrified Farm exhibit. But as a whole there is nothing here that carries American architecture one step further than Europe had reached by 1932. That is not a disgrace to the American architects, who have been doing many admirable things outside the World's Fairs. It *is* a disgrace to the Nice Nellies who run our great American industries and who try to expiate the sin of fostering new technical ideas or manufacturing new materials by either collecting antiques for themselves or by trying to fit their products into a setting as moth-eaten as possible.

In short, the Town of Tomorrow at the Fair, which might have topped the Fair and sent people away with a vision of the future, doesn't even actually come up to the standards of current thought and current design. It remains the bootleg tomorrow that used to be sold a genuine Scotch before October, 1929.

1939~40

Private and public housing was the focus of two "Sky Lines" this season, with Mumford ruminating over the configuration of apartment plans and building heights. In December, Mumford, who did not travel by airplane until he was a septuagenarian, journeyed to Queens to inspect La Guardia Field, the city's new municipal airport. That spring he returned to Rockefeller Center for another look and was surprised to discover that there was much to admire in its completed design.

D URING the last few months a number of apartment houses have been built around the town. There are so many good ones, if one considers only the new façades, that it is hard to single out any particular building for commendation. Fortunately, as Thomas More said of the houses in Utopia, to praise one of them is to praise all. These apartment houses present to the eye the simple vernacular of our period: wide steel casement windows; a plain, unadorned façade of clean, soberly designed entrances; and shops that have been treated as an integral part of the building. That at No. 1 Jane Street is a fine example of what I mean, for the architect, Charles Kreymborg, has given an extra grace to the wall with horizontal bands of brick—a pleasant variation within the pattern. But the point is that these new buildings exemplify a decent, honest, and often quite handsome formula, as good as Bloomsbury was in the eighteenth century or parts of Beacon Hill in the early nineteenth.

It will not do to look too closely behind the fronts of these new houses; in plan they follow the overcrowded pattern of the past. But the important news at the moment is that even the old-fashioned plan is coming in for revision. City commercial building has begun to feel the competition from the more open garden apartment houses that have arisen in the suburbs. The builders likewise have before them the example of the public housing projects in the city, far superior in essentials to anything that mere wealth can purchase. They are beginning to learn a lesson about overcrowding, and it is high time. The practice of building upper-income apartment houses on ancient slum models was rapidly driving most of the population into the suburbs. No one can live by gadgets alone. Light, air, space, gardens—the substance and ornament of all good architecture—are becoming fashionable once more.

O NE of the largest examples of this transformation is the series of apartment buildings along Riverside Drive from 181st to 186th

Street. This rampart of red brick is Castle Village, quaintly so-called mainly because it is neither a castle nor a village. It does inherit the site of the
pseudo-Gothic castle of eighteenth-century fancy that Dr. Charles Paterno,
who, the advertisements tell us, "conceived and constructed" the present
apartments, created for himself a generation ago. But all that remains of the
original mass is the pergola that edges the very fine pleasance above the
river. This was doubtless kept for atmosphere and sentiment, but the
crumbly forms and the shaggy vines of this pergola present a surrealist
contrast to the bright new buildings behind.

The Castle Village apartments are, as the French would say, formidable.
These five great buildings, some dozen stories high, line the west side of
Cabrini Boulevard, known in its pre-Italianate days as Northern Avenue.
Each is in the form of a cross. This open plan gives the buildings complete
exposure on every side. Gone are the courts and air shafts and enclosures
that have done duty so long in New York apartment houses. This new type
of building originally appeared in modern planning in the early theoretical
cities of Le Corbusier; it was one of the first forms he chose for skyscrapers. But isolated examples, like the Fifth Avenue Hospital, came into existence before architects began to play around with apartment plans on the
same lines. Whether it is as logical a form for apartment houses as many
competent architects think, I shall discuss in a moment.

Aesthetically, this X plan is more successful in single units than it is in
repetition. One building, properly supported with minor masses, might
have a superb place in the landscape; five such are just a barricade. In Castle
Village, they conform neither to the hill in plan and placement nor to the
cliffs below in any agreeable transition of color. The contrasting color of
the red brick, indeed, only increases the sense of incongruity. The tans and
honeys of the Medical Center buildings, for example, strike a much better
note in the landscape. To have employed the same color note in this new
apartment project would have shown a firmer sense of city design—a job to
which the individual builder can contribute far more than any municipal art
commission.

Even the architect, George Fred Pelham, Jr., apparently felt that these
five great piles were a little forbidding. How otherwise can one explain the
white shutters that are battened down on each side of the windows on the

three lowest stories, or the cold stone bands that are supposed to tie each building up horizontally, or the iron railing that—all too delicately—breaks into the parapet of the roof? But these feeble attempts at ornament cannot annul the effect of the plan and structure. One cannot make a modest Georgian façade out of a building whose gigantic possibilities spring from another age. The result is that the surface does not achieve the standard of the best modern style. Although the corner windows have been bevelled, the use of heavy wooden sashes takes away no small part of the view that is thus opened up.

W HAT about the X plan itself? Here I find myself criticizing not these particular apartment houses but a dogma that a great many able architects have been building up during the last half-dozen years, a dogma that has already had its effect on various large-scale housing projects. In most new designs, if the site has been big enough to permit real planning, you will find some version of the X plan. Unfortunately, most of them have serious defects; they tend to produce rooms too long in proportion to their width and they create an undue amount of unventilated space, unused or only partly used, in the form of public halls and private foyers.

As the X plan works out in Castle Village, only the rooms on the outer parts of the arm have the advantage of through ventilation or cross-ventilation. But when apartments are planned two rooms deep on each side of the elevator-and-service core, it is possible to give them complete exposure and circulation, and to give rooms the size and shape that represent their function and not just a compromise between the function and what can be carved out of the plan. This straight-line plan—called *Zeilenbau* in Germany—has one other advantage; if properly designed, the size and disposition of the rooms can be altered, and they can be cut up or thrown together as requirements change, whereas all the more complicated and ingenious plans leave the space tied in knots.

I hesitate, as a mere critic, to offer an opinion about a site that Mr. Pelham and the engineer, Victor Mayper, doubtless studied exhaustively before arriving at the X plan. But I nevertheless must record the conviction that a zigzag or sawtooth layout, with apartments two rooms deep, would have utilized the site far better. For the sawtooth plan could have been built up into a unified composition as the plot widened out in its climb up the hill, and it could also have provided a full view of the river and a southeast or southwest exposure for every apartment. The builder of Castle Village is to be congratulated for going as far as he has gone, but he is to be reproached for not going farther, since he had perhaps the finest site remaining in New York for residential purposes.

D ESCENDING from Washington Heights to the depths of Manhattan for a final glance at the new mode, I should like to commend the apartment house at the southwest corner of Sixty-first Street and Second Avenue as probably the finest façade that has been done since the Rockefeller Apartments a few years ago. It is, moreover, an impeccable example of urban good manners. It is next door to the very pleasant First Swedish Baptist Church. The architect, Horace Ginsbern, has accepted the theme set by the color and form of the church and has adapted it in a manner that keeps the apartment building from looking like a parish house and yet gives coherence to the common front. In its use of color through the natural resources of brick, this building compares with the very best work of the eighties, with such a building as McKim, Mead & White's 894 Broadway. One could hardly give it higher praise.

Most of the brick used in this building is lighter than the oranges and mulberry used in the church, but the mulberry is repeated in the brick panel that binds the windows together and the orange is repeated on the corner of the building. The sole ornament on the exterior, apart from the intelligent use of brick, is the long projecting ribbon of lilac-colored stone that runs westward from the avenue and then drops down over the entrance; it serves as a sort of signboard, unconsciously carrying the eye to exactly where the visitor to the building wants to go. The interior of the entrance hall is perhaps a bit overdone, but the panel of glass bricks in the rear, with the yellow Venetian blinds and yellow net drapes, gives it the friendly effect that only daylight can provide; there are chairs and tables for waiting visitors, and it really is a nice place to wait. If one compares the front of the building with the rear, which has not been finished to please the eye, one may get a real lesson in the difference between complete and incomplete design.

E VERYONE is excited over the fact that La Guardia Field, the magnificently expensive new municipal airport at North Beach, may
presently be too small for the traffic. But the thing that makes me
anxious is the fact that the buildings are so large and bulky and visible. The
innocents who designed them must have been dreaming of the time when
airplanes would have the wings of the dove, not of the vulture. Today people ought to know that an airfield should look as guileless as a Long Island
duck farm but be built like the Maginot Line. In fact, an airfield is perhaps
the only place where all the gadgets and fakeries and extravagances of modern building might be introduced freely and rationally justified.

Before I deal with the actual airport, let me draw up the ideal program
for such a place. It should be built from ground level downward. The passengers' waiting rooms, booking offices, and restaurants should be at least
one story underground, to make the traveller feel he is still in his hotel. (A
sour, stale cigar smell should indicate the air-conditioned bar.) Below these
should be the hangars. Passengers should descend to the planes, and the
loaded machines should then be lifted to ground level on a platform, like
the orchestra at a big movie theatre. The control tower, which should be
retractable at will, should have on its roof a neat little garden in boxes, like
those on the Radio City roofs, to complete the camouflage. Such an airport
would be expensive, but why should a country that is laying out more than
a billion dollars a year on armaments haggle about that? The invisible airport would be the last crown of a disappearing civilization. Are we men or
are we moles?

T HE designers of La Guardia Field have conceived their buildings in
the belief that we are still men. All the structures are above ground,
and were designed, hopefully, on the theory that they were meant to be
looked at. At first glance the spectacle is fine. The great hangars are ranged
in groups on either side of the Administration Building; it looks as if the

space between these groups and the central unit will eventually be filled up with other structures. All are done in a dull buff brick. These three buildings, sweeping in a half-circle, face the Grand Central Boulevard and the parking lots and back up on the airfield.

The hangars are pretty good. The roof of each of the hangars—there are three in each group—forms a shallow arch, and on one side the brick wall is shortened to accommodate a panel of green glass between it and the roof to let overhead light into the interior. The window units run in horizontal lines, accentuated by the bands of brown brick that frame them and connect the separate bays. The entrance in the centre of each building breaks this horizontal line, and, like the windows, it is framed in brown brick. These buildings are not conspicuously handsome, but they reach a very decent standard.

I cannot speak with equal enthusiasm of the Administration Building; it is a series of bungles, missed opportunities, and hideous misapplications of ornament. At certain points the round part facing the field comes very close to equalling the all-time architectural low established in the new municipal piers on the North River between Forty-eighth and Fifty-second Streets. This building consists of a central core with wings on each side. From the parking side, the vertical note is emphasized; the front walls are set back and indented for no particular reason, and the grille on the window that lights the stairs only adds to this sense of fussiness. As if to mock this false front, there rises in the rear, above the semicircular main mass, the most important element in the whole field—the observation tower and control room. This is treated almost as an afterthought which had nothing to do with the main design; it has as much aesthetic connection with the rest of the building as the old-fashioned roof water tanks on stilts had with the apartment houses they adorned. In other words, the element that might have been made central in an organic composition is reduced in size and visual importance in favor of a faked entrance.

The core of the building is, as I said, mainly circular, but instead of carrying the form of this circle through the front of the structure as every possible motive should dictate, the architects abruptly terminated the most interesting feature of their composition just at the point where it would be visually most effective. (The double curve that might have been formed by the ramps sweeping upward to the entrance would have been striking.) This failure to make the circular motif a major part of the design was bad enough; it is topped, however, by the way in which this portion is treated on the airfield side. It almost seems as if the same melancholy genius who designed the ornaments for the new North River piers had charge of the decoration of this exterior; the same funeral-parlor motif prevails.

There is something curiously satisfactory in a round wall, whether it is in a windmill, a grain elevator, a gas tank, or the tomb of Hadrian; one must work hard to rob it of its visual pleasure. But the architects of this structure have thoughtlessly introduced, over the tan bricks above the circle of windows, a fringe of black ornament, and they have further spoiled the unity of the mass by placing a rim of black brick around the windows below. It looks as if someone had died. Here is a building close to the earth and sky, irradiated with light—a place beautifully responsive to pure form and clear color. I can imagine a wholly black building that would have looked as handsome as the Adler Planetarium in Chicago, but this dingy black ornament merely gives one the creeps. When one says that this might have looked as handsome as an oil tank, and doesn't, one has said everything.

The interior, by contrast, is better done. The circular plan of the booking hall is both convenient and easy to follow, and the gray-tiled walls are pleasant. But here again the forms are robbed of their native aesthetic vitality by the heavy black columns, edged with white metal, that are ranged around the room; they are designed like funerary torches, with a flame of metal licking upward out of the topmost part. As for Arthur Covey's signs of the zodiac, done in brass sheets and forming a circular frieze in the centre of the hall, and the blue-and-gold pendant globe of the world, they are as unentertaining as they are meaningless. The height of the ceiling makes it necessary to put the kitchen on the floor above not in its logical place (which would be in the central core), but to one side of the semicircular dining room. Given a choice between practical convenience with warm food and inconvenience with the joy of eternally beholding these dubious decorations, I should choose convenience and warm food, and I think the architects should have done so, too.

The treatment of the second floor is just as disappointing. The restaurant, with its round sweep of windows looking north, northeast, and northwest upon the field, was a splendid opportunity for the architects, but they indented the columns a short distance from the exterior wall and thus decreased the outward visibility. If there was any cantilevering to be done here, it should have been done magnificently, from a point at least twenty feet in from the windows. The designers used a vertical type of window, whose upright sashes cut across the line of vision. All this considerably reduces the otherwise perfect delight of dining at the airport, with one of the most spacious views around the city before one—beautiful just by reason of the sweep of unbroken land and sky. The concessionaires of the restaurant proudly announce, in cards set on every table, that the windows, already badly enough crisscrossed by the sashes, will presently be decorated with Venetian blinds and rich drapes. The blinds are for the purpose of getting rid of the sun when it shines too bright, the drapes are designed to completely kill the view. People who can spoil their opportunities to enjoy the meeting of land, water, and sky obviously don't deserve anything better than the bombproof shelter I have outlined.

T HE large parking space between the buildings and the Grand Central Parkway will be none too large for the eventual traffic, if one may judge by a midweek observation made before the airport was really in running order. This parking space was plainly contrived by someone who wanted to prove that walking on land is much more dangerous than flying, for there is no sidewalk for the pedestrian leaving his car, unless he takes to the balks, punctuated by lighting standards, that separate the parking areas from each other and from the roadways. There must be a safe way to handle this problem, and this whole area should be redesigned.

But I can't leave the field still down-hearted. The lamp standards are as excellent as they are simple, and if you don't like the Administration Building's architecture any better than I do, you can at least fly away from it.

THE New York City Planning Commission has been marking out on the map of the city districts that are due to be rebuilt. There are thirty-two areas. If you want to find out what the city would look like if large residential districts in it were done over on the present low-rent-housing models, you'd better make a pilgrimage to the Erie Basin district in Brooklyn, where the Red Hook Houses are, or to the Long Island end of the Queensboro Bridge, where the great housing estate called Queensbridge has been almost completed.

Because I have a few serious criticisms of both projects, I want to make it plain that they are miles above the product of any commercial apartment builder. If our architects and administrators couldn't learn a single trick more, it would still be worth the money and effort needed to rebuild the city after the new open pattern these developments follow. But the architects still have a lot to learn. They are all like prisoners who, after their release, keep on shuffling as if the old ball and chain were still dragging at their ankles.

The Red Hook project is the more conventional one, both in layout and design. It consists of a series of X- and T-shaped apartment buildings grouped on the site to form a series of L's on either side of a main axis. This axis was originally a street, but is now happily transformed into a grass-covered mall. The sweep is almost that of the Versailles water course. Mr. Moses' style of planning evidently went to someone's head.

On the harbor end of the project there is a small row of stores. On the opposite end, in one corner, is another. Behind them are a nursery school and a community house. On what principle the planners put these special buildings near a messy avenue, facing the ugly old district that surrounds these new structures, I am at a loss to explain. Neither the community house nor the nursery school is big enough to serve the whole neighborhood. Indeed, it is very doubtful if they can serve more than a part of their own community. The notion of putting the school in the dustiest and noisiest part of the development was fantastic.

The mistake is all the more annoying because had the school and the community house been placed in the middle of the mall, they would have broken up that drafty alley with its Leningrad formalism, and they would have scaled down the now formidable columns of apartments. In other words, these small buildings, correctly placed, would have done a lot toward giving the entire development the intimate humanizing touch it so badly needs.

Some people have criticized the façades of the individual Red Hook apartment houses because they are devoid of ornament. One might as well criticize the eighteenth-century façades of Bloomsbury for the same reason; in fact, most of the good vernacular architecture of Europe is without ornament. What is wrong with this design is something else—its quite unnecessary monotony. This is the result of taking a single type of unit, six stories high, and repeating it practically without variation throughout the area.

If three-story walk-ups and single-family houses had been included in the development, the contrast of the low masses against the high ones would have provided drama for the eye. How exciting this might have been one can discover in the few places where the shops and the apartments make a varied group. Such a combination of forms would have been better from a human point of view. What is even more important, it would have provided for a greater variety of individual tastes and family sizes. Furthermore, it would have reduced the quite unjustifiable density of two hundred and thirty-six people an acre to a more rational figure.

I APPROACHED the Queensbridge group with skepticism, but on inspection it is much handsomer. Here the unit used forms a Y rather than an X or a T, and the open arms of the Y do away with one of the great objections to T and X units—that on hot summer days every sunny wall forms a perfect bake oven which radiates its heat upon the adjacent wall even when that is in shadow. Moreover, the use of Y units creates a wider angle between opposing walls.

The warm tan of the brick in Queensbridge is a few tones lighter, I should judge, than that used in Red Hook, and the brown tile of the parapet and balustrade copings is a very simple but judicious aesthetic touch. Properly frightened by the cost of garden upkeep in such vast projects, the architects of both developments resorted to paving. Because of the curved design of the Queensbridge walks, the use of contrasting colors and textures here produces a handsome ground pattern. This wholly legitimate decorative device reminds one of the best projects in Amsterdam.

The layout of Queensbridge is distinctly superior to that of Red Hook. The Y units in combination form enclosures which at the same time give the effect of being open and of leading somewhere else—as indeed they do. Each of the major blocks has a large pool of quiet space at the centre, forming a handsome public plaza with a place for children to play, for mothers to walk about in or rest and gossip. This is a mighty edifying contrast to the dusty avenues along which most parents have to air their children, and where they take their rest on a camp stool amid the reek of gasoline and the subtle poison of carbon monoxide.

So far I have been dealing with the community plans of these developments and with their exteriors. On this score, their chief sin is that they overcrowd the sites even though they are in quarters of the city where the price of land was low and the existing buildings had served a population whose density per acre was far smaller.

As a result, both projects are unnecessarily barracklike and monotonous. They are thus on the same level as our worst uniform zoning areas. The authorities who insisted upon this standardization evidently never learned a thing from the pioneer work done by Wright and Stein and Ackerman in Sunnyside Gardens, which isn't much more than a mile from Queensbridge.

But even worse than the repetition of a single-unit plan was the selection of a bad unit to begin with. Because the authorities decided to overcrowd the land, they hit upon six-story elevator apartment houses. Once they committed themselves to elevators, they were forced to focus as many apartments as possible around each elevator landing in the interests of economy, instead of having just two families to a floor, as in a good walk-up apartment. That compelled them to use X and Y units, unfortunately very wasteful, inefficient, and hygienically undesirable plans. Not merely do they make it impossible to provide through or cross ventilation in more than one room in every apartment but they create a pocket of unlighted and unventilated space therein. This space is called the dining alcove, though nobody in his senses would ever dine there.

The practice of giving this waste space a name and then crediting it as half a room in the estimate of costs and rents is a piece of self-deception by the authorities. Our New York City Housing Authority is very proud of the fact—and quite justly, too—that it got such a lot for its money in these projects, for the fixtures are excellent and the workmanship looks extremely sound. But there is no use scrimping in one pocket if money is dribbling out of the other.

If the authorities and their architects had stuck to a simpler, straight-line type of plan, they would have reaped a lot of real advantages. They could have oriented the rows to get the fullest advantage of sunlight; they could have given every room through ventilation; they could have made the inner suites more flexible; and they could have planned living rooms that would really be rooms and not corridors. Such suites could be thrown together or reduced in size with great facility if it were ever found, for instance, that too many four-room apartments existed and not enough twos or sixes. The present designs have no adaptability; they are frozen tight, committed to their mistake till the buildings are demolished.

Yet it is something of a miracle that within three brief years four great municipal housing projects—the Harlem River and Williamsburg developments are the other—have been created whose external spaciousness and comeliness, for all their specific effects, make them already a model for the rest of the city. Each has its internal gardens and playgrounds, each is placed close to a public school, and in both Red Hook and Queensbridge Mr. Moses has handsomely coöperated by providing a bang-up new public playground. Each has its own nursery school, its own community centre, sometimes its own gymnasium, always its own shops; each is an organic unit for living, not a clot of nondescript structures built anyhow, fitted together anyhow. That is a lot, and that is the real reason for demanding a lot more. For it is absurd for our authorities to act today as if they were bound to repeat the mistakes of the past in order to prove they have their feet on the ground.

THE "Versus" show that is now on at the Architectural League is supposed to dramatize the clash between the old and the new in architectural design. On one floor are depicted the monuments of the past: the railroad stations that were modelled after public baths, the suburban country houses that were modelled after palaces, the libraries that were built to resemble pantheons; in short, the dead buildings that were built to resemble other dead buildings. On the upper floor is a vivid array of fresh buildings, evolved fresh—with new plans, new methods of construction, often new materials—out of the needs and tastes of our own day. One floor is a cemetery, the other is a delivery ward. How can they clash? How can there be any question of choice?

It was a kindly thought on the part of the committee which designed this show to keep the two kinds of architecture separated by a whole flight of stairs, but it revealed the fatal open-mindedness which prevents so many good American architects from reaching positive conclusions about their art. To make the exhibition really exciting, the new and the old should have been contrasted side by side, detail by detail. There should have been a picture of our "noble" Public Library when it left Mr. Thomas Hasting's hands, and next to it there should have been a few deadly shots of the Library's interior twenty-five years later, the entrails of its special departments spilling out in the halls, its crowded and cluttered rooms incapable of expansion or alteration.

Alongside the library there should have been a picture of the new Museum of Modern Art—no perfect building either. But the advantage of its steel-cage construction would have been obvious in the facility with which the inept design of the Museum's entrance floor was corrected after the building was opened. Whatever merits the New York Public Library had aesthetically, even as a corpse, have been effectively ruined by the mere transformations of maturity. A similar demonstration might have been made with other pairs of buildings, and it would have shown that the older order is no order at all.

Even on purely aesthetic grounds, of course, the conservatives have no defence. For in architecture, one of the prime marks of good form is coherence; if a building is to have its full meaning for the eye, the street plan and the formal approach, the utilities within the building, the habits and dispositions of the spectator should all speak the same language. If we are to have a harmonious environment, no one can arbitrarily choose the style of his building, making it look like some perfect form of the past, any more than one can arbitrarily choose to speak Ciceronian Latin instead of plain American. The classic renaissance was alive only so long as the rich and the educated peppered their speech with classic allusions, when they read Latin in preference to their own barbarous tongue. That there is still any debate about these matters in architectural circles is a sign of curious intellectual innocence. I suspect that Rip van Winkle was an architect.

WITH all the talk about zoning during the last twenty years, it is odd that so few people understand that it applies in aesthetics as much as it does in any other department of city design. The Swedes long ago realized this, and they have block committees that seek to preserve a harmonious development of buildings. But the east part of Forty-second Street, in particular the strip between two important buildings, the New York Public Library and Grand Central Terminal, already shows alarming symptoms of mistaking itself for the bawdy stretch between Seventh and Eighth Avenues; and the new Sheffield Farms Milk Bar doesn't help matters.

I have nothing against milk. It is a fine drink. Children cry for it, pigs fatten on it, Anna Held used to bathe in it, some of my best friends drink it. I even have a sentimental feeling for Sheffield's, since I can remember, as a boy, the cold, buttery smell of its dairies in the days when they were merely a part of Sheffield, Slawson, Decker, a name to linger over, like Bailey, Banks & Biddle. But this new milk bar is a monstrosity. On the outside, it announces its presence with a huge vertical sign and a great white enamelled signboard with green and red neon lights and a twinkling bottle of milk. It would take a lot of ingenuity to create anything more massively vulgar and out of place than this particular front; the architect probably thought he was all alone in the World of Tomorrow.

As milk bars go, the interior is fairly good: the brilliant red panels at the back of the room soften the cold white glare of the walls, and the use of this red on the subsidiary fixtures, like the mechanical milk-shakers, was a happy inspiration. Even the horizontal tubular lights are not so glaring to stand under as one might think from the outside. But the more playful attempts at decoration, in the form of cutout patterns and especially in a Walt Disney sort of painting, are feeble, and anyway they can hardly be seen by the milk-and-doughnut addicts without a lot of neck-stretching. The one opportunity for effective decoration, the counter signs advertising the various offerings, are graphically and typographically fifth-rate. But the inside could be worse and still pass muster. It is the outside of this particular bar that leaves a sour taste on Forty-second Street.

THE new Essex Street Market, put up by the municipality, is a modest but handsome job, and Mayor La Guardia has every reason to feel good about it. The market stretches for three blocks, from Stanton to Broome Street, covering to the full a shallow strip of land. The main purpose, from the Mayor's point of view, was to rid Orchard Street of the dirty, disorderly, and unhygienic pushcart peddlers' market, which contributed so much to the life and raw color of the East Side. I understand the Mayor's motives and applaud them, but I think the Department of Markets was far too literal in interpreting his wish. For the markets are not merely off the street; they are completely insulated from it by solid brick walls, broken by occasional set-in entrances in plain concrete, which, however, are effectively lettered in gold. The light from the street side comes through long banks of windows, set above the stalls. I have no harsh words for the external design; instead, I want also to praise the admirable use of raised letters on the façades of two of the buildings—an appropriate kind of decoration.

But for the last ten years I have conducted a campaign to persuade merchants to open up the interiors of their shops and to make the life within them the real show window, and I don't propose to abandon this, even out of respect for the Mayor. The Steuben Glass shop on Fifth Avenue is a happy example of this kind of design, and I see no reason the municipal market should not have contributed to the color of Essex Street by opening directly upon it. The entrances are hardly adequate to handle really large crowds; moreover, despite the generous scale of the interior, the extra space gained by uniting the sidewalk and the market would have facilitated circulation during the busy hours. Instead of scaling the market up, it might have been a far better notion to turn the street itself into an open-air arcade. This could have been done even with the provision of permanent stalls and safe, hygienic means of storage.

Granting the Mayor's program, however, there is still one large aesthetic flaw, the incomprehensible failure to control the signs that announce the firms to which the corner frontages in two of these buildings have been rented. The effect of the façade's sober design is flagrantly violated by the neon displays that advertise these shopkeepers—atrociously designed, badly out of scale, altogether obnoxious from any point of view. There is no use taking pains over the design of a building like this unless the Department of Markets has enough aesthetic conscience to prevent such violations. Landlords nowadays often do this, for they have learned that it helps to keep up the value of their property, and the city should have followed suit.

I AM glad to hear that the wave of mild indignation over the Parks Department's proposed improvements of Washington Square has duly registered itself with Mr. Moses and his able assistants. Much might be said for those who wish to keep Washington Square as a reminder of a past whose landmarks are steadily disappearing in other parts of the city. There might even be something to say for someone who stepped forward with a really handsome modern design for this square, one which would create a deeper nostalgia for *our* good old days in the centuries to come. But no one can say anything for the absurd plan that came out of Mr. Moses' office by what was apparently a process of mere sausage-grinding. Some weird formal planning had been done there before this, but the Washington Square project set a new record. Fortunately, this design has been scrapped. But the new one, when it comes, will still bear watching. In intimate designs, the Parks Department somehow loses the human touch it keeps so well in handling large spaces and vast masses of people.

NINE years ago, Rockefeller Center was still on the drafting board. Mr. Rockefeller was referring hopefully to the possibility of giving the buildings an Egyptian touch. Some directors of the Metropolitan Opera House were talking hopefully about a new home. The Center's publicity men, dreaming of larger and more magnificent headlines, had collaborated with the late Raymond Hood to concoct one of the most insipid ideas the project has been afflicted with: hanging gardens. More romantic than anyone else, Mr. Rockefeller's financial advisers were talking hopefully about producing even more rentable space than would be required to create an income on which Columbia University could live in the style to which it was accustomed. About the last thought that occurred to anyone was that a group of office buildings ought to be efficiently designed as offices.

In spite of all these handicaps, Rockefeller Center has turned into an impressive collection of structures; they form a composition in which unity and coherence have to a considerable degree diminished the fault of overemphasis. In other words, they get by. Now, when the project is complete, one can see that the worst mistakes were made at the beginning and that as the decade wore on, the architects, at least, gradually achieved a more rational conception of their problem. But the most gigantic blunders had already been made. Among those blunders one must include the seventy-story R.C.A. Building, because of its seventy stories, the sunken plaza, the hanging gardens, and the—alas!—superfluous motion-picture theatre.

So much has happened since 1931 that most people have probably forgotten the modifications that have been made in the original design, such as the elimination of the oval-shaped building, looking in the renderings exactly like a hatbox, which was originally intended as the central mass for Fifth Avenue. They may also have forgotten that nine years ago the architects were still pondering the idea of using brick and that there was still a chance some "interpretation" of Egypt or the Renaissance might be inflicted on the façades.

One can see that the choice of rough-faced limestone for the façades of the buildings was on the whole a happy one, for the stone has been steadily absorbing soot, so by now both the stone face and the metal plaques are about the same tone and color. Certainly the limestone, combined with the blue of the windowshades, was a safe choice. But now that there is a striking contrast in color between the new and the old façades, one can also see how the architects, by clinging to a single material and color, lost a jolly opportunity. Eventually all the buildings will have the same hue, whereas a positive contrast in color between the central mass and the supporting buildings would have made permanent what is only a temporary effect.

Because the architects went in for façades that were severe and uniform, they doubtless felt doubly bound to relieve this severity with ornament. It only remains to be said that never were so much money and pains spent with so little effect. The hanging gardens were, of course, hardly architectural devices. But even the ornamental sculpture that was used about the entrances is overpowered by the tremendous masses above them. Michelangelo could not have prevailed against this handicap. Furthermore, the most conspicuous murals, those of Sert and Ezra Winter, are aesthetically the worst flops.

The most blatant misuse of sculpture occurs in front of the Fifth Avenue entrance to the International Building. By itself, that entrance, with its absolutely severe rectangular columns framing rectangular glass openings, without a frill, without a fluting, is beyond doubt the finest single architectural element in the whole Center—traditional but fresh, superb in proportion and scale, complete. The beauty of that entrance was marred when the idiotic form of Atlas was placed in front of it.

The architects, too, made a serious muff of the one conspicuous piece of decoration that lay within their direct control: the vertical signs and the marquees which identify the Center Theatre and the Music Hall. This is an art form in which architectural effort has been lacking, yet it is one of the most important features of any modern urban street composition both by day and by night. The Rockefeller Center signs are, I regret to say, failures. They attempt monumentality and merely look elephantine; moreover, the lettering is clumsy and the use of script for "The" and "Theatre" is indefensible. Once the architect breaks away from the old-fashioned street layout, in which the buildings are consecutively numbered, it is important to have distinguishable signs to number and identify the buildings at a distance. It is only when one is close to these buildings—and not always then—that one is told, by lettering or decoration, where one is. This was a chance for organic ornament, so ably used on the office building at 417 Fifth Avenue, at Thirty-eighth. By going in for traditional embellishments, the architects of Rockefeller Center diverted themselves from their real task. (This same failure to identify irregularly placed buildings plagues one on university campuses and in modern housing projects, too, and it drives the casual visitor crazy.)

But the most serious aesthetic error in Rockefeller Center was the original mistake in scale. Except at a distance, one cannot see the top of the R.C.A. Building without tilting one's chin at an uncomfortable angle. At a distance, it is no more impressive than twenty other buildings in the city; not nearly so good, in fact, as the Daily News Building or the Insurance Company of North America's Building. What makes the Center architecturally the most exciting mass of buildings in the city is the nearby view of the play of mass against mass, of low structures against high ones, of the blank walls of the theatres against the vast, checkered slabs of glass in the new garage. All this is effective up to a height of thirty stories. Above that, the added stories only increase the burdens on the elevator system and inflate the egos of great executives.

Employing a unit like the sixteen-story office building that has been put up on Forty-eighth Street, a more compact and economic and efficient use might have been made of the whole site. Like the R.C.A. Building, this latest structure has a broad, low base of two or three stories for exhibition space and shops; and running through the middle of the block, insulated from the streets, set back from its neighbors across the way, is the main mass. This is definitely a new type of building, a substantial innovation and an excellent one. This unit is Rockefeller Center's most conspicuous contribution to the city of the future, unlike the wasteful towers and the dark, overgrown masses of earlier days. It corresponds in plan to the type arrived at in the new Memorial Hospital on East Sixty-eighth Street, and it is not merely a good unit but it makes possible, through the provision of a garage on the lower floors, adequate parking facilities. This structure has not got half the publicity the hanging gardens and the skating rink have received. But it is the real architectural justification of Rockefeller Center.

With a limit of thirty-two stories on the R.C.A. Building, and with units of eight and sixteen stories and theatres flanking this structure, the results would have been stunning, and what is more, every part of the project would have been easy to see. As it is, only from two points—from Forty-seventh Street and Sixth Avenue, and from a third of the way east along the block on Fiftieth Street—can one see the Center at its best. Of course, many of the camera views of the buildings are striking, but then a camera doesn't mind being tilted at a forty-five-degree angle for as much as five minutes, while the human neck does object. Good architecture is designed for the human beings who use or view the buildings, not for publicity men or photographers.

ROCKEFELLER Center is still to be seen as our descendants may see it in another generation. Once we lay out parks and ribbons of open space around such units—the Medical Center is another—they will form a new kind of urban organism. Don't think that the future opening up of the city is just a pipe dream. The parking lots of today, like that on the site of the old Hippodrome, will be the gay playgrounds and squares of tomorrow. Rockefeller Center will look pretty old-fashioned by 1970, but then the Pyramids look old-fashioned now. Seen from quarter of a mile away, the Center group will knock one romantically cold. Even the R.C.A. Building.

INDEX